Democratic Militarism

Why are democracies pursuing more military conflicts, but achieving worse results? *Democratic Militarism* shows that a combination of economic inequality and military technical change enables an average voter to pay very little of the costs of large militaries and armed conflict, in terms of both death and taxes. Jonathan Caverley provides an original statistical analysis of public opinion and international aggression, combined with historical evidence from the late Victorian British Empire, the US Vietnam War effort, and Israel's Second Lebanon War. This book undermines conventional wisdom regarding democracy's exceptional foreign policy characteristics, and challenges elite-centered explanations for poor foreign policy. This accessible and wide-ranging book offers a new account of democratic warfare, and will help readers to understand the implications of the revolution in military affairs.

JONATHAN D. CAVERLEY is Assistant Professor of Political Science at Northwestern University, where he co-chairs the Working Group on Security Studies at the Roberta Buffett Center for International and Comparative Studies. For 2013–14, he is a fellow at the Woodrow Wilson International Center for Scholars. He previously served as a submarine officer in the US Navy.

Cambridge Studies in International Relations: 131

Democratic Militarism

Cambridge Studies in International Relations is a joint initiative of Cambridge University Press and the British International Studies Association (BISA). The series aims to publish the best new scholarship in international studies, irrespective of subject matter, methodological approach or theoretical perspective. The series seeks to bring the latest theoretical work in International Relations to bear on the most important problems and issues in global politics.

Cambridge Studies in International Relations

Democratic Militarism

Voting, Wealth, and War

JONATHAN D. CAVERLEY

CAMBRIDGE
UNIVERSITY PRESS

University Printing House, Cambridge CB2 8BS, United Kingdom

Cambridge University Press is part of the University of Cambridge.

It furthers the University's mission by disseminating knowledge in the pursuit of education, learning and research at the highest international levels of excellence.

www.cambridge.org
Information on this title: www.cambridge.org/9781107667372

© Jonathan D. Caverley 2014

First published 2014

Printed in the United Kingdom by Clays, St Ives plc

A catalogue record for this publication is available from the British Library

Library of Congress Cataloguing in Publication data
Caverley, Jonathan D.
Democratic militarism : voting, wealth, and war / Jonathan D. Caverley.
   pages   cm – (Cambridge studies in international relations ; 131)
ISBN 978-1-107-06398-3 – ISBN 978-1-107-66737-2 (paperback)
1. Politics and war.   2. Democracy.   3. War–Technological innovations.
4. War–Economic aspects.   5. War–Public opinion.   6. Great Britain–History,
Military–19th century.   7. Vietnam War, 1961–1975–United States.   8. Lebanon
War, 2006.   I. Title.
JZ6385.C39   2014
355.02′13–dc23
                                                                2013046219

ISBN 978-1-107-06398-3 Hardback
ISBN 978-1-107-66737-2 Paperback

For three generations of my family

Contents

Figures

Tables

Acknowledgments

Over the long course of writing this book I have enjoyed a tremendous amount of support from within and outside my profession. This book would be impossible without the generosity of many people.

I would first like to thank the members of my dissertation committee for their investment of time and patience in the project that ultimately evolved into this book. I shudder at what this project would have looked like without John Mearsheimer's ruthless paring. As chair, he has provided service after sale; I have turned to him many times for advice, to bounce ideas off him, and for friendship. Charlie Glaser has been a mentor since before I left the Navy, and continues to be the model for the academic and person I aspire to become. Duncan Snidal brought an exacting theoretical knife to the project and continues to help me hone my ideas about politics. Jeff Grynaviski did far, far more than what was asked of him on the committee, and the book is much, much stronger as a result.

Charles Lipson, Patchen Markel, Dan Slater, and Alex Wendt were all integral components of a remarkable graduate school environment for me. In particular, Daniel Drezner, Lloyd Gruber, and Bob Pape all played pivotal roles in the project's early stages. The first two, along with Charlie Glaser, are to blame for my aspiring to a PhD in Political Science. While at Chicago, I was lucky to be surrounded by remarkable peers and friends including Bethany Albertson, Vaidya Gundlupet, Chris Haid, Anne Holtheofer, Jenna Jordan, Adria Lawrence, Emily Meierding, Nuno Monteiro, Michelle Murray, Taka Nishi, Negeen Pegahi, Christian Ponce-de-Leon, Keven Ruby, Frank Smith, Mark Smith, Lora Viola, and Bob Zarate. Bonnie Weir and John Schuessler were particularly indulgent with their time. The University of Chicago's PISP, the Division of Social Sciences, and the Harry Frank Guggenheim Foundation provided much appreciated financial support. This project truly took shape during a pre-doctoral fellowship year at the Belfer Center for Science and International Affairs at Harvard's Kennedy School.

At Northwestern I have been privileged to work with a wonderful collection of colleagues who provided help in a diverse number of ways. I would especially like to thank my colleagues Karen Alter, Jim Farr, Ian Hurd, Steve Nelson, Wendy Pearlman, Will Reno, Jeff Rice, and Jeffrey Winters. Ben Page, Anne Sartori, Jason Searight, and Hendrik Spruyt have provided multiple rounds of feedback. My research was ably assisted by stellar graduate students Olivier Henrepin, Lexi Neame, Jesse Savage, and Mitch Troup. The Northwestern librarians, many only through electronic interface, have helped me acquire reams of books, chapters, and obscure articles from all over the world, usually in wondrously rapid fashion. Finally, I thank the MacArthur Foundation, which sponsored a productive if humbling manuscript conference, courtesy of Dennis Chong.

Outside of Northwestern, Phil Arena, Ivan Arréguin-Toft, Richard Betts, Risa Brooks, Neil Caverley, Monica Duffy-Toft, Matthew Fuhrmann, Sean Gailmard, Sarah Kreps, Matt Kroenig, Chris Layne, David Lektzian, Jason Lyall, Sean Lynn-Jones, Devra Moehler, Jon Monten, John Nagl, Michael Noonan, Daryl Press, Elizabeth Saunders, Todd Sechser, Pascal Vennesson, and Alex Weisiger all presented constructive feedback. Alex Downes, Jack Snyder, and Steve Walt have taken large chunks of time to discuss the argument in great detail. Ben Fordham has been immensely supportive from the first paper that even anticipated this project. Erik Gartzke, Joanne Gowa, and Jenna Jordan generously came to Evanston for a manuscript conference, as did Al Stam who has by now read the full text twice. I have benefited greatly from seminar participants at Chicago, Columbia, Florida State, George Washington, Hebrew University, University of Virginia, and Yale.

I would especially like to thank those who have made my work in Israel even possible, much less fruitful. Here at Northwestern, Ely Reckhas and Wendy Pearlman have given sage advice on a region of which I knew little. In Israel itself, I am grateful to Dima Adamsky, Uzi Arad, Oren Barak, Yehuda Ben Meir, Shlomo Brom, Yair Evron, Chuck Freilich, Efraim Inbar, Avi Kober, Yagil Levy, Benny Miller, Dan Miodownik, Gabi Sheffer, and Gabi Siboni. Udi Eiran gave very detailed comments on my Israel chapter; all remaining errors are my fault, but there would have been many more without him. I especially appreciate the large amount of time Dan Meridor generously spent with me to discuss Israeli grand strategy and military doctrine. I am particularly grateful for a study trip hosted by Israel America

Academic Exchange and the Rabin Center. This research would not have been possible without generous support from the Crown Family Middle East Research Fund at the Buffett Center for International and Comparative Studies.

Parts of Chapters 1, 2, and especially 6 have appeared in "The Myth of Military Myopia: Democracy, Small Wars, and Vietnam," *International Security*, 34(3) (Winter 2010), 119–157; and "Explaining U.S. Military Strategy in Vietnam: Thinking Clearly about Causation," *International Security*, 35(3) (Winter 2011), 124–143.

Working with Cambridge University Press has been very satisfying. I thank the team of John Haslam, Carrie Parkinson, Jonathan Ratcliffe, and Jo North for their combination of feedback, efficiency, support, and attention to detail.

On the personal front, Pat and Richard Light have both provided gentle counsel and family support for which I am most thankful. I'm not sure Andrew and Máire Caverley knew the whirlwind they would reap from weekly trips to the library, time spent abroad, and constant support but I could not have asked for more supportive parents throughout my life. My children, Anja and Felix, have been my greatest joy and distraction. Most of all, I thank Jen Light. In addition to being my most important companion, she has been an exemplar of professional achievement, wonderful parenting, and common sense.

1 | Introduction: sources of democratic military aggression

In wealthy democracies, the preparation for and conduct of military conflict has largely become an exercise in fiscal, rather than social, mobilization. How does this development influence when democracies choose violence as their preferred tool in international politics? When do voters have a moderating influence on foreign policy, and when do they allow or even encourage their leaders to pursue gains through military coercion, even at the risk of overstretch? Why do democracies often pursue a military doctrine ill-suited for the war at hand?

Contemporary political scientists appear optimistic that democracies pursue grand strategies enabling them to be, like George Washington, first in both war and peace. Yet confidence in democracy's superiority at international politics is a relatively recent development. One does not have to look far into the past to see that the current consensus would surprise the more pessimistic appraisals of Cold War thinkers such as Raymond Aron, George Kennan, Walter Lippmann, and Hans Morgenthau. Nor do the classic works of Machiavelli, Rousseau, Kant, and de Tocqueville agree on democracies' relative peacefulness or their ability in war.

Democracies have fought foolish wars, built massive militaries, and have shown a remarkable enthusiasm for imperialism. Democracies account for 17 of the world's 20 largest defense budgets (not counting Russia), with the United States alone responsible for 40 percent of the world's defense spending (SIPRI, 2013b). While these democracies' expenditures remain "affordable" based on the size of their economies, they represent enormous opportunity costs in terms of the provision of domestic public goods or private consumption. Democracies specialize in the acquisition of expensive offensive weaponry; seven of the ten states possessing aircraft carriers are democracies (nine if one counts Russia and Thailand), accounting for 19 (21) of the world's 22 (IISS, 2013). An increasing percentage of the world's "small wars" are fought by democracies. Democracies' participation in new international military interventions rose from less than 15 percent from 1960 through 1989, to 24 percent in the 1990s. From 2000 to 2009, democracies were involved in 30 of the 69 new conflicts, or 43 percent (Themnér and Wallensteen, 2012).

I seek to explain these phenomena with a systematic theory of how and when voters in a democracy will support belligerence in pursuit of international political gains. While Ben Franklin may be right about the certainty of death and taxes, grand strategy shapes how the public feels the burden of each. I focus on the distribution of costs within a democracy, arguing that the average voter will find employing the military instrument more appealing if the costs in blood are minimized and the costs in treasure can be shifted to an affluent minority. Developing a heavily capitalized military allows a democracy to arm and go to war through the mobilization of wealth rather than people. Moreover, economic inequality exacerbates the effect.

Combined, capitalization and inequality produce a form of moral hazard that shapes a democracy's grand strategy. The theory claims that a democracy's average voter (more specifically, the voter of median income) is as likely to choose an aggressive grand strategy as any unitary actor or despot (indeed perhaps even more so) as long as she can get someone else to pick up the tab. Other work has claimed that democracies try to fight wars cheaply. I argue that the average voter's ability to fight wars cheaply, at least for her, implies a democratic state may fight very costly wars indeed.

In this book I offer a theory of how and when voters in a democracy will support military aggression. The more aggressive a state, the broader the range of international political ends for which it will resort to arms. On average a more aggressive state will pursue conflicts with smaller expected values – either through reduced chances of success or lower benefits from victory. Aggressiveness does not always result in war; weak states will often acquiesce when a powerful democracy issues a coercive threat. Nor does aggressiveness always imply a higher likelihood of losing a war should it break out; regardless of the stakes, against very weak opponents a democracy is likely to be victorious. Indeed, aggressive states are likely to pursue many expensive, if victorious, wars for trivial stakes.

1.1 Democratic militarism

In short, I develop a theory of democratic militarism. The term "militarism" commonly describes a condition in which a large portion of society supports the building of an excessively strong military, believes in its superior efficacy as a foreign policy tool, and exhibits a heightened willingness to use it. I treat militarism as a variable describing how heavily military power is weighted within a state's portfolio of investments designed to increase security, its grand strategy. In a highly militaristic state, the use of force becomes increasingly attractive to a large cross-section of the public relative to the employment of other foreign policy tools (or doing nothing).

Alfred Vagts (1959) portrays militarism as inefficient, leading to the construction of a military and its use in ways not designed to win wars at the least cost in blood and treasure to the state. Yet a higher level of militarism is perversely also likely to lead to more military conflicts, ones that are less likely to end well for the state. At extreme levels the state pursues counterproductive policies that ultimately reduce its security.

Conventional wisdom in policy and social science regards militarism to be extremely unlikely in mature, robust democracies.[1] This lack of inquiry into democracies stems from defining militarism as a civil–military relations crisis, a rare but dangerous situation in which the military penetrates the very fabric of society (Van Evera, 2001), and dominates the civilian government in terms of foreign policy decision-making. Liberalism is therefore not only considered militarism's antidote but also its antithesis (Huntington, 1957). This unnecessarily limited definition conflates militarism as an outcome with the process causing it. If a hallmark of democracy is civilian dominance of the military, "democratic militarism" becomes an oxymoron.

In the wake of the 2003 Iraq War, several books have diagnosed and examined a form of militarism specific to the United States

---

[1] Michael Sherry (1995, xi) eschews the term as "too politically charged" in favor of "militarization." While limited to the twentieth-century United States, his subject is much broader than mine, referring to a "process by which war and national security became consuming anxieties and provided the memories, models and metaphors that shaped broad areas of national life."

(C. Johnson, 2004a; Mann, 2003). Andrew Bacevich (2005, 6) attributes the pathology to the perfect storm of

military officers intent on rehabilitating their profession; intellectuals fearing that the loss of confidence at home was paving the way for the triumph of totalitarianism abroad; religious leaders dismayed by the collapse of traditional moral standards; strategists wrestling with the implications of a humiliating defeat that has undermined their credibility; politicians on the make; purveyors of pop culture looking to make a buck.

In these recent accounts, militarism – even in a well-established democratic republic like the United States – remains an elite-driven phenomenon. Indeed the only group excluded from Bacevich's *dramatis personae* is the public. Jack Snyder describes the American public as irrational, passive, but innocent dupes, "psychologically primed" by "the September 11 attack and the easy victory over the Taliban" to support preventive war and ignore the possibilities for quagmire (Snyder, 2003, 39).

This book does not let the public off the hook, and challenges the consensus that militarism can only result from the perverse actions of a selfish elite, taking advantage of personal benefits "without taking fully into account the full range of costs likely to be incurred" (Bacevich, 2005, 206). Political economic theory suggests that voters are just as capable of such self-centered policies. In September 2011, 50 percent of poll respondents thought that, despite a decade of fighting two major land wars in Asia, the conflicts in Iraq and Afghanistan had "made very little difference in their life" (Pew Center, 2011).[2] At the nadir of the American war in Iraq in March 2006, only 39 percent of a poll's respondents cited a negative (14 percent positive) effect on them personally (Gallup/CNN/USA Today, 2006).

Shielding Americans from the costs of war did not start in the new millennium. A 1967 Harris poll shows that only 44 percent of respondents felt that their personal lives had been "affected" by the Vietnam War. Among those affected, more respondents (32 percent) cited inflation than casualties (25 percent). However, responding to the question,

---

[2] Interestingly, only 26 percent thought that military members and their families had "unfairly" sacrificed more than other Americans. In addition, an implausible-to-me 56 percent claimed to have a good friend or family member who served in either of the wars, and thus perhaps we should take public opinion polls with many grains of salt.

"What two or three things about the war in Vietnam most trouble you personally?" 31 percent said the equivalent of casualties or killing; 12 percent said lack of progress; and only 7 percent said rising cost.[3]

Nor is this process limited to the United States. In September 1957, at the height of French mobilization for the Algerian war, although 51 percent of French respondents named the conflict as the most important problem *for France* only 9 percent responded similarly "for you and your family personally" (Merom, 2003, 104). This was by design. By the end of 1955, France had deployed 180,000 French soldiers to Algeria, and the war cost $137 million that year. By 1957, troop numbers, many of them conscripts, had increased by two-and-a-half times to 450,000. But spending on the war had risen by a factor of nearly *eight* (to $1.1 billion, see Spruyt, 2005, 71). Sending conscripts was unprecedented for a French colonial war (Algeria was formally part of the metropole), but the middle class was largely spared through numerous exemptions, and the conscripts themselves largely shielded from the fighting (Merom, 2003). Indigenous recruits made up 90 percent of the units tasked with *quadrillage*, the pacification of the countryside. These *harkis* were supported by a fast-moving, largely professional, reserve force (much of it Foreign Legion), designed to move quickly to the enemy and engage with great violence (Alexander and Keiger, 2002). Even the militarily decisive campaign of 1958 known as the "Challe Plan" only involved about 35,000 (elite) soldiers (Griffin, 2010, 577). Responding to both domestic and international politics, the French developed what historian Jean-Charles Jauffret called a "two-speed army" (Porch, 2008).[4]

This book argues that, if the contemporary United States serves as a poster child for democratic militarism, it is not the result of a set of uniquely American contingencies. Rather, the potential for this

---

[3] The same questions were asked in March 1968, immediately after the high US casualty rates resulting from the Tet offensive. More than half of the respondents thought that the war had affected them personally, and half of these identified inflation and taxes as the principal source. Although only 9 percent knew someone who had been killed in Vietnam, "concern" over the drafting of a son or husband rose to 37 percent. As for the war's other "troubling aspects," 44 percent cited US casualties, and 7 percent cited financial costs. Harris Collection, No. 1734, July 1967; Harris Collection, No. 1813, March 1968.

[4] To the point that elements of the professional army attempted to overthrow the Fourth Republic.

pathology exists in any system where the majority of citizens have an important influence on policy. A suboptimal, militaristic grand strategy can result from rational calculations on the part of the average voter, and no marketplace of ideas will cure it. While taking on a very different appearance than that of nineteenth-century Prussia and twentieth-century Imperial Japan, militarism remains feasible in a state where its military has little connection to society yet remains entirely dominated by the voters' civilian representatives.[5] Indeed, in a democracy this is a prerequisite.

1.1.1 Small wars of choice

While the theory presented in this book enhances our understanding of how democracies prepare for, choose, and participate in conflicts ranging in scale from World War II to the recent Libyan revolution, it primarily seeks to explain influences on democratic involvement and performance in so-called "small wars." The venerable US Marine Corps' "Small Wars Manual" defines these conflicts as "undertaken under executive authority, wherein military force is combined with diplomatic pressure in the internal or external affairs of another state whose government is unstable, inadequate, or unsatisfactory for the preservation of life and of such interests as are determined by the foreign policy of our Nation." As the first phrase implies, small wars do not require national mobilization, although this does not obviate the need for public support. They are fought by a powerful state against a weaker state or nonstate actor ("weak actor" for simplicity). A small war is one of choice; it may be consistent with the strong state's grand strategy but not essential to it.[6] The strong state's aims are limited or political, and success often requires the weak actor's compliance.

Because strong states tend to enjoy overwhelming conventional military superiority, weak actors will often resort to unconventional strategies such as insurgency or terrorism. Fighting an unconventional war is a daunting task even for powerful states. Usually it demands tremendous investments in intelligence gathering and a deep understanding of a foreign culture. Success requires gaining the allegiance, or at least

[5] See Shaw (1991, 14).

[6] For reasons I lay out in the next chapter, this book does not address democracies in their own civil wars, of which there are relatively few (although Colombia and India are glaring exceptions).

acquiescence, of local noncombatants by providing personal security and economic stability. Firepower, when not used with the utmost discrimination, will likely have counterproductive effects. In general, no good substitute exists for boots on the ground.[7]

The principles behind a successful counterinsurgency (COIN) campaign have remained largely consistent over at least the past half century (Gray, 2006; Thompson, 1966). Indeed, there exists a remarkable amount of agreement on how states lose small wars. Ivan Arreguín-Toft (2005) demonstrates how a conventional offensive campaign against a guerrilla warfare strategy will likely result in a win (or at least a "non-loss") for the guerrillas.[8] Jason Lyall and Isaiah Wilson (2009) find that mechanized militaries are less effective because of attendant collateral damage, poor intelligence-gathering ability, and inability to secure the population. Given the unsuitability of a conventional, mechanized military for COIN, Arreguín-Toft seconds Eliot Cohen's (1984) reasonable observation that a state intending to both fight small wars and deter large ones must build two different types of militaries.

Other authors who study counterinsurgency observe that the strong state's regime type makes little difference in the outcome of such conflicts (Mack, 1975; Lyall, 2010), but this finding clashes with the quite strong track record of democracies in conventional wars (Reiter and Stam, 2002).[9] The mosaic plots in Figures 1.1a and 1.1b use two data sets to compare performance in major wars (battle deaths exceeding 1,000) to outcomes of conflicts where a state fights an insurgency outside of the state's territory.[10] Whereas democracies win 62 percent of larger, generally conventional, interstate wars, they only win 47 percent of the counterinsurgencies (non-democracies win 40 and 58 percent respectively). As shown in Figure 1.1b, democracies are no more likely than non-democracies to win, and considerably more likely

---

[7] Friedman (2011) sheds a skeptical light on the traditional 20:1,000 ratio of counterinsurgents to population, but does show, unsurprisingly, that more troops increases the likelihood of a successful outcome.

[8] Arreguín-Toft admits to having little to say on how these choices are made, although the book acknowledges that these are likely to be a function of anticipated costs.

[9] See Desch (2002) and Downes (2009) for empirical challenges to the democratic victory hypotheses.

[10] Figure 1.1a's data are from a source skeptical of democracies' performance in these wars (Downes, 2009). Other sources claim democracies win as much as 93 percent of such conflicts (Reiter and Stam, 2002).

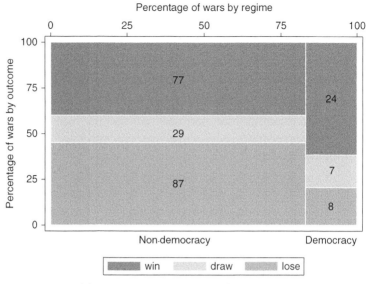

(a) Interstate wars, 1816–1990 (Source: Downes, 2009)

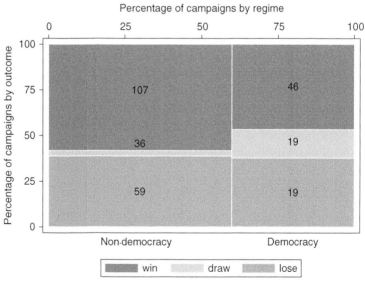

(b) Third-party interventions against insurgencies, 1808–2002 (Source: Lyall and Wilson, 2009)

Figure 1.1 Comparing conflict outcomes by regime

to "draw," against an insurgency. Given the large body of research claiming that democracies deliberately pick unfair fights and tend to win, this is a puzzle.

While arguing that regime type does not affect overall performance against insurgencies, Lyall (2010) also notes that democratic counterinsurgency efforts are more likely to be wars of choice abroad and tend to employ heavily capitalized militaries. Controlling for these and other factors, democracy has little independent effect on war outcome. But if democracies are more likely to select challenging third-party conflicts, and are more likely to use a capital-intensive doctrine while doing so, then regime type may well play a role. The underlying causes of these tendencies remain unexplained.

Finally, this book points out an under-appreciated aspect of small wars: whether or not democracies win more often than non-democracies misses a very important point. Britain used airpower in 1920 to crush the forces of the so-called "Mad Mullah," a figure so ridiculous to Western eyes that he became a punchline in P. G. Wodehouse's novel *The Swoop!* But the resulting British Somaliland protectorate provided few security benefits to Britain, draining the Colonial Office budget to boot (Samatar, 1989). At any given moment for any given war winning beats losing. However, spending blood, treasure, or both to win a war that provides few benefits should not be considered a policy success. But in most empirical work, as the Peninsular War officer and historian William Napier once wrote, "success in war, like charity in religion, covers a multitude of sins." Therefore, in addition to explaining failed campaigns, this book explores when democracies are likely to pursue costly victories for trivial gains.

1.1.2 *Why focus on democracies?*

A remarkable consensus exists within political science (and indeed outside of it) that, when democracy "works," a moderate, effective foreign policy results.[11] The many studies uncovering such findings as democratic peace and democratic victory suggest mechanisms unique to this type of government. Nonetheless enough empirical anomalies exist to justify reexamining democratic foreign policy in order to improve our

---

[11] As I show, even many branches of realism agree on this point, exceptions being Mearsheimer (2001), Desch (2002), and Downes (2009).

understanding of how and why democracies pursue coercion and go to war. Although unconvinced that it is their extraordinary and enlightened foreign policy that distinguishes them from other regime types, I, like much of the field, examine democracies separately.

I also focus on democracies for the same reason Willie Sutton robbed banks: that's where the international politics is. Their number has increased considerably since the end of the Cold War. More importantly, most of the international system's powerful states are democratic, including 18 of the world's 20 largest national economies.[12] Three of the five permanent members of the UN Security Council and two of the four rising "BRIC" powers (Brazil and India) are robust democracies. Democracies have built the world's most powerful militaries and possess the bulk of its offensive and power projection capability. Because of their relative wealth and power, democracies have more opportunities to use their militaries to advance their interests abroad. Even small differences in how democracies conduct themselves internationally relative to other regime types will have important effects on international politics.

1.1.3 Cost internalization and democratic exceptionalism

I use the term "democratic exceptionalism" to describe the large body of research claiming that democracies conduct their security policies differently than do all other regime types. This book challenges and adds to the huge body of work claiming democracies pursue more effective grand strategies compared to other regime types due to the role of the voter, a school of thought inspired by and providing one explanation for the absence of wars between democracies (Doyle, 1986).[13] This book is not about a dyadic peace: democratic, capitalist, or otherwise; and few scholars claim democracies to be innately more

---

[12] Over half of the world's 20 most populous countries are also democracies.

[13] Other posited mechanisms for the democratic peace exist, such as the norm-based arguments (Maoz and Russett, 1993; Owen, 1994; Farnham, 2003; Hayes, forthcoming), and institutional arguments such as the role of democratic transparency (Schultz, 2001; Schultz and Weingast, 2003; Lipson, 2003). Indeed experimental evidence suggests that norms do a better job of explaining democracies' friendly relations than cost–benefit analyses (Tomz and Weeks, forthcoming). However, these explanations have rarely been extended to the other aspects of democratic foreign policy behavior that both cost internalization theories and this book seek to explain. Nonetheless, even these arguments rest on the electorate weighing the merits of the case and

pacific than non-democracies. However, much work has identified other exceptional elements of democratic grand strategy beyond the regime type of their preferred targets.

Many findings of democratic exceptionalism in International Relations (IR) rest on the assumption of cost internalization within the electorate, where "citizens and subjects – rather than presidents and monarchs – fight in wars, die in wars, and pay taxes to finance wars. In most cases, it is not in the citizen's self-interest for the state to go to war" (Chernoff, 2004, 54). Office-seeking executives requiring the support of a large number of voters cannot bribe a small elite with private goods. Instead, democratic leaders "survive on the basis of their public goods performance" including military victory (Bueno de Mesquita et al., 1999, 2003).[14] Since those holding ultimate political power also pay for these public goods, elected leaders must provide these goods efficiently, leaving as much wealth as possible in the hands of the voter for consumption. Democracies thread the needle of providing the voter with both more public goods and lower taxes for these goods compared to non-democracies. In short, democracies get the most bang for their defense buck (Lake, 1992; Bueno de Mesquita et al., 2003).

This mechanism is used to explain why democracies fight shorter wars (Bennett and Stam, 1998; Slantchev, 2004), prefer to negotiate (Bueno de Mesquita et al., 2003; Filson and Werner, 2004), win the wars they do initiate (Siverson, 1995; Bueno de Mesquita et al., 1999; Reiter and Stam, 2002), suffer fewer civilian and military casualties in battle (Valentino et al., 2010), and spend less money on defense in peacetime but more in wartime (Fordham and Walker, 2005; Goldsmith, 2007; Valentino et al., 2010). For the book's purposes, I have consolidated the many findings of democratic exceptionalism into the following implications:[15]

---

making their opinion known, and surely the price of war must be a crucial factor in this.

[14] Like many others including Bueno de Mesquita and Downs (2006) I collapse this arrangement of a large selectorate and winning coalition into the term "democracy."

[15] Note that not every work within the democratic exceptionalist canon agrees on all these points. Reiter and Stam (2002), for example, argue that democracies do not expend more wartime resources, but rather their superior performance is due to their soldiers' tendency to fight with more initiative and better leadership.

(i)   Democracies tend to pursue public goods, including security.
(ii) Democracies tend to win military conflicts, largely due to choosing "unfair fights."
(iii) Democracies expend fewer resources on defense in peacetime, but try harder in wartime.
(iv) Democracies employ their resources efficiently in wartime.
(v)   Democracies are less likely to fight and more likely to negotiate during crises.
(vi) Democracies are more likely to exit expensive wars and accept a negotiated outcome.

The theory advanced by this book addresses all these implications, concluding that some hold, others fail, and still others require qualification. My theory does not contradict many of the preexisting findings of democratic exceptionalism, although it helps us better understand some aspects, such as the "unfair fights" tendency. It accounts for important anomalies to democratic exceptionalism's empirical track record by showing why democracies will persistently fight certain types of wars poorly. Moreover, it shows that certain important international political outcomes result from domestic level mechanisms identified by neither democratic exceptionalism nor its critics.

1.2 Cost distribution theory in brief

Many sources internal to a state can encourage aggression, and this book does not seek to exhaust them. Instead, I examine the effects of one important component intrinsic to democracy: the vote. I assume that the (perhaps retrospective) approval of the voter is a *necessary condition* for democratic aggression.[16] From this starting point, the next chapter lays out my theory of cost distribution.

Using a theory of the preferences of the average voter (more specifically the voter with median income for the state) for security and for consumption, I argue that, like any public good, grand strategy contains redistributive potential and therefore wealth inequality plays a role in its provision. In particular, increased military capitalization lowers the cost of arming and military conflict for the median voter.

---

[16] This is not to say that leaders of democracies do not engage in wars unlikely to be supported by the public, only that democracy is not "working" in these cases.

Having shown theoretically how the costs entailed by grand strategy can vary for the median voter, I go on to explore the implications of this finding for international politics, showing that a redistributive military leads to both increasing military aggressiveness and sub-optimal warfighting. Economically unequal and heavily capitalized democracies are more likely to threaten, initiate, and join small wars; and will often fight them in ways that make winning less likely.

A "small but effective corps of politically expendable Legionnaire forces" combined with copious firepower delivered by Jaguar fighter-bombers enabled France to become embroiled in three African crises (Zaire, Mauritania, and Chad) in a single month under its Gaullist president Valéry Giscard d'Estaing in 1978 (Anrig, 2009, 244). Opposition leader François Mitterrand denounced Giscard for turning France into the "Cuba of the West" (Lorell, 1989, 40). Yet upon taking power in 1981, the first socialist President in the Fifth Republic's history nonetheless continued most of the investments and interventions by previous, conservative administrations (Utley, 2000). Indeed, Mitterrand's Operation Manta in Chad was the largest deployment of French troops since Algeria, but only of a sufficient magnitude to produce a very expensive stalemate lasting over a decade (Utley, 2000, 105), costing 7 million francs a month by May 1984, and requiring special supplementary defense appropriations (Lorell, 1989, 48). Mitterrand's *bouleversement* bears a remarkable resemblance to the great liberal statesmen William Gladstone's invasion of Egypt, addressed in Chapter 5.

To show some evidence beyond historical anecdote, consider the lists of candidates for the "Coalition of the Willing," countries that contributed at least some soldiers to the invasion and occupation of Iraq from 2003 onward. Figure 1.2a lists countries that were members or about to become members of NATO in 2003, while Figure 1.2b shows states in the OECD. Each country's bar length indicates the level of inequality (gini coefficient from Solt, 2009 and OECD, 2012, respectively) and black bars indicate participation. There is little evidence of a pattern below the mean gini coefficient for either figure. However, in Figure 1.2a, only three of the 13 states above the mean gini coefficient did not send soldiers to Iraq, and in Figure 1.2b, five (including Israel) out of 14 failed to join the coalition. Above the mean, states that did not send troops (Turkey, Mexico, and Chile) had extremely high levels of inequality. The participating countries with above-average levels

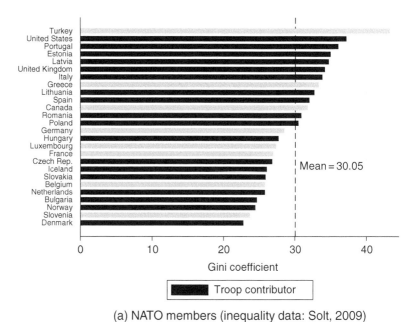

(a) NATO members (inequality data: Solt, 2009)

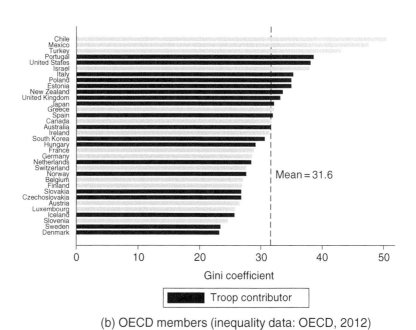

(b) OECD members (inequality data: OECD, 2012)

Figure 1.2 Inequality and "Coalition of the Willing" membership

of inequality do not appear to have much else in common. This book helps explain their decisions to send soldiers to a war of choice against a state that posed little direct threat.

1.2.1 Previous explanations for deviations from exceptionalism

In the process of explaining when democracies will deviate from the behavior predicted by cost internalization (excessive arming, aggressive and militarized grand strategy, etc.), I also address competing explanations.

The suggestion that democracies build militaries in order to avoid casualties and attempt to substitute firepower for labor is not new. One major explanation for why strong states lose small wars is that actors pursuing limited aims can accept only limited costs (Mack, 1975; Mueller, 1980; Maoz, 1989; Sullivan, 2007). Some scholars do argue that democracies are particularly likely to pursue a sub-optimal cost-minimizing strategy. Gil Merom observes a democratic Catch 22 inherent in small wars. By building a firepower-intensive, low-manpower military, "democracies can limit the size and nature of the fighting force and/or reduce the risks soldiers face in combat," but "in order to remain effective in spite of the reduction of the number and/or exposure to risks of soldiers, they must rely on higher and less discriminating levels of violence" leaving the state vulnerable to normative criticism from a vocal "educated middle class" (Merom, 2003, 21–22; see also Kober, 2008).

But this sort of explanation provokes a more essential question: given this tendency, why fight at all? Patricia Sullivan (2007, 497) identifies the problem, arguing that "extant theories cannot explain why militarily preponderant states regularly make poor strategic choices," without supplying a satisfactory answer. Sullivan claims that the war aims frequently associated with small wars can lead to increased uncertainty over the likely costs, but a strategic actor should recognize this and adjust for the larger down-side risk before entering a conflict. Sullivan does not identify a source for this congenital risk acceptance.

One potential source may be the capturing of the state by interest groups who disproportionately gain benefits from a policy while distributing the costs throughout society (Milner, 1997; Moravcsik, 1997). Examining the pathological effects of "domestic coalition politics," Jack Snyder (1991) claims that while democracies tend to experience fewer of these problems due to their governments' reflection of a broader social interest, they can still pursue over-expansion due to a poorly informed electorate or logrolling by narrow special interest groups – sovereign debt holders, the military-industrial complex, a firepower-obsessed military – rather than the will of a majority of rational voters.[17] This approach updates the classical liberal tenet that arming and war only serve the interests of the rich. Militarism and imperialism are, in John Hobson's words, "Irrational from the standpoint of the whole nation" but "rational enough from the standpoint of certain classes," and thus would be absent in "an intelligent laissez-faire democracy which gave duly proportionate weight in its policy to all economic interests alike" (Hobson, 1902, 52).

Elite capture claims in IR are partly buttressed by work, mostly confined to the study of the American case, that the public has relatively little input in the foreign policy of democracies (Jacobs and Page, 2005). Moreover, as inequality rises, political power shifts to upper income individuals, in contemporary parlance the "one percent" (Gilens, 2012; Winters and Page, 2009), as does political engagement (Solt, 2008). Throughout the book, I will address these alternative explanations and why cost distribution theory works better (or at least in tandem) to explain patterns found in public opinion, grand strategy, and conflict involvement.

1.2.2 What this book leaves out

This book does not aspire to present a comprehensive theory of all the forces leading to the decision to fight a war, even in democracies. While democracies may indeed have fundamentally different foreign policy aims than non-democracies, the book remains largely agnostic on this point. Rather, I seek to describe what factors make the average voter more likely to resort to arms to achieve them.

Nor is this book about the United States, although its foreign policy looms large throughout the text. Indeed, comparative politics research suggests that the United States' presidential, majoritarian electoral system inhibits the redistributive mechanism theorized by this book (Brooks and Manza, 2007). While I find that in many important

---

[17] Dominic Johnson (2004) also argues that democracies tend to be more immune to "positive illusions" that bias states towards war.

ways cost distribution theory helps us understand US foreign policy, I candidly admit when it does not.

Of course, democratically-elected leaders are not completely subservient to the median voter specifically or public opinion more broadly. For example, Jacobs and Page (2005) show that many different groups within the United States influence policy-makers, business leaders being the most powerful. However, business leaders exist everywhere, whereas the potential to remove leaders by regular, broad-based elections sets democracies apart from other regime types. Thus if we are to subject democratic exceptionalism to critical examination, we must remain focused on the electorate. If an elite minority can capture the government to decide what military gets built, which countries to attack, and how to fight these conflicts without any influence from the public, then that foreign policy is not particularly democratic.

While I make stark assumptions about how a democracy works in order to get the theoretical ball rolling, in the empirical sections I take measures to control for the progressiveness of taxation, the higher political influence of the wealthy, and the potential for non-linear effects of inequality on my dependent variables. The median voter does nonetheless appear to play an important if not exclusive role in shaping democratic policy, and thus any examination of democratic grand strategy must incorporate it. Much evidence exists that, while the role of public opinion may not be explicitly causal, it constrains and influences policy-makers.[18] Other actors and institutions may play a causal role in an aggressive and militarized grand strategy, they may even be necessary, but I argue that they are not sufficient.

1.3 The book's empirical findings

A theory's worth can be judged by three criteria. First, a good theory explains more than previous attempts or at least explains the same phenomena more plausibly or parsimoniously. Second, a good theory uncovers novel facts. Finally, it should explain important cases. The book seeks to meet these criteria through a diverse array of empirical work.

---

[18] For a thorough overview of research pertaining to public opinion and the United States, see Shapiro (2011).

The quantitative analysis covers a large number of diverse countries over the years 1960 to 2007. Chapter 3 shows that public opinion polling across 37 democracies reveals that the average support for increased spending on the military correlates to a country's economic inequality and military capitalization. Within 20 of these countries, the lower a respondent's income, the more supportive he or she will be for increased military spending. I then take an in-depth look at American (and, in a later chapter, Israeli) foreign policy polling to find that inequality shapes grand strategic preferences, but has little effect on respondents' perception of threats.

Chapter 4 then analyzes statistically the theory's implications for behavior at the state level. Democracies respond to a strategic threat by increasing the percentage of their defense budget devoted to the purchase of military capital. This effect may be exacerbated by inequality, although inequality's role reverses at very high levels, an interesting correlation not predicted by the book's deductive theory (but suggested in Figure 1.2). This analysis puts some empirical flesh on the theoretical bones connecting individual voter preferences to the dependent variable I am ultimately most concerned with: militarized conflict.

Chapter 4 continues by examining the correlation between capitalization, threat, inequality, and conflict behavior. Using hypotheses derived from a formal model (found in the appendix to Chapter 2), I find that economic inequality and especially military capitalization have a striking effect on the probability of a democracy attempting to change the status quo through military force ("aggression" for simplicity). I find that higher levels of military capitalization (measured three different ways) lead to increased military aggressiveness (measured three different ways) by democracies. Inequality also appears to have a positive and significant effect on the likelihood of militarized compellence independent of any role it plays in military capitalization (although again the effect diminishes at high levels). Moreover, the relationships of inequality and military capitalization to aggression differ significantly between democracies and other regime types.

I employ case studies to test the aspects of cost distribution theory that are less amenable to statistical analysis. These cases also demonstrate cost distribution theory's wider applicability by pitting it against important historiographical explanations. In each case, cost distribution theory substantially enhances the conventional understanding in both political science and historiography. While acknowledging the simplifying nature of theory and the complex nature of the past, I make the case for political science's useful contribution to historical understanding by "predicting" new facts not normally associated with current historiographical explanations, and by theorizing important social forces that are no less real despite a dearth of archival evidence.

Chapter 5 examines the simultaneous expansion of the British Empire and the British franchise from 1867 through World War I. I find that a rise in the median voter's relative inequality (thanks to the extension of wealth-based suffrage through the Reform Acts of 1868 and 1884) resulted in the increasingly aggressive expansion of the British Empire, a shifting in British goals served by imperialism, and an innovative shaping of military doctrine in the form of increasingly intensive use of "Native" (mostly Indian) military forces. Rather than a subsidy to provide economic rents for the wealthy, the Empire was a means – expensive for Britain but cheap for the middle-class voter – of maintaining great power status, securing military manpower, and avoiding conscription. In a time when warfare required massive amounts of labor, the British middle-class voter looked abroad, particularly to India, to obtain the bodies necessary for a small, conscription-free island to engage in aggressive international politics and European great power competition. This case takes advantage of clear within-case variation: large, sudden changes in both a key explanatory variable (median voter relative wealth) and in the dependent variables: the extent and form of British imperialism.

Whereas the British study encompasses a large number of conflicts, Chapter 6 focuses in great detail on a single, large war fought for important gains in a way that made success less likely. I ask why, over the course of three different presidential administrations, the United States initiated an obviously risky war, and continued to fight a losing one, in Vietnam. Increased capitalization of the military, commenced under the auspices of the Kennedy administration, allowed the Johnson administration to pursue and prolong an aggressive grand strategy, prosecuting a war whose expected value was low, and continuing to fight even as the expected value dropped. Rather than the hidebound nature of the US military bureaucracy, deliberate decisions by civilian leaders in three administrations based on their assessment of the public's preferences explain poor counterinsurgency strategy in Vietnam.

The final case study in Chapter 7, on contemporary Israel, again shows that socioeconomic status (SES) affects respondents' attitudes towards defense spending. Less wealthy people appear more willing to use the military instrument to ensure Israel's security, and respondents who believe they spend less money per month than the average Israeli household are less inclined to exchange territory for peace. In other words, poorer respondents do not inherently regard the world as a more dangerous place, yet still prefer to invest in military might and are less likely to compromise for peace, suggesting a cost redistributive component. The chapter pivots from public opinion analysis to an in-depth look at important changes in Israeli society and military doctrine culminating in the flawed prosecution of the Second Lebanon War in 2006. Due to its combination of statistical analysis of survey data and process tracing of causal mechanisms leading to poor warfighting, this chapter provides an efficient package of empirical analysis for all aspects of cost distribution theory.

2 | Cost distribution and aggressive grand strategy

The distribution of the costs of arming and war within the state influences the aggressiveness of that state's grand strategy. When all of the state's costs and benefits of a foreign policy decision are accounted for by the actor responsible for selecting the policy, costs are internalized. Shielding decision-makers from some of these costs results in cost redistribution, which can lead to moral hazard. Kant's (1991, 100) famous description in 1795 of the differences between despotic and republican approaches to war epitomizes this condition, "For the head of state is not a fellow citizen, but the owner of the state, and a war will not force him to make the slightest sacrifice so far as his banquets, hunts, pleasure palaces and court festivals are concerned. He can thus decide on war, without any significant reasons, as a kind of amusement."

Kant's suggestion for why a despot might choose war for the most trivial of reasons anticipates contemporary democratic exceptionalism. Unlike democratic exceptionalism, I relax the axiomatic (if often tacit) claim that costs are always internalized within the electorate, arguing instead that costs for the median voter in death and taxes may be much lower than the per capita cost for the state. Thus the same potential incentives for aggression that Kant associates with despotism (in kind if not degree) exist in democracies. With little skin in the game for the average voter, a condition of moral hazard exists. Two specific means distribute away from this voter: *economic inequality* and *military doctrine*.

2.1 Assumptions

To derive this theoretical claim, I begin with four broad assumptions:

(i) Security is a public good.
(ii) Voters weigh security benefits against their personal costs in taxes, conscription, and casualties.

21

(iii) The median voter gets her way in a democracy.
(iv) The existence of economic inequality.

In developing my argument, I choose assumptions that systematically eliminate from consideration many of the extant explanations for aggressive foreign policy; I create a hard theoretical case for democratic militarism. Finding the seeds of aggression within this paragon of democracy poses a severe challenge to the optimism of the current conventional wisdom. Perhaps ironically, I make this claim using the core assumptions of a large research program that *claims this sort of behavior should rarely happen in democracies.*

The book's assumptions accomplish two different tasks. I use them to show that democratic militarism, even under stringent assumptions, is theoretically possible. I then take these same assumptions and use them to derive testable hypotheses showing that the mechanism is empirically plausible. Not finding supporting empirical evidence would not make the logic of my theory any less true – the insights it provides may still help us understand how the world may work under certain circumstances – but the theory would have little explanatory power. Thus I seek to choose assumptions that are sufficiently abstract to be generalizable, but sufficiently realistic to allow for prediction (Mearsheimer, 2001, 30). Because my theory considers the voter's cost–benefit assessment, the domestic politics, and the international system, I divide my assumptions into three sets.

2.1.1 Assumptions about the voter

A theory of democracy and international politics requires a theory of the voter. I assume that individual voters are rational, fully-informed egoists. A policy developed by these hypothetical actors provides the hard case when constructing a theory of democratic militarism. As Kenneth Waltz (2001) points out, previous "first image" explanations for war, from Augustine to Spinoza to Morgenthau, focus on the imperfection of humans. Humanity is either too wicked, too flawed in its ability to reason, or too consumed by an *animus dominandi* to avoid such a wasteful activity as war. First image explanations assume that were all humans able to reason correctly, war would not find a way. I assume the voter has reached this exalted state.

These rational individuals act purposefully, have consistent preferences, and their goal is to increase, in light of these preferences, their well-being by maximizing the good in their lives (security and consumption) and minimizing the bad (casualties, conscription, and taxes).[1] They are capable of perfectly calculating the risks, costs, benefits, and thus the expected value of various policies. They are immune to satisficing behavior and to cognitive biases. These rational individuals are also risk-neutral. They will only pursue riskier policies, those with a lower probability of success, if the potential rewards justify it.[2]

These theoretical voters are fully informed. They cannot know the future with certainty, but they are excellent estimators of probability. They have costless access to any data required to make their decision; elites cannot withhold or distort information. In short not only are these theoretical voters human supercomputers, they are fortunate enough to exist within a perfect marketplace of ideas, a highly idealized scenario that many would argue is structurally impossible (Kaufmann, 2004). Clearly this is a highly conservative assumption, seemingly loading the dice in exceptionalism's favor. In practice, such a level of attention is not required of voters, who can, in the ballot booth, retrospectively evaluate incumbent officials to see if their welfare has increased (Moene and Wallerstein, 2003, 489).

Finally, these actors are egoistic. Scholars often lump this assumption together with that of the rational actor, but it is sufficiently important and controversial to be considered separately. These hypothetical individuals may be motivated by patriotism, duty, or other norms. They may care about the public welfare, and their assessment of a good's benefits may include altruistic values, but they weigh this in comparison to the sacrifices in consumption that the individual must make in order to generate it. Voters perform a cost–benefit analysis that can include everything from the taxes they pay, to concern for volunteers serving in the military, to the balance of power in the international system.

---

[1] In their analysis of conscription using survey experiments, the findings of Horowitz and Levendusky (2011) suggest these microfoundational assumptions to be plausible.

[2] Such a person is indifferent between paying five dollars for a lottery ticket with a one in ten chance of winning 50 or a one in a thousand chance of winning 5,000. More germane for the book, if the ticket price drops to two dollars, then the same rational actor will buy it for prizes as low as 20 dollars, or if the odds of winning decline to one in 25.

I assume that every voter values the consumption of her personal wealth, the enjoyment of any given public good, and the income loss from taxation in the same way. All can offer the same amount of labor and they hold their lives equally dear.[3] In evaluating elected officials' performance, the theoretical voters weigh personal costs against gains in the public good of security when evaluating the type of military the state builds, the way it fights, and the conflicts it enters.

2.1.2 *Assumptions about democracy: median voter theory*

The regular electoral accountability of leaders to the majority of the state's population is the most important element of democratic exceptionalism.[4] By this mechanism, through voters' "rewarding the incumbent government if their welfare has increased and punishing the incumbent otherwise, the parties in government have a strong electoral incentive to adopt policies that raise the welfare of a majority of voters" (Moene and Wallerstein, 2003, 489). Specific to foreign policy, Randolph Siverson (1995, 483) argues that "Because political leaders recognize the possibility of *ex post* punishment in the loss of office, *ex ante* they select policies they believe will be successful and hence lengthen their tenure." Moravcsik (1997, 531) claims that "Liberal democratic institutions tend not to provoke such [aggressive] wars because influence is placed in the hands of those who must expend blood and treasure and the leaders they choose." Given this, we must then develop a theory of what voters want from their leaders.

While I come up with a different answer than does democratic exceptionalism, the theory remains grounded in exceptionalism's assumption that it is difficult for leaders of democratic regimes to collect rents in the form of private gains for themselves or their

---

[3] I simplify the selectorate theory assumption of voters' consideration of both public and private gains from supporting a leader through an election, since in large selectorate regimes, the amount of private goods delivered to the masses becomes exceedingly small.

[4] Indeed, the most ambitious version goes so far as to endogenize other crucial institutional elements of democracy (and alternate theories of democratic exceptionalism) – "independent judiciary, free press, civil liberties, legal constraints on leaders, norms of conduct, and reliance on law" – within a theory of leaders responding to rational voters maximizing their individual welfare (Bueno de Mesquita et al., 2003, 73).

cronies (Lake, 1992). In contrast to the selectorate theory of Bueno de Mesquita et al., the voter – rather than the elected leader – becomes the central actor in cost distribution theory. Also in contrast to Bueno de Mesquita et al., I allow some heterogeneity among voters by employing median voter theory (MVT) as a very simple means of modeling democratic decision-making. Formally, MVT takes on many forms but these approaches result in the same outcome: as long as policy preferences can be ordered along a single dimension (income in this book's case) and are single-peaked, the voter at the median point of this preference (on a tax rate, a spending decision, etc.) will achieve the outcome maximizing her utility, since voters who prefer a different policy will be unable to agree on an alternative to create a new majority.[5]

While MVT requires strong assumptions, its simple, intuitive approach to deciding policies within a democracy makes it a useful tool. Importantly, it is the inherent assumption of the vast majority of democratic exceptionalism, while exceptionalism's critics concentrate on perversions of this rational, democratic ideal to explain flawed foreign policy. MVT thus serves as a parsimonious first cut at considering the democratic provision of defense.

2.1.3 *Assumptions about international politics*

MVT is most appropriately applied to collective goods, such as defense. Economists have long ranked national defense among the

---

[5] Single-peaked implies individuals prefer policies closer to their ideal point than further away. The most straightforward MVT voting rule assumes a direct democracy with no agenda setter, where an odd number of citizens vote on pairs of policy alternatives by majority-rules referenda. Alternatively, one can assume an odd number of voters and candidates from two parties who can credibly commit to policies in advance and are motivated solely by winning the election in a majority rules, winner-takes-all election (Black, 1948; Downs, 1957). To allow for stable equilibria in the presence of more than one issue dimension, we can assume that voters' preferences are only differentiated by one parameter: income or wealth. Alternatively, we can have voters vote probabilistically, vote on each issue sequentially, or divide the citizenry into a small group of wealthy and a large group of non-wealthy people. See Persson and Tabellini (2000) and Acemoglu and Robinson (2005) for reviews of these various approaches. Even works of scholarship that take partisan divides as their starting point find that voters can draw their elected agents to the political center through divided government (Alesina and Rosenthal, 1995) or supermajority requirements (Krehbiel, 1998).

purest of public goods (Kapstein, 1992); it is both nonrival – one's enjoyment of it does not diminish the value for another – and nonexcludable – everyone within the state enjoys it regardless of their contribution to it (Samuelson, 1954; Snidal, 1979).[6] In this sense the government's efforts to provide the state security, its grand strategy, is as much a public goods program as unemployment insurance or a national health service.[7] However, I assume that the basic need for security has a privileged position in the hierarchy of issues, and as the level of threat rises, other issues will become less salient. Therefore, rather than assume multiple public goods, I will subsume for simplicity's sake "peaceful" public goods within the individual's consumption.[8]

I do not claim that states, even democracies, pursue foreign policies for the sole purpose of providing a pure public good. United Fruit Company certainly profited from and lobbied for the 1954 American intervention against the left-leaning democracy in Guatemala. However, Dwight Eisenhower intervened largely to stymy communist expansion, and quite publicly campaigned on the coup in his 1956 reelection effort (Rabe, 1988, 57–62). This theory assumes that in democracies, consideration of voter approval (based on public benefits and private costs) is a necessary component of grand strategic decisions. What dictates the demand for this public good?

I assume that, while in a democracy the voter may have the helm, the ship of state remains the most salient feature on the high seas of international politics. These states interact with each other in an anarchic system where no higher authority can mediate, discipline, or control the actions of states. States possess in varying degrees the potential to harm the vital interests and even the survival of each other, and can

---

[6] An important caveat: the book focuses on the use of the military to provide security at the *international* level. This is because the public good nature axiomatically breaks down when the military is being used to protect some citizens (perhaps even the vast majority) from others. While cost distribution theory will likely help us understand this process, for the purposes of theoretical clarity, this book does not address these important conflicts.

[7] Like these programs, security – or more precisely defense spending – is unlikely to be an entirely pure public good, but rather may be best described as meeting the needs of the politically powerful middle class (Moene and Wallerstein, 2001).

[8] Even if we complicate the theory by allowing public funds to be spent on "butter" as well as guns, as long as the voter regards security as a normal good (i.e. more is better than less), no matter how much she may prefer other goods such as education, the book's theory remains sound.

never be entirely sure of each other's intentions. Given these assumptions, uncertainty is endemic to states within the current international system. Its level varies, but is never zero. In order to reduce this uncertainty, and thus to increase their security, states seek to exert control over the international environment.

I assume that security is valuable, scarce, and costly. The condition of scarcity implies that people want, but can never achieve, perfect or unlimited security and that large amounts of security cannot be obtained without making tradeoffs against other goods. While the demand for security varies with the perceived threat, it is never zero. A state or voter will always prefer more security to less; as its cost drops, the consumer will demand more.

2.2 Grand strategy as public goods provision

Posen (1984, 13) describes grand strategy as a means–ends chain to provide security to the state. More accurately, grand strategy is a calculus of means, ends, and *costs*. A state actor will choose military means to achieve the most political ends at the lowest cost to itself.[9] A grand strategy's cost to a state actor therefore helps determine its ambition. The strong do what they can, the weak suffer what they must, but all states acquire as much security as they can afford.

Military coercion is always a potential means of enhancing a state's security regardless of grand strategy.[10] Consider isolationism, an appropriate grand strategy when threats to vital interests are so low that little need exists to invest in the military, much less use it. Nonetheless, this grand strategy entails a calculated risk – "isolationism is cheap but there is no fallback position should it fail" (Art, 2003, 86) – as long as another state possesses some offensive capability (Mearsheimer, 2001, 30). If costs are especially low, small wars for relatively modest stakes may be pursued regardless of grand strategy. Jack Snyder (2003, 30) identifies the source of great power overstretch through small wars along the periphery of its sphere of influence,

---

[9] I use the term "state actor" to describe the agent in charge of the foreign policy of the state. In a structural realist theory the state actor is the state itself. In a democracy, I assume the state actor is the median voter.

[10] Security dilemma logic implies that some steps a state takes to make itself more safe will make other states feel unsafe, thus triggering security competition. This may well be, and I assume that the median voter will consider this as much as any other actor.

"Imperial rulers feared that unchecked defiance on the periphery might cascade toward the imperial core."

At some point, however, the gains from an increase in security are no longer worth the costs. The marginal costs outweigh the benefits; the more security one has the less one is willing to pay for an additional amount. As Robert Powell (1999, 75), citing Arnold Wolfers (1962), points out "military allocations thus reflect a balancing of marginal costs and benefits and not a maximization of power." This book establishes whose marginal costs matter, focusing on what happens when these costs can be shifted within the state.

2.3 Independent variable: internal cost distribution

The distribution within the state of the costs of arming and war is my theory's independent variable. In a democracy, when the median voter accounts for all of a grand strategy's costs and benefits, costs are internalized. Shielding her from some of these costs results in cost redistribution and moral hazard. Two specific factors distribute costs away from the median voter: *economic inequality* and *military doctrine*.

2.3.1 Inequality

Because most theories incorporating economic inequality and international relations focus on the inordinate power of the wealthy, my focus on the relatively poor as the source of aggression may seem counterintuitive. By giving every citizen an equal say in the affairs of the state, inequality can lead to the shifting of resources from the relatively wealthy to the relatively poor through policy.

Even in democracies, wealth is never distributed equally; the person with median income is less well off than a person with the mean income. If the median voter can set a tax rate and spend the government revenue on a service available to all citizens, she can take advantage of the potential for redistribution, a proposition known as the Meltzer–Richard hypothesis (Meltzer and Richard, 1981; Persson and Tabellini, 2000). Even with a flat income tax, the wealthy will pay a larger portion of the costs for a public good enjoyed equally by all.[11]

---

[11] The assumption that income is taxed at a flat rate is a conservative assumption, as even the least redistributive of tax systems in OECD democracies are at least

A relatively poorer median voter will support a higher tax rate since the benefit she enjoys from the public good outweighs the relatively small amount she loses to taxes.[12] For similar redistributive reasons, the median voter will prefer to tax capital rather than labor (Persson and Tabellini, 2000, 117–122). Both redistribution mechanisms influence the production of military power.

In both of these cases, the resulting level of public good provided exceeds that of a utilitarian benchmark that sums up and maximizes the welfare of every individual citizen (Persson and Tabellini, 2000, 49).[13] Median voter theory predicts that if – as many democratic exceptionalists claim – the security provided by the use of the military is a public good, then democracies should be prone to "overprovide" this as well. The effect can be intensified if militarism provides private benefits beyond security, as is often the case. The interwar French left advocated settling massive numbers of pensioned World War I veterans in Morocco, for example (Knight, 1937, 62). Importantly, the median voter need not be deliberately soaking the rich; all the theory assumes is that voters retrospectively assess what they are getting in return for what they are paying in terms of (potential) death and taxes.

Investigations of MVT's domestic policy implications receive mixed empirical support.[14] In this book, I argue that defense spending should be considered when examining the role of inequality and redistribution. Scholars object to MVT on the empirical grounds that the

---

    somewhat progressive (OECD, 2011, 228). In the empirical section, measurements of inequality will factor in the effect of income redistribution.

[12] A regressive taxation system would have a different incentive structure, but this simply does not exist in the developed democracies discussed in this book. For example, according to the Congressional Budget Office, in the United States the fifth of the population with the highest incomes were responsible for 69% of all federal tax revenue. The middle quintile paid only 9% and the lowest paid less than one (Harris, 2007). A recent survey reported that, across 29 developed economies, the top quintile provided on average 47% of the country's tax revenue. Switzerland had the lowest percentage at 37% (OECD, 2011).

[13] While utilitarianism is not necessarily the correct normative standard for many policy decisions, in terms of international politics I will argue for its appropriateness.

[14] While evincing overall skepticism in their review of the Meltzer–Richard mechanism, Kenworthy and Pontusson (2005, 450) find broadly that "countries that have experienced greater increases in market inequality also exhibit larger increases in redistribution."

wealthy exert more influence than the non-wealthy (at least in the United States). Larry Bartels (2008, 82–94), finds, for example, that elected leaders' partisan identity and the wishes of their wealthiest constituents appear to have greater influence on policy than does the median voter. However, Bartels also argues that defense is both highly salient among all income levels in the United States, has grown increasingly so from 1984 through 2004, and is weighted most heavily by middle income voters in presidential elections.

Indeed, in many ways, the provision of "guns" rather than "butter" should conform closest to the Meltzer–Richard story. At least in the United States, strong bipartisan support exists for considerable amounts of military spending (Betts, 2005), and defense spending appears responsive to public preferences expressed in opinion polls in the United States and elsewhere (Wlezien, 2004; Eichenberg and Stoll, 2011). Because foreign policy is often considered a realm apart (at least rhetorically), it may be less prone to the chaos resulting from voting over multiple issue dimensions (Gowa, 1998; Wlezien, 2004). Military preparation requires long planning windows which can dampen any cycling among political parties or voters. Successful military coercion by democracies generally requires consensus among political elites (Schultz, 2001).

2.3.2 *Capitalization and the importance of military doctrine*

While inequality is an essential prerequisite for security to contain a redistributive element, it is not necessarily the portion of cost distribution theory with the most explanatory power. How military capability is produced – the choice of military doctrine – has profound consequences for the distribution of costs, and it is the book's principal focus. Barry Posen (1984, 7) defines military doctrine as the act within a grand strategy of setting "priorities among various military forces and prescrib[ing] how those forces should be structured and employed to achieve the ends in view." Democracies' bias towards capitalized militaries represents a doctrinal preference on force structure, while firepower-intensive warfare is a form of force employment. Both the structural and employment aspects of doctrine can have distributional effects.

Military doctrine operates in tandem with inequality but, since every state has a skewed distribution of wealth, much of the "work" in explaining variation in militarism is done by the former. Whereas relative wealth fluctuates within a relatively narrow band over time, with long periods of increase and decrease, for at least the past century military doctrine, aided by technology, has allowed the average voter to lighten her burden of war considerably. This leads to the central claim of my theory: the more military coercion becomes an exercise in fiscal rather than social mobilization, the more prone a democracy will be to what the British socialist Sidney Webb called in World War I "the conscription of riches" to fund an increasingly aggressive foreign policy.[15]

The provision of security through military doctrine unfolds over multiple steps. The actor in charge of the state – facing an environment of varying threats, risks, and insecurity – first decides how much to spend on the military (i.e. the tax rate), then what form this military should take, and finally whether to use it for coercion.[16] A forward-thinking individual will anticipate these subsequent decisions when setting the tax rate.[17] She will consider the sorts of hostilities her state may encounter and construct a military to be as effective as possible for the lowest cost. And of course, in the midst of military conflict, she should adjust her military to perform more effectively given the feedback from any fighting.

Military power can be stylized as the output from a production function consisting of the two factors of capital (tanks, planes, ammunition, even human capital provided by training) and labor (soldiers, sailors, etc.). One factor of production can serve as a substitute for the other. For example, a heavily capitalized military can make up for a small population. However, capital and labor are imperfect replacements and show diminishing returns; given a hundred tanks and ten soldiers, adding another tank will not produce as much military power as another soldier. In economic terms these factors exhibit a declining marginal rate of technical substitution. Until it is possible to

---

[15] For work linking defense spending to left-leaning governments, see Narizny (2007) and Whitten and Williams (2011).

[16] Even status quo powers can use a military for coercive gains through extended deterrence.

[17] If we wish to complicate the theory by assuming voters only evaluate candidates retrospectively, then the forward thinking will be done by the elected official anticipating reward or punishment at the polls (Moene and Wallerstein, 2003, 489).

build a military made entirely of robots, defense requires some of both factors.[18]

Conscription as a flat tax, casualties as a public bad

Tax revenue can pay for both the capital and labor inputs. Personnel also can be supplied through conscription, a taking of property in the form of a citizen's labor and, potentially, life (Horowitz et al., 2011). Even in the United States, the possibility of conscription remains salient and reduces support for war (Horowitz and Levendusky, 2011). A "flat tax" form of conscription – every citizen has an identical risk of being drafted – means that every person contributes equally to the military labor force, while a flat tax on income would result in the wealthier paying a higher share of the fiscal costs of defense. Therefore, even if the odds of being conscripted are equally distributed, the median voter will demand that a larger amount of the military budget go towards the purchase of capital, thereby reducing her risk of conscription. Consequently, as many people believe, the shift from a conscript to an all-volunteer military lowers the cost of conflict for the median voter, all things equal. In July 1946, only 44 percent of Dutch respondents favored sending conscripts to Indonesia, but 74 percent favored military action as long as the force was limited to professionals and volunteers (Spruyt, 2005, 166).

Margaret Levi (1997, 36–37) usefully distinguishes between small and large demand military scenarios, concluding that in the former, the public will prefer an all-volunteer military, whereas in the latter the public will prefer conscription without elite exemptions. I argue that a capitalized military results in more scenarios meeting the small demand category, and also reduces the risks to the median voter in a large demand scenario. The median voter normally will be happy with an expensive, all-volunteer force; but once the level of threat creates a demand for labor that reaches into the middle class, the voter will support a military supplied through a fair draft whose conscripts are protected by large amounts of capital (Vasquez, 2005). During the heyday of its empire, the French almost never used conscripts in its territories, preferring (like Britain) to rely on indigenous fighters

---

[18] Even then this is likely to be prohibitively expensive and may very well result in a war between humans and machines programmed to enslave us all, a public bad.

and the Foreign Legion. The development of France's nuclear *force de frappe* – largely adopted to make up for the losses in prestige and military manpower as the French empire dwindled – illustrates the political potential and the strategic tradeoffs in the mechanism of substitution. Charles de Gaulle, along with the French left and right, was dedicated to conscription for political and cultural reasons. This military of draftees was unlikely to fight anywhere, including central Europe. The nuclear deterrent was, in part, an extremely expensive means of ensuring these conscripts would never see battle (Clayton, 1988, 46; Horne, 1984, 386).

While the assumption of the draft is a useful simplification for theoretical purposes, there are many other reasons for the median voter to favor a capital-intensive military. Casualties are also a public bad; people do not want to see their fellow citizens killed. Additionally, in reality the less wealthy are more likely to be drafted, are more likely to join an all-volunteer force, may gain jobs from domestic weapons manufacturing, and often regard military service as a means of acquiring human capital (Appy, 1993; Cooper, 1977; Kriner et al., 2010). US military personnel are one of the few types of labor that enjoy solid and secure benefits that have far outpaced inflation and the larger labor market thanks to a series of pay raises granted by the government over the past decade (Congressional Budget Office, 2012). The median voter will therefore accept a higher tax to build highly capitalized militaries in both peace and in war, since such militaries redistribute money and skills through jobs and training as well as reduce the risk of conscription and casualties. In short, a capitalized military not only results in the median voter doing less of the fighting herself, but also will generally allow someone else's resources to fund the costs of war.[19]

While I theorize that democracies prefer capitalized militaries and capital-intensive doctrine, clearly a state's capital and labor endowments play a crucial role in determining military structure and success. Nor do I claim that inequality is the sole source of capitalization in a modern democratic military. Multiple causal paths besides the median voter's redistributive preferences can lead to this. Wealth, population age, level of education (itself a form of capitalization), and

---

[19] Geys (2010) shows that public opinion responds to both casualties and the financial cost of war.

geography all influence the form a military takes and correlate with democracy. The United States and its allies built high quality militaries to counteract the Soviet Union's quantitative advantage, and continue to focus on deterring conventional threats from countries like China. However, whether or not one treats the emergence of capital-intensive militaries as exogenous to median voter preferences, such a military reduces the median voter's likely costs of conflict, thereby making coercion more attractive. Regardless of their origins, capital-intensive militaries create incentives for the average voter to pursue an aggressive grand strategy, keeping her private costs modest even as the state's costs mount. In the famous words of Robert McNamara about the exorbitantly priced anti-infiltration barrier planned for Vietnam, "Get on with it for God's sakes, it's only money!" (Halberstam, 2001, 630).

Substitutability through doctrine

The ability to replace military labor with capital, shifting the burden of defense further onto the rich, is constrained in part by the available substitution technology, a broad concept that includes both tools and techniques, what Posen describes as "structure" and "employment," respectively. The right tools can increase the output of military power with the same amount of inputs, or increase the effectiveness of one's favored factor of production. A bulldozer makes one person much more effective at moving earth, but for the purposes of archaeology it is a disastrous substitute for several individuals wielding small chisels and brushes.[20] Nuclear weapons bring a lot of bang for the buck, but their usefulness for operations other than deterrence in service of the most vital of interests is limited.

The Rif Rebellion in Morocco aptly illustrates how different combinations of capital, labor, and doctrine (and regime types) produce military power. Prior to 1923, non-democratic Spain relied on an under-equipped and poorly trained conscript force to hold down its last major colonial possession. Rifian forces, under the remarkable Abd el-Krim, massacred up to ten thousand Spanish soldiers in the

---

[20] I am less concerned with substitution of one form of capital for another in the pursuit of lower savings, as this does not vary across regimes. Both Khruschev and Eisenhower used nuclear weapons to avoid the capital and labor costs of large-scale conventional forces (and despite the two states' different capital endowments).

battle of Annual. The rebel artillery may actually have been superior in quality to that of the Spanish (Laqueur, 1998, 185).

The military dictator Primo de Rivera seized power in 1923 after the disaster, scaling back Spain's ambitions and renewing its capability. With fewer ties to the Church and associated oligarchs, he quickly reformed the army by replacing many conscripts with indigenous *Regulares* and the newly formed, and misleadingly named, Spanish Foreign Legion – a professional force that was 90 percent Spanish (Alvarez, 1999, 82). Rivera curtailed Spain's Moroccan commitments with a policy of "semi-abandonment" and may have left altogether had el-Krim, flush from mauling Spain, not attacked French Morocco.

While less appalling than Spain's casualties, the Rifian army handed the undermanned French forces a series of stinging defeats and losses of up to 20 percent to their deployed soldiers (Thomas, 2005, 212), numbers that were censored in France (Harris, 1927, 203). France promptly entered the war, and with its new and powerful French ally, Rivera initiated a reconquest and pacification campaign, with a division of labor among the allies.

While securing the Rif through an amphibious assault had been mooted since 1909, the pre-dictatorship Spanish army did not have the equipment. The eventual landing at Alhucemas was an ambitious masterpiece of combined arms warfare, skillfully employing airpower, naval gunfire support, and armor (Alvarez, 1999; Woolman, 1968). Casualty rates for Spanish legionnaires approached 40 percent over the campaign (Alvarez, 2001, 235). Spain's ally France provided naval and air support, but no soldiers, for the landing.

On the French front, the socialist *Cartel des Gauches* government in Paris replaced the legendary colonial warrior Louis Hubert Lyautey (who coined the term "oil spot") with Philippe Pétain, who had no colonial experience but did have a famous love of firepower.[21] The French army (which contained significant numbers of metropolitan troops along with the Foreign Legion and colonial forces) cautiously but inexorably advanced northward over fall and spring campaigns (Pennell, 1986, 198). A disgusted Lyautey described "the military organization, doctrines, methods and programs currently installed in Morocco" as "heavy, slow, inappropriate for the country and too

---

[21] Thomas (2005, 216–217) discusses the political jockeying of the socialist parties over the Rif War, and the fear of losing bourgeois voters.

costly for the French budget" (Gershovich, 2000, 138–139).[22] In late 1925, French prime minister Paul Painlevé could report to the French legislature that while 2,176 French soldiers were killed in Morocco, only 632 were actually French (Harris, 1927, 247).

The past century has seen a rise in labor-augmenting technologies favoring the use of capital over labor in conventional warfare (Biddle, 2004), as it has in most forms of production.[23] But, even in earlier times when labor formed a much larger portion of a military force, democracies found ways to let their money rather than their voters do the fighting, such as France's use of Senegalese troops, augmented by airpower, to put down rebels in Syria (Thomas, 2005). Chapter 5 makes the case that labor substitution in part underpinned the British obsession with protecting India.

Improvements in precision-guided munitions, airpower, and armor have all made a given amount of capital increasingly lethal, thereby shifting modern military force structure's capital-to-labor ratio.[24] In World War II and Vietnam, an individual infantryman cost about $1,900 (2010 dollars) to equip. Investments in Iraq and Afghanistan have increased to $17,000 per infantryman. The ratio of killed to wounded in small-unit action in these earlier wars was about 1 to 3.4. The killed-to-wounded ratio is now about 1 to 9. Likewise, the casualty rate has decreased from 3 percent to less than a third of 1 percent within close-combat small units (Scales, 2010).

Force employment (the "software" versus "hardware" of doctrine), or how one employs the personnel and materiel given the constraints of the available tools, is an equally crucial element of substitutability. Tanks and airplanes are structure; *blitzkrieg* is employment. Germany's mechanized forces performed spectacularly during the Battle of France, but the French main battle tank was technically superior, and the average French armored division had a much higher ratio of tanks to infantry, relative to the Wehrmacht. Germany employed its capital and

---

[22] In turn, one inspecting general, reporting to the prime minister, "charged Lyautey as being reluctant to 'employ all the powerful modern materials at our disposal', such as planes, tanks and machine-guns" (Gershovich, 2000, 138).

[23] Much of it the result of innovation by democratic powers.

[24] This is not a unidirectional trend across time; in an earlier time the invention of close order drill made the average peasant a much more effective fighting force and resulted in an emphasis on large, labor-intensive armies rather than capital-intensive professionals (McNeill, 1982).

labor inputs efficiently *given the nature of the conflict*: a conventional offensive against a largely static line of defense with little strategic depth.[25]

As the *blitzkrieg* example implies, war type is of equal if not greater influence on substitutability as technology. It is largely determined by the weak state's strategy, which I divide into two categories: conventional and unconventional (Arreguín-Toft, 2005). A capitalized military will be much more effective against a conventional opponent than an unconventional one. Such a fighting force dispatched Iraq's conventional forces with ruthless efficiency in both 1991 and 2003, but was poorly suited for the counterinsurgency campaign that followed the second conflict. For COIN, better tools are of minimal value in making a capitalized military more effective, and technique, while crucial, only goes so far when faced with labor constraints. Little can be accomplished without boots on the ground, yet democracies never seem to "learn," continuing to embark on these conflicts with a heavily capitalized approach.

2.4 Moral hazard

Grand strategic externalities arise when decision-makers do not bear all of the costs inherent in the choice, but instead shift some of them to third parties outside of the transaction. This can lead to moral hazard, a perverse incentive for risky behavior. The term "moral hazard," widely used in the wake of the recent global financial crisis, is often applied to incentives within an insurance policy for the insured "to change their behavior in a way that increases claims against the insurance company" (Rauchhaus, 2006, 65). For example, drivers insured against auto theft will more likely park on the street than pay for secure parking. Many domestic public policies merge the Meltzer–Richard effect with moral hazard.[26] Deposit insurance ensures that every individual's bank deposits are safe up to a certain limit (a redistributive

---

[25] France's inefficient use of its assets in building an overly capitalized military was largely the result of domestic politics, and thus is in keeping with cost distribution theory (May, 2000).

[26] Moral hazard arguments have been used in IR theory before. Extended deterrence may result in more aggressive behavior on the part of the "protégé" because the sponsor will come to its aid (Fearon, 1997; Crawford and Kuperman, 2006).

policy). Because the insurance applies regardless of the bank, an individual has little motivation to consider the bank's solvency. Indeed, she is likely to choose the higher interest provided by a bank making risky investments. I apply similar logic to building a military and its employment as a tool for coercion.

Of course, voters will not support conflicts with no prospect for benefits. Conflict remains costly for the median voter, who still pays some taxes and may be conscripted (a deductible of sorts). Rather, moral hazard increases the likelihood of entering conflicts whose expected value in increased security is outweighed by the likely total costs for the state, which are borne inordinately by the wealthy. The median voter's risky behavior is in effect being subsidized.

Second, the incentive to use the capital-intensive military exists for conflicts where substitutability is low because the decreased likelihood of winning is outweighed by the lower costs of fighting in such a manner. The result is the continued application of an inefficient military doctrine in pursuit of modest war aims, a low likelihood of victory, or a combination of the two. Indeed, the median voter will continue to support building the "wrong" type of capitalized military in anticipation of fighting small wars compared to a counterfactual cost internalized actor. The US Army's famous "AirLand Battle" doctrine of the 1980s, developed in the wake of the Vietnam War, was a conventional maneuver strategy, sometimes interpreted as the Army's ploy to avoid another counterinsurgency quagmire (Crane, 2002). Then again, the manual itself stated flatly "While AirLand Battle doctrine focuses primarily on mid- to high-intensity warfare, the tenets of AirLand Battle doctrine apply equally to the military operations characteristic of low-intensity war" (quoted in Lock-Pulla, 2004, 95).

Redistribution-induced moral hazard explains what other rational choice approaches to small wars have not, the initiation and continuation of small wars when the costs of fighting do not appear worthwhile for the democratic state. Figure 2.1 illustrates the different choices made by both a cost internalized ("unitary") actor and the median voter given a capital-intensive, and therefore redistributive, military. The y-axis describes the potential public good value provided by choosing to fight ("war"), while the x-axis describes the likely strategy of one's opponent. When the security gains are high (a vital national interest is at stake), both actors will pursue a war, and will fight it as efficiently as possible, regardless of the weak actor's

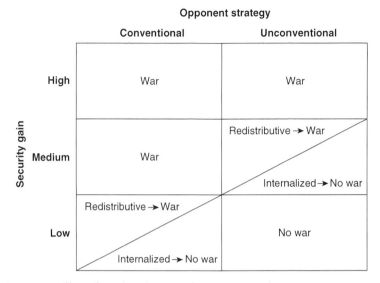

Figure 2.1 Effect of a redistributive military on war selection

strategy.[27] However, when the potential gains are modest the unitary actor will enter a war only against a conventional opponent where a capital-intensive military is likely to be highly effective. The cost internalized actor will avoid using a highly capitalized military against an unconventional opponent even for moderate security benefits. Low benefits do not justify choosing war, regardless of how effective the strong state's military doctrine might be.

The two divided boxes – "conventional-low" and "unconventional-medium" – in the median voter's decision matrix show the conditions of moral hazard. The median voter will choose wars using an efficient strategy against a conventional foe for low gains that a cost internalized actor would eschew, the bottom left box in Figure 2.1. The strong state's success may be assured, but the stakes are trivial. In Chapter 5, I argue that these conflicts characterize much of British imperial expansion in the late nineteenth century.

---

[27] Note that my theory would still suggest that the median voter would prefer to fight these wars in a way that minimizes cost without jeopardizing success. For example, Franklin Roosevelt certainly fought World War II in a deliberately capital-intensive manner. However, the differences between democracies and non-democracies are likely to be less pronounced, especially as resources are employed to the maximum.

More importantly, the median voter will use an inefficient strategy against an unconventional opponent in pursuit of moderate aims because the reduction in costs outweighs the sacrifice in expected value. My theory predicts that under the right circumstances, democracies will take steps that *will make success less likely* even in relatively important conflicts, the middle right box of Figure 2.1.

I claim in Chapter 6 that this explains why the United States fought a losing strategy for so long in Vietnam, and why Israel did not achieve its stated goals during the Second Lebanon War (Chapter 7). Conversely, while cost distribution theory suggests that democracies fight insurgencies poorly, they should excel at *instigating* them. Think of this as the Lawrence of Arabia model: a single Englishman with lots of cash helps to lop off a sizable chunk of the Ottoman Empire.

In addition to deciding *whether* the state initiates a fight, in a wartime democracy the median voter has an important say in *how* the state fights and whether it will continue fighting. Capitalization therefore serves as an independent and a dependent variable in both peace and in war. Figure 2.2 lays out the roles of capitalization and inequality in a democratic military during peacetime up to and including the decision to enter into a war, as well as in wartime when the state must continually decide *whether* and *how* to continue fighting.

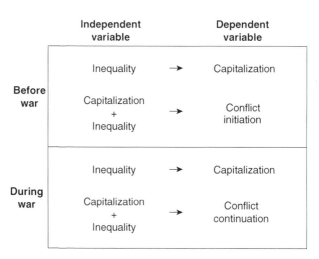

Figure 2.2 Roles of inequality and military capitalization

Some redistributive attempts to provide security combine these two ideal types. The "substitution" of the Royal Air Force and indigenous forces for the British Army not only enabled Britain to fight a trivial conflict against the Mad Mullah in Somaliland, but it was also used to secure Iraq's oil reserves in Basra, an important goal to be sure. In the 1920 rebellion in Iraq, Britain doubled the number of Royal Air Force squadrons deployed; a smaller percentage, a little over 29,000 soldiers, reinforced the existing 60,000 troops in Iraq, and 24,508 of these soldiers came from India. The operation cost the Treasury a shocking 40 million pounds. By 1922, all British Army troops were removed, with the Air Force retaining operational control, supported by Indian Army forces (Corum and Johnson, 2003, 55–57). The strategy derisively referred to by Chief of the Imperial General Staff Henry Wilson as "Hot Air, Aeroplanes & Arabs" (Omissi, 1990, 18) encouraged the Cabinet to reject the army's conservative plan of holding oil-rich Basra alone in favor of the more costly and much riskier aim of controlling all of Iraq and Palestine (Ferris, 1989, 86–97).

Finally, inequality and capitalization have powerful effects on the ability of democracies to signal their resolve to other actors. By definition if a signal becomes less costly, then it conveys less information (see this chapter's appendix). The Vietnam War shows these countervailing effects of redistribution within the United States (as well as what results when two redistributive militaries meet). The American median voter may have attempted to buy more security for herself at the least personal price, but this undermined the costliness of the international signal being sent to the opponent. American planners sought to communicate American resolve to North Vietnam (and the Soviet Union), but were limited to means, such as bombing, that were of limited cost to the American public. Not only did this degrade the costly signal, it also allowed the public to support a lengthy war. The opponents in the war fought in ways that were quite redistributive given their regime types. The United States substituted capital for labor, while the North Vietnamese General Giap, according to a close observer, regarded "any cost in Communist lives as bearable so long as a sufficient number of his troops continue to be available. His [was] not an army that sends coffins north" (Mueller, 1980, 512). The result was a prolonged and costly war, fought by extremely inefficient and (for the United States) ultimately unsuccessful means. Given the implications of cost distribution theory, it is not clear the average voter would want it another way; a Harris poll in the summer of 1967 showed that a slight majority of Americans did not feel affected by the war in any meaningful way (Lorell and Kelley, 1985, 25).

2.4.1 Strong and weak versions

The stark theory laid out above can lead to two versions in terms of democratic grand strategic behavior, depending on how direct the median voter's influence on the state may be, and how much less responsive are non-democracies. Cost distribution theory may simply describe a permissive condition: with no skin in the game, the voter passively allows the executive (or some other privileged elite actor) to conduct the state's foreign policy, including war, as it sees fit. Alternatively, the median voter may exert sufficient pressure on leaders to pursue the public good of security more aggressively. I characterize these as "weak" and "strong" versions of cost distribution theory, respectively. One's preference regarding these versions should be based on both the plausibility of the assumptions and mechanism as well as their empirical performance. Refereeing between the two, which align with the two great traditions of realism and liberalism, is of substantial interest for IR theory and public policy.

The weak version undermines the so-called "selection effects" argument (Reiter and Stam, 2002) by removing the conservative element checking executive excesses in democracy: the voter. This may be more plausible because the average voter generally does not pay much attention to foreign policy, and her opinions are strongly shaped by the executive and other elites. In a modern democracy, there is no direct way for the average voter to demand an executive start a war. Richard Sobel (2001) finds that public opinion in democracies can constrain but not provoke government involvement in foreign adventures, and thus making the cost of war cheaper for the median voter creates a more permissive environment for aggression. If increased capitalization merely removes a check on the executive, we should see more variance in conflict behavior, but not necessarily an increase.

Put differently, the weak version of the theory suggests that leaders of democracies will act no differently than those of any other regime type if left to their devices by the voter. In this case, one will be unable to reject the null hypothesis that democracies act no differently than non-democracies. While it is interesting that different states can turn themselves into billiard balls by different means, in terms of international politics it is of secondary importance. In the weak version of the theory, military capitalization leads to a realist world in which regime type "hardly matters" (Desch, 2002).

Of course, the balance of the field's empirical work claims that democracies *do* appear to work differently in important ways. The strong version of the theory delineates the circumstance under which democracies act *systematically* more aggressively than non-democracies. It rests on the claim that the average voter, approximated by the median voter, plays a pivotal role. This would provide support for many of the core principals of liberalism; at the very least regime type matters. On the other hand, the role of democracy in international politics is likely to be much less benign than democratic exceptionalism suggests. Finding empirically systematic differences of inequality, capitalization, and conscription between democracies and non-democracies, as I do, lends credence to the strong version.

2.5 Classical liberalism and alternate explanations

The most powerful alternate explanation for a link between inequality, capitalization, and militarism is the classical liberal tenet that the relatively poor have little value for arming and war, a variant of the Kantian cost internalization argument. Perhaps policies in highly unequal states, even democratic ones, favor the rich, a venerable claim in social science. John Hobson (1902, 52) famously contends that:

Irrational from the standpoint of the whole nation, [imperialism] is rational enough from the standpoint of certain classes in the nation. A completely socialist State which kept good books and presented regular balance-sheets of expenditure and assets would soon discard Imperialism; an intelligent laissez-faire democracy which gave duly proportionate weight in its policy to all economic interests alike would do the same.

Even when, goes the logic, the less wealthy spend fewer tax dollars than the rich for a given amount of defense, the marginal utility of those tax dollars for essentials such as food and shelter grossly outweighs any additional benefit from aggression. Relatedly, the marginal utility for an additional unit of defense spending will be higher for the wealthy, who have more to protect.

A variant of this argument argues that the less well-off inherently prefer "butter" rather than guns. This is not terribly problematic for the theory. Allow the median voter/consumer to distribute her income between a private good (untaxed income) and two different public goods (security and welfare). Unless welfare is strictly preferable to security at all times, the consumer will spend her money on a mixed basket of goods that reflect her preferences and the goods' prices. If her income rises, she will enjoy more of all three. If the cost of providing the two public goods drops (due to higher inequality, increased tax progressivity, etc.), she will consume more of both security and welfare (in the same proportion to each other as before). If the price of security falls relative to welfare (which I argue is the case with military capitalization), she will consume more security and less welfare.

Summing up the classical liberal logic, any correlation of democracy and inequality to military spending and aggression found by this book is best explained by the disproportionate power of the rich rather than voting by the poor.

2.5.1 Elite capture

The distortionary aggression resulting from state capture is an age-old concern of both classical liberals and Marxists dating at least to the turn of the twentieth century. John Hobson lays the blame for the Boer War squarely at the feet of Cecil Rhodes, "who used the legislature of the Cape Colony to support and strengthen the diamond monopoly of De Beers, while from De Beers he financed the [Jameson] Raid, debauched the constituencies of Cape Colony, and bought the public press, in order to engineer the war" (Hobson, 1902, 213; see also Lenin, 1987).[28] Moravcsik (1997, 517) presents this logic more systematically and less pungently. These explanations revolve around powerful elites, usually the wealthy, capturing the state apparatus and employing foreign policy as a tool for personal economic advancement, such as securing a location to invest surplus capital. Recent efforts have linked the military policy of states to the rising and declining political and economic fortunes of certain subgroups within the state (Narizny, 2007; Rowe, 1999; Rowe et al., 2002; Rowe, 2005).

---

[28] The Jameson Raid was an 1895 attempted insurrection to overthrow the government of the Transvaal in favor of British interests.

Jack Snyder (1991) describes how log-rolling between narrow economic interests can overcome the more diffuse but larger interests of the state as a whole. According to Snyder, democracies tend to experience fewer of these pathologies because the government reflects a broader social interest.[29] Democracies are therefore less prone to two forms of rent-seeking that lead to "imperialist bias" – rent-seeking by the state itself (Lake, 1992) as well as by privileged groups within the state.

2.5.2 *Failure in the marketplace of ideas*

Distorted foreign policy deliberation can also bias a state towards aggression. Many argue that democracy's superior "marketplace of ideas" makes it more immune to this. If voters have a stake in generating an optimal outcome and freedom of speech guarantees the public airing of the pros and cons of all possible policies, then opposition parties will point out the flaws in the government plan, the public will mobilize against narrow special interests, and consequently the best ideas will rise to the top.[30] This is the preferred democratic exceptionalist mechanism of structural realists, who start by deriving an objective security demand from assumptions about the international system. Given the existence of such an objective strategy, the more deliberative the society, the more likely it is to pursue this course (Snyder, 1991; Van Evera, 1999, 2001; Reiter and Stam, 2002).[31]

At least in the United States, faith in the marketplace of ideas has taken a beating recently. In Chaim Kaufmann's (2004) analysis of the Iraq War, "median voter logic can often be bypassed by elite manipulation of how issues are framed in debate," such as by emphasizing Saddam Hussein as a "madman" or linking Iraq to Al Qaeda. Government officials can mislead a reluctant public in order to bring the state

---

[29] Olson (1982) argues that concentrated interests have an inherent advantage due to the electorate's collective action problem combined with the smaller party's large gains relative to the small losses of any given voter. It is not clear why democracies would be so much worse at this than non-democracies however.

[30] As an extra benefit, these deliberations send signals to potential enemies, reducing the incentives for war due to private information (Schultz, 2001).

[31] For a compelling criticism of objective security functions, see Narizny (2007).

into a conflict they assess to be necessary (Schuessler, 2010). Sebastian Rosato (2003, 595) argues that voters are easily manipulated by the powerful, who can "drum up nationalistic fervor, shape public opinion, and suppress dissent despite the obligation to allow free and open discussion." This approach is often coupled with the theories of elite rent-seeking described above; one means of state capture is for interest groups to promulgate "imperial myths" (Snyder, 1991). If one's susceptibility to these myths correlates to income, one would see many of the same regularities predicted by cost distribution theory.

2.5.3 Civil–military disintegration

A range of explanations for aggression, particularly ill-advised aggression, blame flawed civil–military relations for poor integration between a state's grand strategy and its military doctrine. Posen (1984) argues that when international competition is high and few allies are available, a state's political forces will overcome resistance by the military and other parties to tightly bind military doctrine to the political aim of survival. According to Posen, one should observe improved integration over the course of a war, if not before one; and yet learning appears to occur quite slowly if at all in many cases. Perhaps in wars of choice, structural pressures are insufficiently strong to force integration. In either case, Posen's balance of power theory does not explain systematically poor performance in small wars by democracies or any other type of regime.

Organizational and cultural theories argue that without sufficient pressure from political leaders, elements of the national security structure, particularly the military, will pursue their own ends with little regard for grand strategy. Posen and Jack Snyder (1984) claim that bureaucratic forces push militaries towards offensive doctrine. Elizabeth Kier (1997) finds that a military's culture cannot be limited simply to a preference for the offense but again emphasizes the inability of civilian and military leaders to reconcile their differences. Deborah Avant (1996) argues that when civilians cannot agree, military leaders are more conservative in choosing war. Work specifically addressing US conduct of small wars often locates blame within its military culture. Cohen (1984, 165) argues that "The most substantial constraints on America's ability to conduct small wars result from the resistance of the American defense establishment to the very notion of engaging in such conflicts, and from the unsuitability of that establishment for fighting such wars." This area of attack has been popular within the American military intellectual community (Krepinevich, 1986; Nagl, 2005; Yingling, 2007; McMaster, 2008). This culture's existence, however, does not answer the central question: why does culture not adapt in response to repeated failure, or barring that, why do civilian planners not at least adapt to the stubborn culture?

All of these "military myopia" approaches seem to require the same solution: enhanced civilian control of the military. Poor integration of strategy and doctrine appears to be largely a function of the military being allowed to "do its thing" (Komer, 1973). Firm subordination of the military to the civilian leadership and therefore ultimately to the voter, a prerequisite for a healthy democracy, would seem to render this argument moot.

2.5.4 Non-rational explanations

All of these approaches share a commitment to the idea that aggression is rarely the average voter's fault. At worst she is simply a hapless bystander as elites and other forces set the state's foreign policy. The one research program that *does* fault the capacity of voters and their role in aggression relies on non- or extra-rational explanations for state behavior. Many versions of structural realism, a generally rational choice approach to international politics, argue that hypernationalism, clearly a socially constructed concept, must play a role in encouraging democracies to act aggressively (Mearsheimer, 1995; Van Evera, 1999; Rosato, 2003; Miller, 2007). Other approaches extend the concept of strategic culture to the public, castigating the average American in particular as suffering from a "self-delusion about the character of future conflict" (McMaster, 2008, 19), or an "optimism" which leads "US policy, including its use of armed force, to attempt the impossible" (Gray, 2006, 33). By reflecting the will of an irrational people (including the average voter), in this sense one can say that democracy is the "cause" or at least the transmission belt for risky behavior. Strategic culture approaches surely have their place in studying conflict behavior, but they also risk tautology – i.e. the United States fights a certain way because it is the United States. American exceptionalism and French *spécificité* look awfully similar; in 1978 France found its finely honed system of heavy airpower in tandem with small ground contingents engaged in three crises (Zaire, Mauritania, and Chad) simultaneously (Lorell, 1989, 40). This book identifies the underlying influences on this strategic culture common to many democracies.

2.6 Empirical implications and strategy

The theory laid out above suggests the following testable implications:

- Military capitalization reduces the costs of arming and war for the median voter
  - A democracy will respond to an increased threat by developing a more capitalized military.
  - As economic inequality rises, a democracy will develop a more capitalized military in response to a threat.

Having established that capitalization shifts the costs away from the median voter, I test the effects that redistribution has on conflict behavior. As this chapter's appendix demonstrates formally, an increase in redistribution through capitalization may not have clear effects on the outbreak of fighting. A more redistributive democracy would build a bigger military to deter a potential aggressor, thus making conflict less likely. The state would also more aggressively extend its deterrent threats to more states, potentially raising the likelihood of being involved in a conflict. In social science terms, the relationship between redistribution and war is non-monotonic. However, the theory laid out above and its formalization below do clearly show that a redistributive state is more likely to attempt to compel others for low stakes and aggressively practice extended deterrence for increasingly peripheral prizes where it prefers the status quo. Therefore, I claim:

- When internal costs are shifted away from the median voter, a democracy will act more aggressively
  - The more capitalized its military, the more coercion attempts a democracy will initiate.
  - The more economically unequal its electorate, the more coercion attempts a democracy will initiate.

Finally, I examine the roles that cost distribution plays in *how* a democracy fights during wartime. I claim that the median voter can pursue inefficient military doctrines under redistributive circumstances.

- The median voter will favor using more of the states' resources for a less effective capital-intensive wartime strategy to produce the same amount of military power as a more effective labor-intensive strategy.

In other words, in an economically unequal state with a heavily capitalized military, both war and peace will be expensive.

To empirically evaluate cost distribution theory, I first turn to statistical analysis of both the microfoundations of the theory (that is public opinion on defense spending and foreign policy) and evidence of militarism at the state level (arming and aggression). These tests evaluate the role of my explanatory variables – threat, inequality, and military doctrine – against the democratic exceptionalist null of cost internalization. Finding significant effects of substantively interesting values in the predicted direction will give us confidence that the theorized relationships hold across a wide variety of states and years.

The "large N" analyses of Chapters 3 and 4 are designed to show the theory's applicability across many cases, to take advantage of the full range of values of the dependent variables, and to overcome other potential case selection biases. The book's qualitative chapters complement the statistics rather than duplicating them via an "intuitive regression" through cross-case analysis (Collier et al., 2004; King et al., 1994). These chapters instead examine the transmission belt between the voter and foreign policy, the democratically elected government. Focusing on the grand strategic deliberations of leaders, I determine whether and how they responded to the pressure of the electorate in reacting to international threats, and why they chose a given element of grand strategy (military force) over others. If my theory is correct, elites will often choose grand strategies that will minimize costs to voters, pursuing means and ends that the elites acknowledge in their deliberations to be risky and potentially costly for the state overall. With qualitative analyses, I can more directly pit competing explanations for aggression (elite rent-seeking, lack of civilian control, etc.) against each other, primarily by zeroing on the deliberations of democratically elected leaders, and their dismay with electoral pressures. Examining decisions on military doctrine made in the midst of fighting makes sense because they are less likely to be based on wealth, population age, and maritime strategy and therefore control for the overdetermined nature of military capitalization.

Each case reflects one of the two facets of aggression hypothesized by cost distribution theory: the pursuit of many small, unfair fights for trivial gains or choosing and fighting poorly in an important war. The cases are deviant cases for democratic exceptionalism, "wildly discordant observations," that may challenge our confidence in a theory's power (Rogowski, 2004, 82). They cannot test democratic exceptionalism, since I have intentionally chosen where it has obviously failed. Rather, the process tracing allows me to find microevidence rendering other explanations for democratic aggression less plausible, while inspiring confidence that my mechanism is a necessary cause for important cases. Guided by the deductive theory, I use primary (as well as secondary) source material to uncover new evidence and revisit historical data previously not featured in IR. If one measure of a social scientific theory's worth is its ability to provide counterintuitive understandings of important cases, then this is a valuable exercise.

2.7 Conclusion

As the introduction notes, this book addresses how democracies select and fight small wars. To do so, this chapter has derived a voter preference for a capitalized military from four major assumptions: security is a public good; voters weigh security benefits against taxes, conscription, and casualties; median wealth is less than mean wealth in every state; and democratic leaders heed the preferences of the median voter. Like the democratic exceptionalist research program, the book's empirical section will find evidence that the American public weighs the benefits of limited war against the costs. Although one recent study of American public opinion assigns expectations of success as the most important factor in the public's support for a conflict (Gelpi et al., 2006), it also points out that the public more generally carries out relatively competent cost–benefit analysis. This chapter extends this logic by arguing that when the ability to substitute materiel for personnel is low, as it is against unconventional opponents, democracies may still prosecute wars using an ill-suited military doctrine (and thus a lower chance of success), because the costs remain modest for this pivotal voter.

Democratic exceptionalism's cost-internalization mechanism provides an overly optimistic assessment of democracies' discretion in how and even when they fight small wars. Neither an apolitical public, nor a dysfunctional military culture, nor a military doctrine divorced from grand strategy causes a flawed warfighting strategy. Rather, it results from political leaders' assessment of the average voter's preferences. Although claiming that democracies substitute capital for labor to reduce the costs of war for voters is not news, tying the pursuit of such a strategy to a rational voter has several novel and important implications for understanding their conduct of small wars. The most important implication of the theory (formalized in this chapter's appendix) is that an increase in redistribution, akin to Jackson and Morelli's (2007) "positive bias," will result in increased attempts at coercion, even to the point of pursuing them where the costs for the state outweigh the gains.

2.A Appendix: formalizing the theory on conflict

The formal model below, while not necessary to understand the theory for understanding cost distribution theory's explanation of conflict behavior, makes three contributions. First, it demonstrates rigorously the theory's sound internal logic. Second, formalization accounts for countervailing forces affected by cost redistribution (which raises the expected value for war, makes an opponent more likely to back down without a fight, and undermines a democracy's ability to send a costly signal). Third, the formal model helps derive hypotheses amenable to quantitative testing.

My interest in cost–benefit analysis of conflict naturally dovetails with a research tradition fundamentally motivated by the costliness of war. Bargaining models are especially appropriate for limited wars, what Clausewitz called "real" versus "absolute" wars. The bargaining model of war assumption that state policy is set by a rational actor capable of subtle calculations in an information-rich environment conforms closely to the ideal case for democratic exceptionalism, which is after all a rational theory at its core.[32] A formal bargaining model can succinctly address the influence of redistribution on several important parameters that in turn may have offsetting effects on international conflict behavior. For example, redistribution may allow the median voter to pursue more attempts at coercion, thereby increasing the probability of war. On the other hand, redistributive militaries tend to be bigger, which in turn is likely to force the opponent to back down without a fight, thereby reducing the probability of war.

While the costliness of war, and thus the logical preference by conflicting parties for a negotiated settlement, is the underlying motivation for rationalist models of war, few works in the field dwell on the role that varying levels of costs have on conflict behavior. Instead, thanks largely to the work of James Fearon (1995), rationalist research has concentrated on the factors that overcome this ex post inefficiency – imperfect information, low credibility of commitments, and indivisibility of disputed goods. In many of these models, when costs are invoked it is generally due to their informative role. Fearon (1997) divides these costly signals into two. The first, "sinking costs," involves the equivalent of burning money to convey how much an actor values a prize,

---

[32] See Reiter (2003) for a comprehensive review.

but does not enhance the actor's commitment (the costs are incurred regardless of whether one backs down from a bluff or fights). The second, "tying hands," only incurs costs if the actor backs down from threats, and is thus a sign of commitment.

Many previous models view a state's military power as exogenously given. This entails considerable sacrifice in explanatory power; arming is costly, conveys information, and raises the expected value of a war. In his examination of the "guns and butter" tradeoff vis-à-vis conflict, Robert Powell (1999) is a notable exception that suggests a reduction in the costs of war for both sides results in an increased risk of war. Branislav Slantchev (2005) develops a model in which arming serves to both tie hands and sink costs, from which this appendix borrows extensively. However, while Slantchev's model incorporates the costs (and benefits) of arming as well as war, like Powell and others it does not stray from the cost internalized actor assumption.

Indeed, few models relax the unitary actor assumption when it comes to the objective security function and thus do not allow for redistribution and other biases. One exception incorporates the concept of "political bias," the ratio of the share of benefits from war compared to the share of costs for the country's pivotal agent (Jackson and Morelli, 2007). War is possible when at least one state in a dyad is led by a leader with "positive bias," and as the bias grows, the more likely war becomes. One of the model's many important implications is that such cost–benefit biases can result in war even under perfect information, because the total pie of rewards associated with avoiding war is no longer necessarily greater than the potential gains from fighting (Jackson and Morelli, 2007, 1361).[33] Like the lion's share of the literature addressed in this book, it assumes "a negative correlation between political bias and the level of democracy."[34]

The model presented in this appendix incorporates elements of all these previous versions in a way that parsimoniously corrects some of each individual model's weaknesses. First, like Slantchev (2005), it endogenizes the decision to arm, considers the buildup of military

---

[33] Another of the model's most intriguing propositions is that it is sometimes rational for unbiased actors within a state to choose a positively biased agent who will aggressively pursue transfers, but this is only in the absence of war. Also see Leventoglu and Tarar (2005).

[34] Jackson and Morelli (2007) refer to the possibility of differential tax rates as being a source of bias for the median voter in a democracy.

54 Cost distribution and aggressive grand strategy

power to be more than a signal, and treats arming and fighting as interdependent decisions. However, unlike Slantchev, the model here relaxes the assumption of an unbiased actor. Unlike Jackson and Morelli (2007) it focuses on internal shifting of costs rather than biases in benefits, and treats security as a public good. The "action" of this appendix's model is therefore found in the distribution of costs of arming and coercion.

According to Slantchev (2005, 24) the danger of war is greatest when an aggressive state has the resources to arm for war but not enough to separate itself from the less resolved through costly signals. In this appendix I show under what circumstances an increase in redistribution increases or decreases this danger, ultimately finding that it increases the amount of resources required to signal resolve but will encourage the median voter towards more aggression anyway.

2.A.1 What must the model capture?

An information deficit is one means of making a war "rational," and sources of information asymmetry have corralled much of this research program's attention. In this appendix however, it plays a role akin to Alfred Hitchcock's MacGuffin: necessary for war to occur, but not the model's focus. Rather, I accept an information deficit as given, and concentrate on the cost–benefit analysis of the agent with control over a given state's foreign policy (the "state actor").

Since the redistribution of the costs of arming and of war will have several effects on coercive diplomacy, I choose a model encompassing all of them. Arming must be costly, but an increase in military power also changes the likely outcome of any war, and thus contains the potential to provide benefits. Arming also provides a signal to an opponent regarding one's value for the disputed asset. Finally, since redistribution should change a state actor's assessment of the feasibility of compellence and deterrence, the model should incorporate both types of coercive diplomacy.

For these reasons, I construct a model based largely on Branislav Slantchev's (2005) "Military Threat Model" (MTM). The MTM is in turn a variation of the "ultimatum game," the basis of many rational models of war. The MTM acknowledges that the mobilization of forces not only serves as a costly signal (Fearon, 1997), but is likely to increase the payoffs of a war by improving the odds of victory. The

model combines in a straightforward manner the decisions to arm and
to use coercion in the pursuit of both deterrent and compellent goals.
While in practice it is difficult to distinguish between deterrence and
compellence,[35] we can use these concepts to analyze varieties of grand
strategies, ones seeking to maintain the status quo versus revising it.
The MTM and its antecedent ultimatum game also have the benefit
of being well established, allowing me to explore nuances relevant to
this book's research question rather than prove the propositions of the
baseline model.

Redistribution

I add one element to the Slantchev model by assuming that, while the
gains from military victory are public, the state must fund arming and
war through private costs in blood and treasure (Bueno de Mesquita
et al., 2003). In turn these costs are not distributed evenly within the
state, and therefore the model assigns a crucial role to the portion
of the costs paid by the agent in charge of a state's foreign policy
("state actor"), the median voter in the case of a democracy. To do
this, I include a simple, exogenous "redistribution parameter."

Given the plausible assumption that the income or wealth (income
from now on for simplicity) of the voter at the median y_m varies
inversely with the extent of the franchise, one could consider three
generic types of "median voters" with respect to the mean (i.e. per
capita) wealth of the state $\bar{y}$. In a democracy, $y_m < \bar{y}$, in a plutarchy
$y_m > \bar{y}$, and in an egalitarian society $y_m = \bar{y}$.[36] For any non-zero level
of inequality, an increase in substitution technology – or any other factor allowing for increased military capitalization – will distribute costs
away from the average voter. In the empirical sections, I will tease out
the specific explanatory variables covered by cost distribution theory –
military doctrine and economic inequality – but for parsimony and
tractability I will assume a single redistribution parameter. The added
benefit of using a single term is that it makes the model generalizable
to other forms of redistribution and other regime types, an implication
to which I will return at the end of this appendix. The ability of the

---

[35] Was the United States trying to compel North Vietnam to cease activity in
South Vietnam, or deter it from escalating? What about vice versa?

[36] One can even go so far as to imagine an autocracy where a despotic actor
considers all the state's wealth to be her property, $y_m = N\bar{y}$ (Olson, 1993).

state actor to shift the costs of arming and war, that is to increase the redistribution parameter, undermines the quality of this costly signal, makes more instances of coercion attractive, and encourages states to pursue inefficient strategies.

2.A.2 Laying out the model

As in the original MTM I assume that only two international political actors exist. Since I am interested in part in how military spending serves as a signal, like Slantchev I will assume the target is uncertain regarding the compeller's value for the prize in the target's possession. I do not allow for multiple rounds of bargaining. I seek to calculate when the redistribution of costs makes coercion generally more attractive rather than its role in the initiation, conduct, and termination of a war-as-bargain over multiple rounds. Nonetheless my arguments should apply to these more complex games. Because the state actor is the median voter, audience costs play no role in the game.

I am more concerned with the development of foreign policy on a grand strategic level than with the signaling effects of costly mobilization for a given crisis, Slantchev's focus in the original model. For this reason, there is no "distribution of power" at the beginning of the game; a state makes an arming decision from a baseline of zero with only the other actor in mind. This arming decision is also a threat, inherently taking into consideration the military's use as a tool for deterrence or compellence. Additionally, I assume that all military spending is equally useful for both offense and defense, and, contrary to the claims I make about the diminishing returns of capitalization, I assume no inefficiency in choosing a heavily capitalized military.

The game consists of two strategic state actors with identical populations and resources, players D (the Deterrer) and C (the Compeller).[37] D possesses some asset, whether it be a disputed territory or a policy stance, that provides a valuable public good to each player of the amount V_i. The value of this asset may differ for each player, but its

[37] Identical populations allow me to focus on per capita defense preparations and the private cost–benefit calculation of the state actor. A larger population at the same per capita wealth would make the individual cost of providing the public good lower and should thus lead to more aggressive foreign policies.

maximum per capita public good value is normalized to 1. In order to defend the status quo, D possesses some exogenous military capability M_D.[38] One could make M_D a strategic decision, adding another round to the game, but the mathematical complexity of the resulting solutions overshadows any additional insight it might provide. While I assume that all parties know the defender's value for the prize, V_D, only the Compeller knows her value, V_C.[39]

Unlike the original version of the MTM, I do not assume that the costs of producing military power or of going to war are evenly distributed or internalized by a unitary state actor. Rather, the distribution of the costs of arming can vary based on a redistribution parameter $\theta_i \geq 1$. When $\theta_i = 1$, costs are internalized. When $\theta_i > 1$, costs are shifted away from the state actor. The cost of arming/mobilizing for the median voter in the potential compeller state is therefore m_C/θ_C. If $\theta_C = 2$, C's actor pays only half the per capita costs of the desired military effort.

In the first round of the game, C will consider attempting to compel D into transferring the asset. Should the Compeller find that a revision of the status quo is not worth its associated costs, she will invest no resources in making a militarized threat, $m_C = 0$, and the Deterrer retains the public good, giving a payoff of $(V_D, 0)$. This is a successful *Deterrence* outcome. Alternatively, C chooses a level of mobilization greater than 0, threatening D in order to compel him to transfer the public good.

Given $m_C > 0$, D must then decide whether to resist the compellence attempt. If D backs down, the outcome is successful *Compellence* and her payoff will be $V_C - m_C/\theta_C$. However, should the Deterrer choose to resist, C is then faced with the decision to fight, resulting in *Capitulatation* or *War*. In the case of war the outcome is decided probabilistically by the relative level of arming. I assume that the likelihood of victory is determined only by the level of military effort made by both sides; for example the probability that C will prevail is $m_C/(m_C + M_D)$. Following Fearon, war is an inherently costly enterprise entailing a per capita cost k_i for each side, but I assume that the costs of

---

[38] In the interests of clarity I will refer to the Compeller as "she" and the Deterrer as "he."

[39] See Slantchev (2012) for analysis of two-sided arming and two-sided uncertainty and much, much more.

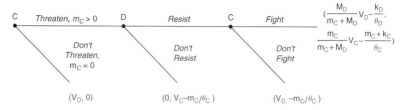

Figure 2.3 Deterrence compellence game

war can also be redistributed by the median voter. Therefore the state actor's cost of war is k_i/θ_i, and the payoff for the *War* outcome is $(V_D M_D/(m_C + M_D) - k_D/\theta_D, V_C m_C/(m_C + M_D) - (m_C + k_C)/\theta_C)$. *Capitulation* by C in response to D's resistance results in a payoff of $(V_D, -m_c/\theta_C)$. The extensive form game is illustrated in Figure 2.3.

The first thing that is clear from the game's final node is that when $\theta_i > 1$, actor *i* will be willing to go to war for an expected value less than the per capita costs of arming and of war. Conceivably then, a state-actor may pursue conflicts in which the costs to the state as a whole outweigh the overall benefits to the state. Thus the number of attempts at both deterrence and compellence will increase as the level of redistribution in D and C rises, respectively.

Proposition 1. *For any given levels of armament (m_i) and prize values (V_i), an increase in redistribution (θ_i) will increase the expected value of war relative to capitulation (in C's case) or being compelled (in D's case).*[40]

While this proposition is a modest one set up by the assumptions of the model, its implications are not. The larger model builds on this insight to show under what circumstances these coercive attempts succeed, and when war is likely to result.

2.A.3 *The decision to attempt compellence*

Again from Slantchev, two sets of equilibria exist, based on several important cutpoints. Starting with the final node, by subgame perfection, C is indifferent between fighting and not fighting when:

---

[40] The proof is by inspection of the payoffs in the final two nodes.

$$V_C = \frac{k_C(m_C + M_D)}{m_C \theta_C} \equiv \gamma(m_C) \qquad (2.1)$$

Note that the lowest value of the prize for which the Compeller will fight is strictly decreasing with both m_C and θ_C, even before we take into account that redistribution will influence the level of arming in the game's first round.

Knowing this, D can assess the expected benefit of resisting at the second node based on a posterior belief regarding C's value for the prize characterized by the distribution function $G(\gamma(m_C))$, which I assume is uniform and with a feasible range $[0, 1]$, and whether it falls above or below the threshold $\gamma(m_C)$. C's mobilization thus conveys information about the lowest possible value she places on the prize. The Deterrer, taking into account the arming of C at the first node, will resist when the payoff of risking war is greater than that of backing down or:

$$G(\gamma)(V_D) + (1 - G(\gamma)) \left(\frac{V_D M_D}{m_C + M_D} - \frac{k_D}{\theta_D} \right) \geq 0 \qquad (2.2)$$

At the first node, the Compeller can achieve assured compellence by choosing $\overline{m}_C$ such that D will find not fighting just preferable to fighting based on equation (2.2). This is the upper limit of what C is willing to invest, since any greater expenditure provides no additional benefit.

In addition to the level of arming that assures compellence, a second important value exists: the amount necessary to maximize the Compeller's payoff in the event of certain war. Let m_C^* be the level that maximizes her wartime payoff (from Figure 2.3) or:

$$m_C^* = \sqrt{V_C M_D \theta_C} - M_D \qquad (2.3)$$

Clearly, more redistributive states will always "try harder" in war time.

Proposition 2. *Military effort m_C^* is always increasing in the Compeller's redistribution θ_C.*[41]

I now characterize a series of Compeller "types," cutpoints for V_C where C is indifferent between two actions, in addition to γ of equation (2.1). Let β be the type of Compeller, given M_D, indifferent

---

[41] Proof: $\frac{dm_C^*}{d\theta_C} > 0$.

between war (where C spends m_C^*) and assured compellence (where C spends $\overline{m}_C$):

$$\beta = \frac{\left(\overline{m}_C + M_D - k_C\right)^2}{4\theta_C M_D} \tag{2.4}$$

All $V_C \geq \beta$ prefer assured compellence to war.

Let α characterize the type of Compeller indifferent between being deterred (and therefore not arming) and successful compellence. Therefore:

$$\alpha = \frac{\overline{m}_C}{\theta_C} \tag{2.5}$$

It must be emphasized that for the unitary actors in Slantchev's model $\overline{m}_C$ must be less than 1, which is the maximum public good value of the disputed asset. Thus when $\alpha > 1$ in Slantchev's model, no type of C would invest in a military. This is no longer the case once we relax this assumption of cost internalization and allow for the redistribution of arming and war costs. Since C is willing to invest up to $V_C\theta_C$, when $\theta_C > 1$ the value for which C will assure compellence lowers.

Finally, there exists a cutpoint δ where the Compeller is indifferent between being deterred and going to war (factoring in m_C^* from equation (2.3)):

$$\delta = \frac{M_D + k_C + 2\sqrt{M_D k_C}}{\theta_C} \tag{2.6}$$

Slantchev demonstrates that there are only two sets of equilibria, one occurring when $\alpha < \delta$ and the other where $\delta < \alpha < \beta$. In the first case lower value types of C will be deterred, and the higher value types will invest $\overline{m}_C$ and achieve compellence. War is not a possibility, although bluffing (making a compellent threat, but backing down in the face of D's resistance) on the part of C is.[42] In the second case a set of types exist in which C is not willing to invest $\overline{m}_C$, but the expected value of war is greater than that of being deterred. The expected value of war, even with the additional costs that make war ex post inefficient, outweighs the expected value of compellence. What is more, for similar reasons D resists C's threat, knowing that a war is certain to result. How does the redistribution parameter shape these equilibria?

[42] The bluffing equilibrium rightfully gets significant attention in Slantchev (2005), but is less interesting in the context of this appendix.

Assured compellence or deterrence

In the first of the two sets of equilibria, war is not possible. Bluffing, however, is; the Compeller will mobilize even though she is unwilling to fight, i.e. $V_C < \delta$. Recall that $\overline{m}_C$ is the maximum the Compeller will ever invest, because it is the smallest amount required to guarantee that the Deterrer will capitulate. In this set of equilibria we can imagine two different values of $\overline{m}_C$ for assured competence based on whether $V_C > \delta$. The first would reduce $G(m_C)$ in equation (2.2) to zero, war would be guaranteed, and sufficiently unpleasant for D that he backs down; let us characterize this as $\hat{m}_C$. The second would be a bluff in which some types of C will choose a level of m_C that, while less than the level of arming a player of type $V_C > \delta$ would choose, will still make the expected value for the Deterrer's risking war by resisting just less than that for not resisting (see equation (2.2)).[43]

The value of $\hat{m}_C$ for a genuine compeller is much simpler to solve since $G(m_C) = 0$. Assured compellence must then only make the benefits of compellence slightly outweigh that of certain war:

$$\hat{m}_C = M_D \left(\frac{V_d \theta_D}{k_D} - 1 \right) \tag{2.7}$$

Note that in equation (2.7), the level of redistribution for C has no effect on $\hat{m}_C$, which is simply the level of arming that makes war unpalatable for D under any circumstances. θ_D does play a role however. Not surprisingly, the more the costs of arming and war are redistributed away from the state-actor D, the more expensive it will be for C to guarantee successful compellence.

Proposition 3. *For any given level of D's arming (M_D) and prize values (V_D), an increase in the Deterrer's redistribution (θ_D) will require increased arming (m_C) to ensure compellence.*[44]

However, since α is strictly increasing with θ_D, fewer types of C will pursue successful compellence against the redistributive Deterrer.

---

[43] Solving to see how θ_C influences the probability of bluffing versus going to war shows that it is not a monotonic relationship but depends on the other parameters' values. Assuming that the distribution of possible types is uniform, one can solve, using equations (2.1) and (2.2), for $\overline{m}_C$ in the bluffing equilibrium using equation (2.1). I use Mathematica to do this and simulate scenarios depicted later in the chapter.

[44] Proof: from equation (2.7) $\frac{d\hat{m}_C}{d\theta_D} > 0$.

A more redistributive state will be better at deterring not because of increased capability, but because the cost of fighting has gone down.

Should the Compeller be of the type where the costs of bluffing do not outweigh the gains, she will invest nothing in her military, and the game ends in C's being deterred (i.e. "Don't Threaten") at the first node of Figure 2.3. Under no circumstances in this set of equilibria is war possible. The more redistributive the state, the more unlikely this scenario becomes. Redistributive compeller states are harder to deter. When war becomes a possibility, this is a problem.

Risking war

The second set of equilibria in the Slantchev model results in a risk of war but no bluffing by the Compeller (therefore $\overline{m}_C = \hat{m}_C$, one of the MTM's key counterintuitive insights). This occurs when $\delta < \alpha < \beta$. As in the first equilibria, all $V_c < \delta$ are deterred, and all $V_C \geq \beta$ invest $\hat{m}_C$ to achieve compellence. In the intermediate category, that is all $V_c \in [\delta, \beta)$, C will allocate m_C^*, the Deterrer will resist, and war occurs. Note that this decision is made with full information that war will certainly result, but the potential benefits of war still outweigh its costs for both parties.

As long as the possibility exists that $V_c > \beta$, that is $\beta < 1$, the ex ante probability of war is $\Pr(\delta \leq V_c < \beta)$. As the likely cost of compellence rises for C, that is if $\delta \leq \alpha < 1 < \beta$, war is certain if C chooses to compel. In this case the ex ante probability of war is $\Pr(V_C \geq \delta)$. When the costs of war continue to climb for the Compeller, for example for very high levels of M_D, the only outcome in equilibrium is deterrence.

How does redistribution affect the probability of war and competence? First, as in the first set of equilibria, it is easy to show that the number of types of V_C that pursue successful compellence attempts always increases with θ_C. There are also a larger number of compeller types that prefer war over being deterred. However, possible cases do exist in which the probability of war, that is $V_c \in [\delta, \beta)$, declines (when D is heavily armed, values the prize at low levels, and has high costs of war). Thus θ_C has no monotonic relationship to the probability of war. However, the combination of successful compellences and wars in pursuit of revisionist aims, that is when $V_C > \delta$, increases.

Proposition 4. *The Compeller will make more threats as redistribution* (θ_C) *increases.*[45]

Finally, because θ_D only affects $\hat{m}_C$, but has no effect on δ, in this model, the number of successful compellences declines, and the probability of war rises.

Proposition 5. *An increase in the Deterrer's redistribution* (θ_D) *decreases the chances of successful compellence and raises the probability of war.*[46]

Implications through simulation

The value of each cutpoint (and therefore the probability of each outcome) is illustrated in Figure 2.4. For simplicity's sake, I assume that the Deterrer is a unitary actor with perfect cost internalization ($\theta_D = 1$). I then chose two values for θ_C, a cost internalized Compeller ($\theta_C = 1$), and a redistributive Compeller. For the redistributive actor, I set $\theta_C = 2$, in which the state actor only pays half the costs of arming and war relative to the mean for the state. The y-axis depicts the range of values of V_C for each possible equilibrium outcome, for any given level of M_D. Within Figure 2.4, graphs (a) and (c) show the entire range of V_C and M_D, while (b) and (d) highlight the points at which C will bluff.

The dark gray areas in (a) and (c) show the combinations of V_C and M_D in which war is the equilibrium outcome, that is $V_c \in [\delta, \beta)$. In the redistributive case (c), the area bounded by δ and β is larger than that of (a). In the face of modest levels of M_D, C will go to war for relatively low values of the prize. Similarly, C will enter in a war even in the face of significant military investment by D if the prize is sufficiently valuable. Likewise the space in which C will successfully compel D is similarly large in the redistributive case. In terms of bluffing, in the redistributive case (d) the range of V_C at which C will bluff rather than spend the resources necessary for a genuine compellent threat are lower than in the cost internalization case (b).

---

[45] Proof: From equation (2.6) $\frac{d\delta}{d\theta_C} < 0$.

[46] Proof: From equation (2.7) $\frac{d\bar{m}_C}{d\theta_D} > 0$. Therefore from equation (2.4) $\frac{d\beta}{d\theta_D} > 0$.
Since $\frac{d\delta}{d\theta_D} = 0$, $\Pr(\delta \leq V_c < \beta)$ is increasing in θ_D.

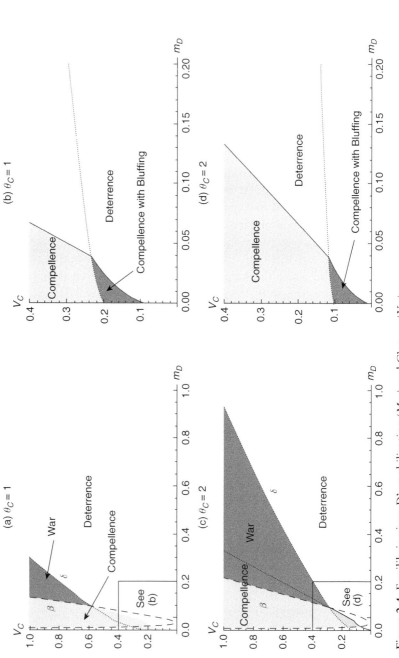

Figure 2.4 Equilibria given D's mobilization (M_D) and C's type (V_C)

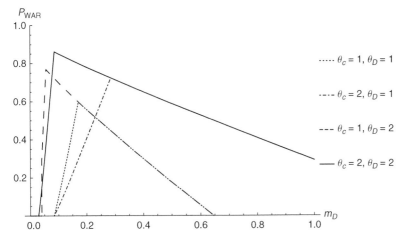

Figure 2.5 Ex ante probability of war

Figure 2.5 highlights the likelihood of war for various combinations of redistributive/cost internalized Compeller and Deterrer (four in all). The probability of war is a function of C's "type," and here I assume a uniform distribution of $V_C \in (0, 1)$.[47] The probability of war is therefore $\Pr[\delta - \beta]$ for equilibria where compellence is possible, and $\Pr[1-\beta]$ where D cannot be peacefully compelled. The two effects of an increase in θ_C displayed in Figure 2.4 are readily apparent here as well. As in Figure 2.4, the shift from cost internalization to redistribution in the Compeller makes war more likely for moderate to high levels of M_D, but also shifts the probability curve to the right, since for more (low) values of M_D a redistributive Compeller will achieve her ends without resorting to war.

Figure 2.5 also shows the effect of increased redistribution for the Deterrer on the ex ante probability of war. This is indeed a monotonic relationship (as we assumed that M_D is fixed). War becomes possible, even likely for quite low levels of M_D. Not surprisingly, the most volatile scenario occurs when a redistributive Deterrer meets a redistributive Compeller. Treating M_D as exogenous and concentrating on the decision of the Compeller does not capture important strategic behavior. While in many cases a low level of M_D will make war quite

---

[47] $V_D = 0.8$ and $k_C = k_D = 0.1$.

likely, if the Deterrer can choose m_D it is correspondingly unlikely to select this arming level.

That noted, the one-sided arming case can shed light on important types of interstate crises. For example, while it is safe to say that the United States military spent the last decade of the twentieth century largely preparing for "Desert Storm II," Saddam Hussein developed and employed his military to minimize an internal coup (Gordon and Trainor, 2006). Additionally, states arm in response to an overall level of danger, a portfolio of threats, or against other states entirely. For example, the US military that fought in Desert Storm in 1991 was not designed with the Iraqi Army in mind, but rather that of the Soviets.[48] Finally, compellence is generally a luxury good more readily available to great powers, which, as in the Vietnam War, have discretion over how much effort to expend relative to the smaller deterrer who is likely to expend all of its resources or none at all.

2.A.4 Redistribution and conflict

The relationship between Deterrer and Compeller presented here is quite complex. Nonetheless, the model provides several valuable insights that can be expressed in relatively simple fashion. The model shows clearly the potential for moral hazard. Moral hazard does not necessarily lead to war, but it will lead to a very expensive peace. A redistributive state is likely to attempt to compel others for low stakes and aggressively practice extended deterrence for increasingly peripheral prizes where it prefers the status quo. Any compellence attempt will also require a larger military effort, even setting aside the inefficiency concerns suggested earlier in this chapter.

The MTM suggests that military capitalization, coupled with inequality, allows democracies to be more aggressive in their grand strategy. Redistributive states are likely to attempt coercion for lower prizes compared to the state in which all costs are internalized. However, when costs are not internalized, coercion attempts, while likely to be successful, may entail large costs for the state that outweigh

---

[48] Although planning to counter an Iraqi attack on Kuwait and Saudi Arabia did supplant a Soviet invasion of Iran as the principal concern for the Defense Department from the end of 1988 onwards, this did little to change overall American force structure.

the smaller benefits of conflict that the median voter is willing to pursue. The appendix does support the claim of Bueno de Mesquita et al. (2003) and others that democracies will try harder in war, but, from a cost internalization perspective, harder does not always entail smarter. Under extreme circumstances democracy allows the pursuit of a policy that has a negative expected value for the state, but remains rational for the median voter.

While many propositions derived from strategic models are difficult to evaluate due to the non-monotonic relationship between many of the independent variables and dependent variables such as the outbreak of war (Signorino, 1999), testing the implication that redistribution leads to more coercion attempts is straightforward. The probability that C will successfully compel D in a compel-or-deter equilibrium is $1 - \alpha$. In equilibria where war is possible the probability that C will initiate an attempt at compellence (which will either succeed or result in war) is $1 - \sigma$. From equations (2.5) and (2.6), in both cases θ_C has a positive, monotonic relationship with the probability of compellence. When expressed logarithmically, there is no interaction between θ_C and other variables on the right hand side of these equations. The effect of military capitalization on the probability that a player would initiate a compellence attempt can be analyzed using logistic regression.

While equation (2.7) shows that the Compeller's assured compellence level of arming ($\hat{m}_C$) does not vary with θ_C, when a compeller decides to arm in order to maximize her payoff from war, she chooses m_C^*. From equation (2.3), the relationship of θ_C to this effort is always positive and monotonic. On the other hand, both m_D and θ_D have non-monotonic effects on C's behavior and are thus more challenging to estimate statistically.

Some implications regarding the strategic interaction of two states will be explored in the qualitative section. The model claims that for a redistributive state bluffing can be harder for multiple reasons, not the least of which is the fact that the value of a given unit of military power as a costly signal is attenuated. We shall see in Chapters 6 and 7 that this can have tragic consequences, especially if two redistributive actors meet in combat.

3 | *Analyses of public opinion*

Public opinion data can provide microfoundational evidence for defense's redistributive potential, and determine what role one's relative wealth plays in grand strategic preferences. A classical liberal (or Marxian) analysis might agree that inequality leads to militarization, but explain it as a result of the wealthy's superior political power. However, if the public good of defense actually has redistributive implications then an individual's relatively low wealth should correlate to *support* for higher defense spending and more aggressive policies, and this does not fit competing explanations.

The first section tests four hypotheses across a broad array of democracies. The most direct test of the Meltzer–Richard hypothesis is to see if one's relative income (wealth, SES, etc.) affects one's attitude towards defense spending:

H_1 *Respondents with lower income are more disposed to support higher defense spending.*

The theory also suggests hypotheses for state-level independent variables:

H_2 *Higher state-wide inequality will result on average in higher support for defense spending.*

H_3 *Increased public good value for defense will result on average in higher support for defense spending.*

H_4 *Higher military capitalization will result on average in higher support for defense spending.*

In addition to the cross-national data, I employ a second data set derived from a survey which asked American respondents to assess foreign policy goals and threats as well as defense spending. These data allow me to competitively test cost distribution theory against explanations resting on a wealth-based perception of threat

68

(that is, less well-off respondents are more likely to be seduced by "myths of empire"):

H_5 *Income affects respondents' assessment of threats.*

Failing to reject the null of H_5 removes consideration of wealth-specific threat inflation as a possible causal mechanism. The remaining hypotheses provide positive tests of cost distribution theory's predictions:

H_6 *Respondents with lower income are more disposed to support military force over diplomacy.*

H_7 *Respondents with lower income are more disposed to support military force to advance foreign policy goals.*

While the chapter finds much support for these theoretically derived hypotheses, it also finds, perhaps not surprisingly, that the relationship between inequality and grand strategy is more complex than the theory depicts. In particular, the empirical relationship between inequality and my dependent variables does not appear to be linear. While acknowledging where the deductive theory disappoints and incorporating inductive findings into a richer explanation leaves me open to the accusation of ad hoc theorizing, the result is a better understanding of democracies and war.

3.1 Cross-national public opinion on defense spending

To test H_1 through H_4, I use a series of cross-national surveys of 37 countries from the International Social Survey Program on the Role of Government (ISSP, available for years 1985, 1990, 1996, and 2006).[1] The surveys provide high quality data at the micro-level (i.e. the individual survey respondent) as well as allow for some testing of state-level factors. To measure an individual's support for defense spending, each survey asks respondents, "Please show whether you would like to see more or less government spending in the Military and Defense. Remember that if you say 'much more', it might require a tax increase to pay for it." Responses ranged along a five-point scale with

[1] Note that all the country-years included in the data set are (at least by one definition) democratic, in that they have all received a "Polity" score of 6 or higher (Gurr et al., 2002).

one being "spend much more," three "spend the same as now," and five "spend much less." I reversed the original coding so that a higher value represents a more hawkish attitude towards defense spending.

3.1.1 Explanatory and control variables

The independent variable of greatest interest is a micro-level one: the respondent's *Household Income.*[2] Since each survey recorded income in different incremental categories as well as in the local currency, I divided the data into income quintiles for each state to allow for cross-national comparison. Income quintiles do not capture any skew in income distribution; I operationalize this important factor with a state-level variable, economic *Inequality*, measured by the Gini coefficient. When dealing with inequality data, researchers must choose between scope and consistency. The most consistent source, the Luxembourg Income Study (LIS), contains limited numbers of observations, primarily of wealthy, developed states. Therefore, in addition to LIS I use the Standardized World Income Inequality Database (SWIID) developed by Frederick Solt (2009), which employs a missing-data algorithm to generate inequality measurements comparable to LIS. It should be noted that, while the theory simply assumes that every voter's income is taxed at the same rate, this conservative assumption is rarely the case. State taxation regimes generally feature some degree of progressiveness, and this varies across countries. Both the LIS and SWIID data report inequality after taxes and income-related government transfers, and thus to a large degree control for this variation.

As a first cut, Figures 3.1a and 3.1b graphically depict the difference between the middle and upper income quintiles' mean responses (and whether a difference of means test reported that the probability of the difference not being greater than zero was less than 0.05) for each country-year. The differences are arranged along the x-axis by the level of inequality in each state as coded by LIS and SWIID, respectively.[3] The predominantly negative values suggest that wealthier respondents

---

[2] I used individual income for Israel in 1996 due to data availability.

[3] If we run separate logistic models 58 out of 67 coefficients are negative, 37 significantly so. Note that Israel 2006 (-0.10 coefficient and 0.046 standard deviation) and Japan 2006 (-0.026 coefficient and 0.043 standard deviation) are not plotted on the figures due to an absence of state-level inequality data.

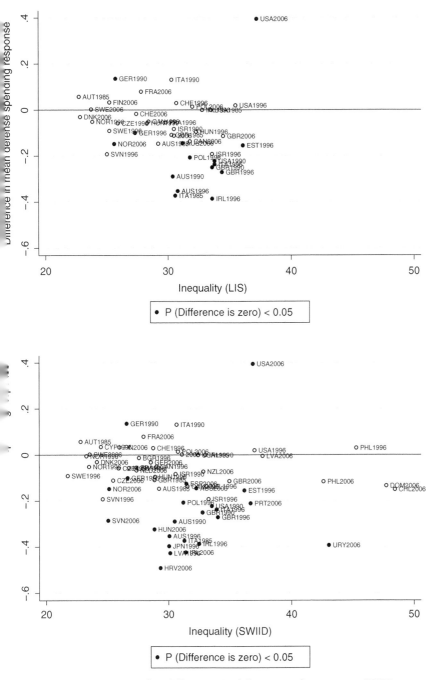

Figure 3.1 Income quintiles' differences in defense spending support (ISSP)

are on average more dovish. Furthermore, the downward slope in the observations suggests the relationship is exacerbated by state-level inequality. However, in Figure 3.1b, which contains a number of less-developed states with quite high levels of inequality, the relationship appears curvilinear; that is, at very high levels of inequality the differences between income quintiles appears to decline (although largely remain negative).

Not surprisingly, respondent *Education* tends to correlate with income. Indeed it is often used as a proxy for income in research (Dion and Birchfield, 2010). However, education may also exert an independent influence on one's assessment of international politics and the need for defense spending, i.e exposure to more information (or to academics) shifts one's opinion against defense spending. I include it as a control variable, although this will likely reduce the coefficient of my primary explanatory variable, *Household Income*. I also include demographic variables: *Age*, gender (*Male*), and a measure of how respondents choose a political party affiliation (*Party* ordered from leftmost to rightmost).

Outliers such as the United States in 2006 as well as the broad range in the difference between median and top household income quintiles (for states at roughly the same level of economic inequality) suggest that macro-level factors affect individual attitudes considerably. One clearly cannot directly compare survey responses across states due to the presence of a number of state-level factors (an "about the same" response in Israel is not comparable to the same response in Ireland). Given the theory, one would ideally employ a cross-sectionally comparable measurement of a respondent's assessment of defense spending's benefits (such as an evaluation of threats facing the state), but this does not exist. However, a recent history of military conflict should shape attitudes towards defense. I therefore incorporate a *Conflict* dummy variable if the state has participated in an armed conflict in the last five years.[4] Given the theory's highlighting of the draft as a tax on labor (Horowitz et al., 2011), I introduce *Conscription* as a categorical variable based on whether a state's military contains no conscripts,

---

[4] Armed conflicts involve one or more states in which 25 deaths have occurred (Gleditsch et al., 2002). As an alternative measurement of threat, I included a dummy variable, *Terror* for whether the state (or its nationals) endured a fatal terrorist attack the previous year (RAND Corporation, 2011); the (largely insignificant) results are in the online appendix.

fewer than half conscripts, between 50 and 66 percent conscripts, and greater than 66 percent conscripts (Gifford, 2006).

While this chapter focuses on the role played by individuals' relative income, I take advantage of the opportunity presented by the data to test the plausibility of the theory's other explanatory variable, *Military Capitalization*. For decades, casualty-averse warfare has been synonymous with air campaigns and so I include the logged ratio of fixed-wing combat aircraft (fighters, bombers, command and control, and electronic warfare; but not transport, training, or helicopters) and ground personnel (all army, and any naval or marine infantry forces), all taken from *The Military Balance* published by the International Institute for Strategic Studies (2013).[5]

Finally, I introduce a state-level variable likely to affect both independent and dependent variables: *logged GDP per capita* from the UN Development Program.[6] Even with these state-level variables included, unobserved factors no doubt affect the dependent variable, and the data set contains only a modest number of poor quality data at the country-year level (both threat and inequality are notoriously difficult to measure consistently). In addition to eliminating state-level variables altogether through fixed effects, this section also employs multi-level models to incorporate all the theory's state-level variables and to account for these sources of bias (Anderson and Singer, 2008).[7]

3.1.2 Results

To intuitively portray the effects of substantively interesting changes in the micro-level variables, Figure 3.2 shows first differences in predicted probability of each possible response of a fixed effects model,

---

[5] The next chapter uses several different operationalizations of capitalization to explore its effect on state-level behavior. I only use aircraft per soldier here for simplicity's sake. Including other versions of capitalization has little effect on the coefficients and standard errors of the micro-level explanatory variables. See the online appendix for these regressions.

[6] Both GDP per capita as well as its constituent parts possess plausible links to the independent and dependent variables. For example, the larger the population, the lower a public good's per capita cost. I report results models using logged population and GDP in the online appendix.

[7] I incorporate random intercepts describing the average response for each combination of year and country, and assume my explanatory variables (income), education, and political identification contain a random component and differ between country-years.

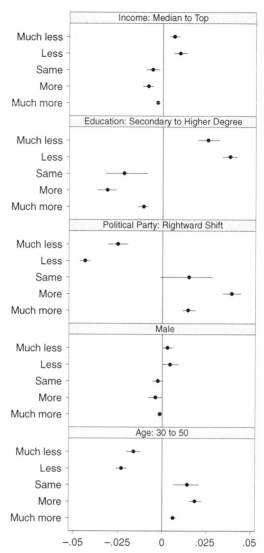

Ordered logit with country and year fixed effects. 95% confidence intervals depicted. N (respondents) = 46,723; N (state-years) = 57; Pseudo R^2 = 0.10. Simulations conducted using Clarify (Tomz et al., 2001).

Figure 3.2 First differences, probability of defense spending support

which avoids state-level omitted variable bias at the cost of making no effort to test these factors' effects. Of all the models presented in the appendix, Figure 3.2 depicts the smallest, most conservative estimate of *Income*'s coefficient.[8] The graph shows, with 95 percent confidence intervals, the change in likelihood of a specific change in an independent variable's value, depicted above each box. For example, the predicted effect of increasing a respondent's age from 30 to 50 years would result in an approximately 2 percent increase in the likelihood of favoring "more" defense spending, and reduces the likelihood of responding "less" by more than 2 percent.

Figure 3.2 makes clear that one's relative income is negatively and significantly related to support for defense spending; that is, shifting from the median to the top income quintile increases the probability of desiring less defense spending by 1.6 percent, and reduces the probability of supporting more spending by 1.1 percent. A higher level of *Education* is also associated with increased dovishness (shifting from a high school diploma to a college degree reduces the probability of supporting more spending by 4.2 percent), even when controlling for *Income*, although we cannot conclude that this is entirely due to redistribution. On the other hand, increased *Age* correlates to hawkishness. This may capture another redistributive element, but then again, older people are less likely to be drafted or serve in the military. Not surprisingly, respondents locating themselves further to the political right are more hawkish. Gender has a very small effect, although *Male* correlates, perhaps surprisingly, to more dovish responses.

It is unlikely that any particular multivariate investigations of public opinion can identify the "true" substantive effect of any given variable, and thus one should compare the effects with extreme caution. For example, we know that education and income are tightly correlated, and so part of education's effect (in the theoretically predicted direction) is probably due to wealth, rather than knowledge or deeper political awareness. The models do provide compelling evidence of a significant effect for income despite loading the dice against cost distribution theory by inserting all of the covarying control variables.

---

[8] The appendix reports the results of this model, an identical model using imputed data, and a hierarchical ordered logit model. Income's coefficient is in the predicted direction and is significant at conventional levels in all three models.

Table 3.1, which contains the results for a series of hierarchical linear models, shows that income quintile continues to have the predicted relationship with support for increased defense spending. More importantly, the table allows us to examine the effects of state-level factors.

Turning to the state-level variable of *Inequality*, while respondents in more unequal states are on average more supportive of increased defense spending in the models using LIS, the relationship weakens in models incorporating SWIID. Models 6 and 7 incorporate a squared term for inequality to see whether extremely high levels of inequality dampen the average respondent's enthusiasm for defense spending.[9] The poor, high-inequality countries (many with a recent history of domestic repression by the military) present in SWIID but not in LIS – Chile, Dominican Republic, Philippines, and Uruguay – appear to have less clear preferences regarding the marginal utility of increased military spending. Figure 3.3 shows the joint effect of the Gini coefficient and its squared term, and includes a histogram of the distribution of inequality among the country-years. The average response within a country becomes increasingly hawkish until about a standard deviation above the mean Gini coefficient (30.9). An interesting and plausible explanation in the spirit of cost distribution theory would be that less wealthy countries are unable to capitalize their militaries, thus mitigating its public good value.

Military capitalization, that is the logged ratio of combat aircraft to ground personnel, correlates to an increase in the mean support for defense spending. A 10 percent increase in aircraft per soldier, holding all other factors constant, would produce a 0.011–0.014 increase in the mean response on defense spending within a country-year. An upward shift one standard deviation above the mean (logged) capitalization value produces a more impressive 0.1 increase in the mean response on defense spending. Recent involvement in a military conflict also results in more hawkish attitudes towards defense spending The extent of the draft correlates to more hawkish attitudes in all the models (but not at significant levels). One must interpret these state-level coefficients cautiously, given the relatively small number of state-years in the data set (33 when using LIS and 54 for SWIID). Nonetheless,

---

[9] F-tests of the log-likelihoods support including the square term in the SWIID models, but not in the LIS models.

Table 3.1 *State-level inequality and defense spending opinion (ISSP)*

Inequality measure	(1) None	(2) LIS	(3) SWIID	(4) LIS	(5) SWIID	(6) LIS	(7) SWIID
Individual level							
Income Quintile	−0.0188***	−0.0155*	−0.0179***	−0.0161*	−0.0196***	−0.0161*	−0.0196***
	(0.00511)	(0.00646)	(0.00521)	(0.00651)	(0.00538)	(0.00652)	(0.00536)
Age	0.00373***	0.00452***	0.00413***	0.00457***	0.00406***	0.00457***	0.00405***
	(0.000287)	(0.000352)	(0.000294)	(0.000353)	(0.000300)	(0.000353)	(0.000300)
Male	−0.0173*	−0.0277*	−0.0197*	−0.0297**	−0.0285**	−0.0297**	−0.0283**
	(0.00875)	(0.0109)	(0.00901)	(0.0109)	(0.00928)	(0.0109)	(0.00928)
Education	−0.0679***	−0.0835***	−0.0698***	−0.0821***	−0.0703***	−0.0821***	−0.0704***
	(0.00745)	(0.00975)	(0.00765)	(0.0100)	(0.00791)	(0.0100)	(0.00796)
Party (l to r)	0.164***	0.191***	0.165***	0.192***	0.172***	0.192***	0.172***
	(0.0157)	(0.0200)	(0.0160)	(0.0208)	(0.0166)	(0.0208)	(0.0166)
State level							
Inequality		0.0532***	0.0204*	0.0430*	−0.00512	−0.0351	0.179*
		(0.0153)	(0.00919)	(0.0168)	(0.0103)	(0.221)	(0.0626)
Inequality^2						0.00131	−0.00267*
						(0.000367)	(0.000916)
Capitalization				0.152*	0.114+	0.144*	0.135*
				(0.0612)	(0.0581)	(0.0625)	(0.0555)
ln (GDP pc)				−0.296*	−0.393***	−0.326*	−0.353***
				(0.142)	(0.0980)	(0.155)	(0.0938)
Conflict				0.298*	0.277**	0.302*	0.204*
				(0.117)	(0.0900)	(0.119)	(0.0861)

Table 3.1 (*cont.*)

Inequality measure	(1) None	(2) LIS	(3) SWIID	(4) LIS	(5) SWIID	(6) LIS	(7) SWIID
Conscription				0.0528	0.0122	0.0502	0.0365
				(0.0799)	(0.0496)	(0.0857)	(0.0496)
Pop. % > 65				−0.112***	−0.0545**	−0.113***	−0.0666***
				(0.0319)	(0.0207)	(0.0325)	(0.0198)
Var: Income	0.000758***	0.000740***	0.000732***	0.000741***	0.000760***	0.000741***	0.000753***
	(−0.000128)	(−0.000158)	(−0.00013)	(−0.000156)	(−0.000133)	(−0.000159)	(−0.000133)
Var: Education	0.00235***	0.00237***	0.00231***	0.00240***	0.00238***	0.00239***	0.00242***
	(−0.000299)	(−0.00039)	(−0.000309)	(−0.00039)	(−0.000317)	(−0.000393)	(−0.000322)
Var: Party	0.0125***	0.0117***	0.0120***	0.0119***	0.0123***	0.0119***	0.0123***
	(−0.00135)	(−0.0017)	(−0.00134)	(−0.00173)	(−0.0014)	(−0.00173)	(−0.0014)
Respondents	46723	29882	43655	29482	41011	29482	41011
States	58	33	54	32	51	32	51
L.L.	−63370.469	−40313.309	−58954.351	−39683.638	−55308.442	−39688.293	−55311.45

Hierarchical linear models using Stata's "xtmixed" command. Constants and covariances not reported for space reasons. Standard errors in parentheses. ***p < 0.001, **p < 0.01, *p < 0.05, +p < 0.1.

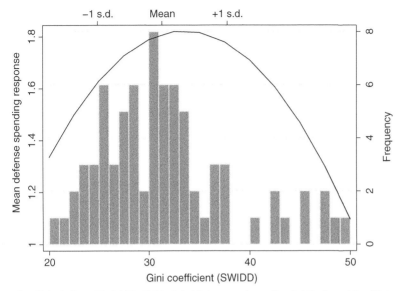

Coefficients from Model 7 in Table 3.1. Histogram shows the distribution of the Gini coefficient by country-year with frequencies along the righthand axis.

Figure 3.3 Mean defense spending response as a function of inequality

given the low likelihood of a type I error, the significant results provide important support for the macro-level aspects of the theory.

Taken together, analysis of the ISSP surveys provides evidence in favor of the microfoundational H_1, and some support for H_2–H_4. These results substantiate the theory's claim that defense spending contains a redistributive element. However, while recent involvement in an armed conflict appears to have a statistically significant (and unsurprising) effect on attitudes about defense spending, we cannot say with great confidence how perceptions of increased benefits can affect the voter's calculation, H_3. Likewise, voter preferences and military capitalization should be endogenously related. The former encourages the latter, but a voter should be more willing to spend more money on a capitalized military. We should therefore view this section's tests of H_2–H_4 as suggestive.

3.2 US public opinion on threats and military force

The cross-national analysis above does not allow us to test any dependent variables beyond relative support for defense spending. In addition to providing additional support for H_1 and H_3, I turn to US public opinion to establish two facts. Showing that income does *not* affect one's perception of threat undermines an explanation based on elite threat-inflation targeted at the less sophisticated (i.e. less wealthy), or H_5. Second, and more positively, these public opinion data allow us to determine whether relative wealth shapes perceptions of the utility of force, H_6 and H_7. All data for this section are taken from the 2010 Chicago Council on Global Affairs (CCGA) survey of American public opinion on foreign policy (Bouton et al., 2011), which contains a host of questions on the use of military force and the assessment of threat.[10]

3.2.1 Measuring threat

To determine whether relative income shapes one's assessment of threat, rather than one's desired means to address these threats (i.e. H_5), I examined responses to the following CCGA prompt: "Below is a list of possible threats to the vital interest of the United States in the next 10 years. For each one, please select whether you see this as a critical threat, an important but not critical threat, or not an important threat at all." I excluded threats that are unlikely to have military solutions (or do not have an associated military action in the survey), such as "US debt to China," and incorporate respondent opinions on the following "possible threats":

- "The development of China as a world power"
- "Islamic fundamentalism"
- "The possibility of unfriendly countries becoming nuclear powers"
- "Disruption in energy supply"
- "International terrorism"
- "A confrontation between mainland China and Taiwan"
- "Violent Islamist groups in Pakistan and Afghanistan"
- "Military conflict between Israel and its Arab neighbors"
- "Iran's nuclear program"

To test a more general attitude towards threat, I also took the mean of an individual's responses to each threat to create a *threat index*. The index's value takes on a value of zero if a respondent assessed

---

[10] Readers interested in the theory's applicability to other states should also look at the similar analysis (and results) for Israeli public opinion in Chapter 7.

every threat as "not important," and two for a person evaluating every threat as "critical." The index's mean is quite high, 1.46 with a standard deviation of 0.38 (recall that "2: critical threat," is the highest response).

3.2.2 Measuring militarism

As in the previous cross-national analysis, I begin by examining responses to a question on whether *defense spending* "should be expanded, cut back, or kept about the same." The CCGA also lists "Maintaining superior military power worldwide" as one of the 11 possible "foreign policy goals that the United States might have" and asks whether this goal is very, somewhat, or not important; *military superiority* is the second operationalization of militarism.

As the cost of a capital-intensive campaign drops for the respondent, one becomes more likely to "overweight" it in one's preferred portfolio of foreign policy tools. No survey question assesses US attitudes towards firepower or military capital. Nonetheless, encouraging the respondent to choose between two tools, only one of which is theorized to have redistributive implications, helps to determine whether the marginal rate of substitution of military might for economic power changes with income. I include a dependent variable of respondent assessments of the importance of *military versus economic strength* embodied in the survey question "Which of the following do you think is more important in determining a country's overall power and influence in the world: a country's economic strength, or its military strength?" The fourth operationalization of militarism uses the survey question that best embodies an ambitious, militarized foreign policy, *world policeman*: whether the respondent agreed or disagreed with the following statement: "The US is playing the role of world policeman more than it should be."

I developed a *troop use index* which, like the threat index, takes the mean response to eight different scenarios prefaced by the question "There has been some discussion about the circumstances that might justify using US troops in other parts of the world. Please give your opinion about some situations. Would you favor or oppose the use of US troops?" I then tested each of these scenarios individually as a dichotomous variable, as well as any other question in the survey that specifically mentions the use of force. For example, CCGA separately asks whether respondents would support the use of "US air strikes" and "Attacks by US ground troops" against "terrorist training camps and other facilities." I pair each potential military use with an appropriate threat assessment. In some cases, the troop use scenario directly matches an explicit threat listed above. In other cases, I operationalized threat by the best fitting measure available in the survey. Table 3.2 presents the specific troop use scenarios, the mean response (from 0 to 1, as all questions are dichotomous), and the associated threat assessment question.

3.2.3 *Explanatory and Control Variables*

To facilitate comparison to the cross-national ISSP surveys, I divided the respondent population into household *Income Quintiles*.[11]

The statistical models also include potential confounding variables, ones that competing explanations suggest can cause a predilection for force or an aggressive grand strategy. The Chicago survey includes important questions unavailable in the cross-national ISSP. The most important factor, the assessment of threat, has already been discussed. Multiple IR realists suggest that militarism correlates to lack of knowledge about foreign affairs. I therefore included two measures of political knowledge and interest: a dummy variable for whether the respondent correctly identified South Korea as a democracy (*ROK Democracy*) and the level of *News Interest* he or she has "in news about the relations of the United States with other countries." I also include dummy variables for respondents who identify themselves as *"Black"* or *"Hispanic"* as identification with these groups correlates to income, and might also correlate to foreign policy preferences.

I also include covariates similar to those in the previous cross-national section. Including *Education* in the analysis will likely reduce the effect of income, but is nonetheless essential given its potential confounding effect. One's self-placement on a "political spectrum" from left to right (*Conservative*) likely correlates to income and the

---

[11] I also created an *income* variable in which I took the midpoint of each of the survey's income categories (i.e. $13,750 for the category "$12,500 to $14,999"). I coded the top category, "$175,000 or more," the top 3.2% in income as $287,686 based on estimates from the United States Census Bureau. I then ran the same series of regressions using this value as well as its log, and found similar results. These are reported in the online appendix.

Table 3.2 *Troop use scenarios and associated threat* (CCGA)

Troop use scenario	Mean	s.d.	Threat measurement
"US air strikes against terrorist training camps"	0.816	0.388	"International terrorism"
"US ground troops against terrorist training camps"	0.737	0.44	"International terrorism"
"A US military strike against Iran's nuclear program"	0.461	0.499	"Iran's nuclear program"
"Military action" against terrorists "operating in Pakistan"	0.743	0.437	"Violent Islamist groups in Pakistan"
"Use of US troops to ensure the oil supply"	0.552	0.497	"Disruption in energy supply"
"Use of US troops if N. Korea invaded S. Korea"	0.431	0.495	"How important is S. Korea to the United States?"
"Use of US troops if China invaded Taiwan"	0.266	0.442	"Confrontation" between China and Taiwan
"Use of US troops to enforce an Israeli–Palestinian peace"	0.51	0.5	"Military conflict . . . Israel and its Arab neighbors"
"Use of US troops if Israel were attacked"	0.494	0.5	"Military conflict . . . Israel and its Arab neighbors"
"Use of US troops to stop . . . genocide"	0.72	0.449	Importance of "defending human rights"
"Use of US troops . . . to stop the killing in Darfur"	0.560	0.497	Importance of "defending human rights"
"Use of US troops to deal with humanitarian crises"	0.708	0.455	Threat index

dependent variables, as does membership in a major political party (operationalized as *Republican* and *Democrat*). I include *Age* and a *Male* categorical variable as well.

3.2.4 Results

Income should influence one's willingness to use military force, but not one's assessment of the need for it. Regressions on each of the nine threat assessments (reported in the appendix) described above show that one's relative income is unlikely to play a significant role in influencing one's assessment of threat. If anything, the higher one's income, the more likely one will identify various foreign policy challenges as "critical" or "important" threats (albeit only significantly so in one model). The more highly educated and politically left-leaning find threats less salient and dangerous, and those "uninterested" in foreign policy news are also much more likely to have lower threat estimates as well. Older respondents and Republicans have higher threat estimates, but so do Democrats compared to those without a party affiliation (not at conventionally significant levels). One's race/ethnicity appears to have little relationship with the dependent variables. Interestingly, men are more likely to have lower threat estimates.

Having undermined the competing income-based myth argument, I then regressed the same independent variables on the five measures of militarism. In each model, the coefficient for income is negative, that is wealthier respondents are more dovish. The easily interpreted OLS regression on the troop index shows that a shift from the median to the top quintile reduces the average response on the use of troops in various scenarios by 0.04. While all coefficients are reported in the appendix, as with Figure 3.2, I depicted the first differences in predicted probabilities for substantively interesting changes of the explanatory variables in Figure 3.4. Defense spending has the weakest relationship with income (the null hypothesis has a probability of 0.19 of being correct). In every other model income quintile has significant effects that are quite large relative to the other variables. A shift from the median to the top quintile results in an increased likelihood of a more dovish position roughly equivalent to shifting from high school to a bachelor's degree. Indeed, few other explanatory variables even achieve statistical significance consistently besides education, ideology, and Republican affiliation. On balance, income quintile is a

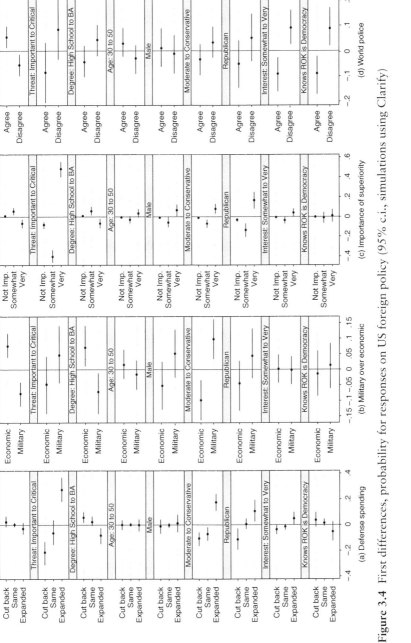

Figure 3.4 First differences, probability for responses on US foreign policy (95% c.i., simulations using Clarify)

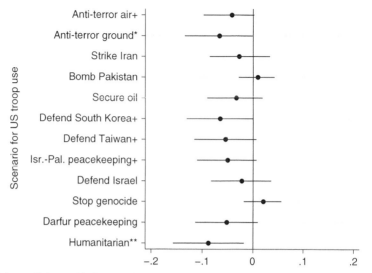

Beta coefficients with 95% confidence intervals for income quintiles reported for each dependent variable, ** $p < 0.01$, * $p < 0.05$, + $p < 0.1$.

Figure 3.5 Logit coefficients for income quintile on support for specific military scenarios

better predictor of one's attitude towards the use of the US military than most intuitive factors. Overall, the results strongly support the theoretical prediction that the costs of the military's use are not spread evenly throughout the American public.

Finally, the section turns to the specific scenarios under which the CCGA asks for opinions on the use of the United States military. For reasons of space, Figure 3.5 reports only the coefficient for income quintile for each of 12 scenarios (tables with full results can be found in the appendix). Support for cost distribution theory is more ambiguous here. Ten of the 12 coefficients are negative, half achieving a level of statistical significance beyond the (two-tailed) 90 percent confidence interval. Wealthier respondents are less inclined to use airpower or US troops to attack terrorist bases. Surprisingly, the largest income effect is for the use of US troops "to deal with humanitarian crises."

On balance, we have strong reason to suspect that income affects grand strategy preferences but not one's assessment of threat. Income correlates somewhat to respondents' attitudes towards defense spending, but less wealthy people appear to be much more willing to use the military instrument in abstract scenarios. The relationship weakens to some degree when specific "proper nouns" are used.

3.3 Beyond casualty aversion to democratic militarism

In this chapter I have submitted cost distribution theory to a battery of micro-level tests. I find that, across a wide variety of countries, the more skewed the distribution of wealth within the country, the more likely the average voter will support higher defense spending. Looking more closely at American public opinion (and Israeli public opinion in Chapter 7), the lower one's household income the more likely one is to take a militarized approach to foreign policy. As importantly, there is little evidence that those with lower incomes in the United States find the world a more threatening place.

Given the small number of country-years examined here, and the unaccounted intermediating effect of government policy for each state in the cross-national survey, we can only take the findings at the macro-level to be suggestive. Nonetheless, the state-level effects predicted by the theory are largely confirmed. Not surprisingly, if a state has been recently involved in a conflict, respondents on average support more defense spending. A higher ratio of military aircraft to ground personnel also correlates to more enthusiasm for defense spending by the average respondent within each state. The somewhat counterintuitive finding that conscription correlates to more support for defense spending supports the theory as well.

The curvilinear relationship of economic inequality with approval for more defense spending was not explicitly anticipated by Chapter 2's theory. It seems that, for most countries in the survey, larger values of the Gini coefficient result in a more hawkish average response. The effect, while still positive, diminishes at very high levels of inequality. Defense may be something of a luxury good. I consider this further in the next chapter, as well as in the book's conclusion.

Nor do the surveys, particularly the cross-national ones, capture the benefit side of respondent calculations. While this chapter undermines the claim that the less wealthy are more susceptible to being manipulated by "myths of empire," it is equally clear that the public's perception of the need for security plays an important role in its cost–benefit calculus.

The relationship between the government and public opinion is, to say the least, complex (Berinsky, 2007; Baum and Potter, 2008). Nonetheless, large amounts of evidence suggest that the role of the average voter in shaping the incentives for a state's foreign policy is an important one, and in a democracy it plays a normatively essential one. The fundamental insight of the median voter theorem is that the will of voters in the center of an issue preference aggregation exerts a powerful pull on elected officials and therefore on the state's foreign policy. By relaxing the selectorate theory's assumption that all citizens are identical, this chapter takes a first step beyond the observation that democracies are "sensitive to costs" and begins to delineate what these costs may be and who pays them (Filson and Werner, 2004). Even if one argues that the rich are far more politically influential, the results from this chapter suggest that making government more representative of the less wealthy will not reduce the level of militarism.

3.A Appendix: statistical results

Table 3.3 lists the countries and years for which cross-national public opinion on defense spending from ISSP is available. Coefficients obtained from a pooled sample of all countries' respondents are likely to be biased, leading to underestimated standard errors, and I address this problem a number of ways. Table 3.4 reports results from three models incorporating only the micro-level variables. Model 8 employs an ordered logistic regression with fixed effects for each combination of year and country. Model 9 reports the same estimation technique using multiply-imputed data.[12] Fixed effects avoids state-level omitted variable bias at the cost of making no effort to test these factors' effects. Model 10 reports the results of a hierarchical ordered logit, assuming that both the state-year constants and income contain a random component.[13] Income's coefficient is in the predicted direction and is significant at conventional levels in all three models. The large variance term for income relative to its fixed effect coefficient, suggests, as expected, that state-level factors have considerable influence on income's effect.

Table 3.5 examines the influences on respondent assessments of the severity of various threat scenarios, and shows that income quintile has little effect. Table 3.6 presents the regression results depicted in Figure 3.4, while Tables 3.7 and 3.8 provide the results presented in Figure 3.5.

---

[12] Imputations and analyses performed using Amelia (Honaker et al., 2009) and Clarify (Tomz et al., 2001) software respectively.

[13] Hierarchical model was analyzed using GLLAMM (Rabe-Hesketh et al., 2004) for Stata.

Table 3.3 *Number of ISSP respondents by country and year*

Country	Year				Country	Year			
	1985	1990	1996	2006		1985	1990	1996	2006
Australia	1,295	2,168	1,993	2,435	South Korea				1,554
Austria	868				Latvia			1,341	703
Bulgaria			907		Netherlands				922
Canada			1,040	864	New Zealand			1,075	1,216
Chile				1,210	Norway		1,404	1,155	1,219
Croatia				795	Philippines			966	1,108
Cyprus			899		Poland			1,114	1,161
Czech Rep.			862	890	Portugal				1,132
Denmark				1,326	Russia				2,166
Dominican Rep.				2,034	Slovenia			695	521
Estonia			1,830		South Africa				2,235
Finland				1,002	Spain				1,851
France			1,152	1,165	Sweden			1,109	1,037
Germany		3,034	2,653	1,328	Switzerland			2,169	756
Hungary		764	1,276	837	Taiwan				1,845
Ireland		895	887	779	United Kingdom	1,338	1,011	886	812
Israel		944	731	815	United States	356	1,085	1,235	1,443
Italy	1,247	873	1,096		Uruguay				973
Japan			810	1,065					

Boldfaced figures have available state-level inequality data.

Table 3.4 *Ordered logistic results for defense spending opinion (ISSP)*

	(8) Ologit	(9) Ologit (imputed)	(10) Ologit (multilevel)
Income Quintile	−0.0357***	−0.0483***	−0.0527*
	(0.00666)	(0.00585)	(0.0229)
Age	0.00837***	0.00626***	0.00811***
	(0.000559)	(0.000459)	(0.000564)
Male	−0.0332+	−0.0693***	−0.0349*
	(0.0172)	(0.0147)	(0.0172)
Education	−0.138***	−0.124***	−0.138***
	(0.00687)	(0.00574)	(0.00679)
Political Party	0.316***	0.301***	0.315***
	(0.00898)	(0.009)	(0.00901)
Constant 1	−1.514***	−1.517***	−1.452***
	(0.120)	(0.117)	(0.110)
Constant 2	0.104	0.0140	0.168
	(0.120)	(0.117)	(0.110)
Constant 3	2.119***	1.88***	2.187***
	(0.120)	(0.117)	(0.110)
Constant 4	3.824***	3.466***	3.893***
	(0.121)	(0.1189)	(0.112)
Variance: Income			0.0946***
			(0.0105)
Variance: Constant			0.853***
			(0.124)
Respondents	46723	69784	46723
State-years	58	58	58
pseudo R^2	0.102	0.092	
log-likelihood			−61845.966

A1, A2: ordered logit, state-year fixed effects.
A2: imputed values using Amelia and Clarify.
A3: Hierarchical ordered logit using GLLAMM. Covariances not reported.
Standard errors in parentheses, ***$p < 0.001$, **$p < 0.01$, *$p < 0.05$, + $p < 0.1$.

Table 3.5 *Income and US threat assessment (CCGA)*

	(11) Proliferation	(12) Nuclear Iran	(13) Energy	(14) Islam	(15) AfPak	(16) Terror	(17) China	(18) Taiwan	(19) Threat Index
Income	0.106*	0.0638	0.0547	0.0363	0.00982	0.0261	−0.0134	−0.00344	0.0113
	(0.0435)	(0.0432)	(0.0397)	(0.0390)	(0.0401)	(0.0468)	(0.0392)	(0.0396)	(0.00699)
Education	−0.155***	−0.192***	−0.0506	−0.0200	−0.0918**	−0.0723+	−0.138***	−0.0924**	−0.0262***
	(0.0386)	(0.0388)	(0.0339)	(0.0329)	(0.0346)	(0.0404)	(0.0336)	(0.0335)	(0.00593)
Age	0.00819+	0.00247	0.00679+	0.0102**	0.00388	0.00882+	0.00807*	0.00858*	0.00193**
	(0.00425)	(0.00424)	(0.00385)	(0.00382)	(0.00388)	(0.00454)	(0.00377)	(0.00390)	(0.000676)
Male	−0.307*	−0.268*	−0.0909	0.128	−0.208+	−0.430**	−0.397***	−0.139	−0.0596**
	(0.135)	(0.133)	(0.123)	(0.120)	(0.124)	(0.145)	(0.120)	(0.123)	(0.0216)
Conservative	0.107*	0.140**	−0.0123	0.178***	0.103*	0.177**	0.162***	0.0939+	0.0319***
	(0.0520)	(0.0518)	(0.0473)	(0.0469)	(0.0480)	(0.0561)	(0.0467)	(0.0482)	(0.00834)
Republican	0.317+	0.505**	−0.136	0.162	0.386*	0.541**	0.148	0.112	0.0590*
	(0.173)	(0.177)	(0.155)	(0.155)	(0.159)	(0.192)	(0.153)	(0.157)	(0.0275)
Democrat	0.372*	0.000179	0.229	−0.193	0.231	0.304+	0.0437	−0.0180	0.0330
	(0.164)	(0.160)	(0.152)	(0.146)	(0.152)	(0.172)	(0.148)	(0.152)	(0.0266)
"Black"	0.321	0.134	0.573*	−0.106	−0.126	−0.126	−0.223	−0.0975	0.00795
	(0.282)	(0.263)	(0.258)	(0.235)	(0.240)	(0.277)	(0.242)	(0.251)	(0.0429)

Table 3.5 (cont.)

	(11) Proliferation	(12) Nuclear Iran	(13) Energy	(14) Islam	(15) AfPak	(16) Terror	(17) China	(18) Taiwan	(19) Threat Index
"Hispanic"	0.172	0.380	0.166	−0.165	0.115	0.362	0.236	−0.0246	0.0365
	(0.238)	(0.243)	(0.214)	(0.207)	(0.216)	(0.264)	(0.207)	(0.210)	(0.0370)
Uninterested	−0.325***	−0.353***	−0.367***	−0.367***	−0.492***	−0.418***	−0.254**	−0.332***	−0.0984***
	(0.0848)	(0.0843)	(0.0796)	(0.0775)	(0.0816)	(0.0900)	(0.0780)	(0.0798)	(0.0139)
ROK	−0.0385	0.0435	0.126	0.0789	0.000571	−0.135	−0.238+	0.184	0.00527
	(0.140)	(0.138)	(0.126)	(0.124)	(0.128)	(0.150)	(0.124)	(0.128)	(0.0223)
Democracy?									
N	1149	1151	1153	1142	1148	1153	1146	1137	1161
pseudo R^2	0.037	0.047	0.027	0.042	0.034	0.050	0.036	0.024	0.102

Models 11–18: ordered logit; 19: OLS. Constant coefficients not reported. Standard errors in parentheses, ***p < 0.001, **p < 0.01, *p < 0.05, + p < 0.1.

Table 3.6 *Income and support for US military use* (CCGA)

	(20) Def. Spending	(21) vs. Economic	(22) Superiority	(23) World Police	(24) Troop Index
Threat Index	1.348***	0.254	2.264***	0.508	0.195***
	(0.229)	(0.273)	(0.201)	(0.363)	(0.0331)
Income	−0.0734	−0.273***	−0.139**	−0.191**	−0.0208**
	(0.0565)	(0.0697)	(0.0434)	(0.0736)	(0.00706)
Education	−0.123**	−0.132*	−0.0969**	0.0967	−0.0106+
	(0.0472)	(0.0574)	(0.0360)	(0.0684)	(0.00597)
Age	−0.000185	−0.00454	0.00733+	−0.00841	−0.00110+
	(0.00543)	(0.00664)	(0.00413)	(0.00785)	(0.000652)
Male	0.0651	0.278	0.291*	−0.0696	0.0363+
	(0.169)	(0.208)	(0.136)	(0.234)	(0.0216)
Conservative	0.391***	0.271**	0.174**	0.101	−0.0135
	(0.0763)	(0.0867)	(0.0530)	(0.0878)	(0.00829)
Republican	0.587**	0.275	0.690***	0.340	0.0996***
	(0.215)	(0.258)	(0.179)	(0.314)	(0.0282)
Democrat	−0.0608	−0.213	0.0416	0.272	0.0597*
	(0.218)	(0.268)	(0.155)	(0.282)	(0.0278)

Table 3.6 (cont.)

	(20) Def. Spending	(21) vs. Economic	(22) Superiority	(23) World Police	(24) Troop Index
"Black"	−0.189	0.0716	0.805**	0.710+	−0.0219
	(0.388)	(0.395)	(0.289)	(0.398)	(0.0460)
"Hispanic"	0.386	0.0107	−0.0368	−0.179	−0.0582+
	(0.294)	(0.364)	(0.244)	(0.440)	(0.0333)
Uninterested	−0.224+	0.00133	−0.170*	−0.499**	−0.0347*
	(0.117)	(0.137)	(0.0866)	(0.171)	(0.0150)
ROK Democracy?	−0.255	0.0722	0.0434	0.660**	0.0967***
	(0.180)	(0.215)	(0.136)	(0.254)	(0.0225)
N	575	592	1148	554	574
pseudo R^2	0.114	0.076	0.148	0.070	0.183

Models 20 and 22: ordered logit; 21 and 23: logit; 25: OLS.
Standard errors in parentheses, ***p < 0.001, **p < 0.01, *p < 0.05, + p < 0.1.

Table 3.7 *Income and support for US military scenarios, part 1 (CCGA)*

	(25) Terror Air	(26) Terror Ground	(27) Strike Iran	(28) Bomb Pakistan	(29) Troops for Oil	(30) Troops for ROK
Issue Importance	0.801***	0.696***	0.936***	0.704***	0.629***	0.408***
	(0.215)	(0.200)	(0.180)	(0.165)	(0.156)	(0.0861)
Income Quintile	−0.154+	−0.153*	−0.0572	0.0386	−0.0707	−0.132+
	(0.0809)	(0.0718)	(0.0628)	(0.0667)	(0.0605)	(0.0681)
Education	−0.0833	−0.143*	−0.207***	−0.141*	−0.105*	−0.0341
	(0.0680)	(0.0613)	(0.0567)	(0.0579)	(0.0536)	(0.0596)
Age	0.00296	−0.00371	−0.0132*	0.00823	0.00577	−0.00623
	(0.00762)	(0.00672)	(0.00616)	(0.00654)	(0.00566)	(0.00623)
Male	0.353	0.530*	0.597**	−0.0190	0.0478	1.039***
	(0.243)	(0.215)	(0.195)	(0.206)	(0.184)	(0.204)
Conservative	0.240*	0.285***	0.225**	0.00905	0.0515	0.115
	(0.0933)	(0.0835)	(0.0729)	(0.0751)	(0.0718)	(0.0796)
Republican	0.303	0.117	0.681**	0.289	0.901***	0.679**
	(0.313)	(0.277)	(0.240)	(0.270)	(0.239)	(0.261)
Democrat	0.320	0.180	−0.208	−0.0713	0.00569	0.633*
	(0.287)	(0.257)	(0.238)	(0.244)	(0.230)	(0.261)

Table 3.7 (cont.)

	(25) Terror Air	(26) Terror Ground	(27) Strike Iran	(28) Bomb Pakistan	(29) Troops for Oil	(30) Troops for ROK
"Black"	−0.308	−0.728+	0.210	0.163	0.183	−1.065*
	(0.457)	(0.391)	(0.390)	(0.395)	(0.353)	(0.417)
"Hispanic"	−0.315	−0.287	−0.0954	−0.0403	−0.0677	−0.985**
	(0.382)	(0.354)	(0.329)	(0.362)	(0.295)	(0.345)
Uninterested	−0.528***	−0.597***	−0.133	−0.0996	0.0101	−0.467***
	(0.145)	(0.136)	(0.131)	(0.126)	(0.120)	(0.137)
ROK Democracy?	0.557*	0.0434	0.148	0.523*	0.0318	1.027***
	(0.254)	(0.223)	(0.199)	(0.212)	(0.190)	(0.207)
N	552	553	578	587	564	564
pseudo R^2	0.111	0.104	0.137	0.064	0.063	0.193

Ordered logit. Constant coefficients not reported.
Standard errors in parentheses, ***p < 0.001, **p < 0.01, *p < 0.05, + p < 0.1.

Table 3.8 *Income and support for US military scenarios, part 2 (CCGA)*

	(31) Troops for Taiwan	(32) Isr.-Pal.	(33) Defend Israel	(34) Genocide	(35) Darfur	(36) Humanitarian
Issue Importance	0.560***	0.537***	0.831***	0.808***	0.962***	0.795***
	(0.164)	(0.151)	(0.162)	(0.127)	(0.153)	(0.130)
Income Quintile	−0.123+	−0.104+	−0.0470	0.0721	−0.102	−0.188**
	(0.0705)	(0.0602)	(0.0650)	(0.0686)	(0.0630)	(0.0698)
Education	−0.0522	−0.0456	−0.0667	−0.158*	−0.0290	−0.0120
	(0.0606)	(0.0532)	(0.0572)	(0.0622)	(0.0559)	(0.0601)
Age	−0.00244	−0.00151	0.00843	−0.0128+	−0.0150*	−0.0100
	(0.00643)	(0.00565)	(0.00600)	(0.00655)	(0.00599)	(0.00636)
Male	0.657**	−0.0910	0.416*	−0.314	−0.110	−0.149
	(0.215)	(0.184)	(0.196)	(0.208)	(0.192)	(0.206)
Conservative	0.120	−0.213**	0.200**	−0.232**	−0.194**	−0.0759
	(0.0823)	(0.0718)	(0.0745)	(0.0834)	(0.0749)	(0.0811)
Republican	0.703**	0.556*	0.629*	0.406	0.0331	0.0538
	(0.266)	(0.236)	(0.251)	(0.262)	(0.244)	(0.252)
Democrat	0.171	0.286	−0.0481	0.164	0.255	0.758**
	(0.281)	(0.231)	(0.245)	(0.262)	(0.241)	(0.274)

Table 3.8 *(cont.)*

	(31) Troops for Taiwan	(32) Isr.-Pal.	(33) Defend Israel	(34) Genocide	(35) Darfur	(36) Humanitarian
"Black"	−0.311	−0.0812	−0.0180	0.761	−0.0591	−0.413
	(0.441)	(0.358)	(0.375)	(0.464)	(0.380)	(0.432)
"Hispanic"	−0.143	−0.298	−0.402	0.0965	−0.647*	−0.300
	(0.355)	(0.302)	(0.318)	(0.348)	(0.311)	(0.336)
Uninterested	−0.139	−0.0161	−0.254+	−0.293*	−0.228+	−0.219+
	(0.143)	(0.121)	(0.130)	(0.131)	(0.124)	(0.129)
ROK Democracy?	1.013***	0.315+	0.842***	0.202	0.277	−0.0806
	(0.228)	(0.190)	(0.202)	(0.216)	(0.198)	(0.213)
N	557	561	559	570	565	565
pseudo R^2	0.120	0.049	0.147	0.117	0.118	0.114

Ordered logit. Constant coefficients not reported.
Standard errors in parentheses, ***p < 0.001, **p < 0.01, *p < 0.05, +p < 0.1.

4 | *Analyses of arming and war*

I take the previous chapter's empirical insight of foreign policy as redistribution to examine the roles of inequality and, most especially, capitalization in allowing democracies to act quite boldly to change the international status quo. To do so, I have developed a new data set incorporating three new measurements of the state's ratio of military capital stock and military personnel.

In spite of recent strides (Signorino and Tarar, 2006; Signorino, 1999), the challenges inherent to statistical analysis of strategic behavior are by now well known, particularly when exploring the factors leading to war or successful deterrence (Fearon, 2002; Schultz, 1999). To paraphrase Mark Twain, often the best a substantive researcher can achieve is to find estimators that rhyme with rather than replicate the formalized relationships between the variables. For this reason and that of data availability, I do not test all the theory's empirical implications. For example, while cost distribution theory suggests that in important conflicts a democracy can experience incentives to fight in a suboptimal manner, the formal model shows that the relationships between capitalization and "winning" or "losing" a conflict are far from straightforward, and are therefore better tested in case studies. Testing whether democracies try harder in terms of defense spending is marred by the non-stationary nature of the data (Lin and Ali, 2009).

Faced with these constraints, the preeminent goal of this chapter's quantitative analysis is demonstrating that redistribution in the form of military capitalization has a significant effect on a democratic state's grand strategy. I aggressively control for biases inherent in the data. I subscribe to the philosophy that, when in doubt, simpler statistical approaches are better. I seek to show convincingly that certain essential elements of cost distribution theory receive strong empirical support, allowing us to have confidence in the theory's usefulness in its entirety.

4.1 States' military capitalization

If a capitalized military tends to reduce the costs of defense for the median voter (and thus raises support for more defense), then:

H_8 As the military threat to a state increases, a democracy will develop a more capitalized military.

H_8 is a novel deviation from the finding of many works of democratic exceptionalism that democracies try harder in war, and spend less on the military in times of peace. Instead of arguing that democracies respond to a threat by spending more on defense, I argue that democracies also respond to threats by shifting their resources to different things, namely military capital.

A number of plausible explanations – casualty aversion, high per capita wealth, and an aging population – exist for this relationship between threat and military capitalization. To demonstrate the redistributive element of military preparation, I look to another factor within the state:

H_9 As economic inequality increases, a democracy will develop a more capitalized military.

Finally, the theory explicitly incorporates the risk of being conscripted as a public bad, and therefore I test the following hypothesis:

H_{10} A democracy with a conscripted military will develop a more capitalized military.

This last hypothesis may appear counterintuitive, because we normally associate all-volunteer militaries like that of the United States with a high-tech "Revolution in Military Affairs" (RMA) form of warfare. More deductively, when labor is artificially cheap (as in a conscripted military) one will use more of it (and use it less efficiently, see Horowitz et al., 2011). On the other hand, finding support for H_{10} is not ironclad proof for cost distribution theory, as one could explain this finding if the money that would be devoted to market wages in a volunteer military can instead be invested in equipment. Nonetheless, while finding significant evidence of this relationship does not provide exclusive support for cost distribution theory, it remains an interesting finding.

The unit of analysis is the state-year. I analyze two complementary sets of data, both of which represent considerable updates to the capitalization data analyzed by Erik Gartzke (2001). The first includes 60 states that have filed reports for the Military Expenditures Database of the UN Office for Disarmament Affairs (n.d.).[1] The second data set consists of the democratic members of NATO with observations from 1971–2010 (NATO, 2011).[2] Because the two organizations have different accounting procedures, the data sets are not easily reconcilable and are thus analyzed separately. I operationalize military capitalization as the portion of the defense budget devoted to "Procurement and Construction" (UN) and "Equipment" (NATO).[3] More direct measurements of mechanization such as the number of armored vehicles per soldier (Sechser and Saunders, 2010) do not vary much over time and give no sense of these platforms' quality. For example, North Korea and the US have roughly comparable numbers of submarines, but I have good reason to believe the latter's fleet is more capital-intensive and effective.

Both data sets exhibit selection effects. Figure 4.1 shows clearly that the number of countries making reports to the UN rises steadily over time. Figure 4.1 also makes clear that there is, unsurprisingly, a great deal of overlap between the states that submit reports to NATO and the UN.[4]

Regime type is clearly endogenous to the data generating process. NATO members have been largely democratic, even before it was a membership requirement. Figure 4.2 shows clearly that one's Polity score is also a very good predictor of submitting a report to the United

---

[1] Fifteen other states have submitted a single year's worth of data, and are thus dropped from the data set due to the need for fixed effects.

[2] States in both data sets were coded as democratic with a Polity 2 score of 6 or higher according to the Polity IV data set (Gurr et al., 2002).

[3] These measures factor in the relative prices of capital and labor and account for purchasing power differences. Of all the potential measurements of a state's capital spending priorities, the defense budget proportions are the least likely to exhibit non-stationarity that plagues defense spending data (Lin and Ali, 2009, 302–304). Tests show little evidence of integration for either data set's measure.

[4] There is, however, surprisingly *little* overlap between either of these data sets and the country-years represented in the ISSP surveys. I ran versions of the multi-level models in Table 3.1. The coefficients for both NATO and UN data sets were positive, as predicted by the theory, but not significant. Then again, there were only 19 state-years covered by the UN data set, and a mere 10 in the NATO data set.

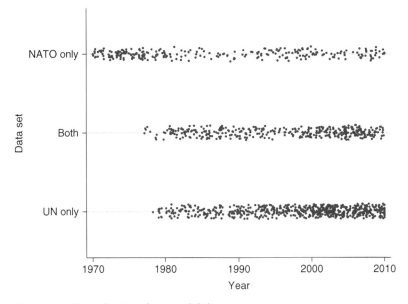

Figure 4.1 Capitalization data availability over time

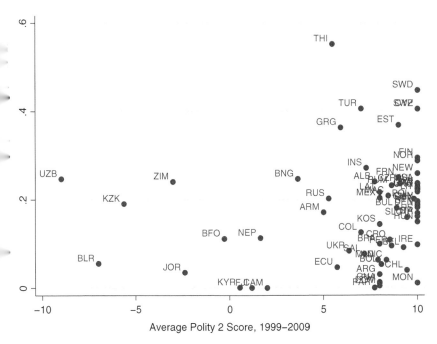

Figure 4.2 Regime type and procurement as % budget (UN)

Nations. Since almost no observations of capitalization are available for countries with a Polity score of less than 6, we cannot use these data to test the strong versus weak versions of cost distribution theory.

The two data sets complement each other. The NATO data are most likely of higher quality and consistency, not only because NATO tracks and reports military spending in significant detail, but also because these states generally report aspects of their population and economy in a transparent and effective manner. Many NATO member states are also among the world's wealthiest and most mature democracies, and thus represent "easy cases" for democratic exceptionalism (Mansfield and Snyder, 2005). NATO members report annually the percentage of their defense budget spent on *Equipment*.[5] The UN data set contains more observations and allows for comparisons across a wider array of countries.[6] The graphs in Figure 4.3 give a sense of the differences in percentage between these two measures, the distribution of the percentages for each year, as well as the names of the countries with especially high capital spending. NATO countries were steadily increasing their capital spending up to the end of the Cold War, but there appears to be little systematic movement over time since then. There appears to be a similar pattern in the UN data set, but the drop after the Cold War appears much sharper.

---

[5] In later years, NATO members also report "infrastructure" spending. However, in order to maximize the number of observations, and because in later years the reports from these countries overlap a great deal, I decided to focus only on equipment even if this understates how much a country spends on military capital.

[6] It also collects more fine-grained data, including a top-line value for the percentage of the defense budget spent on "Procurement and Construction." The other categories are "Operating Costs" – which includes the subcategories "Personnel" and "Operations and Maintenance" – and "Research and Development." The "Procurement" subcategory covers the tools of war – aircraft, missiles, vehicles, electronics, and ammunition – whereas "materials for current use" and "maintenance" are excluded from this category. The "Construction" subcategory covers air bases, naval bases, and missile sites; as well as personnel, training, and medical facilities. Both subcategories are likely to have redistributive aspects (both in security and in pork) and so I employ the sum of the two. Many countries only report a top-line "Procurement and Construction" figure, which makes isolating the "Procurement" component impossible. Furthermore, some countries simply reported a "Procurement" value in a simplified report format that appears to have little relationship to the longer report categories that make up my data set. These states have been excluded from the data set.

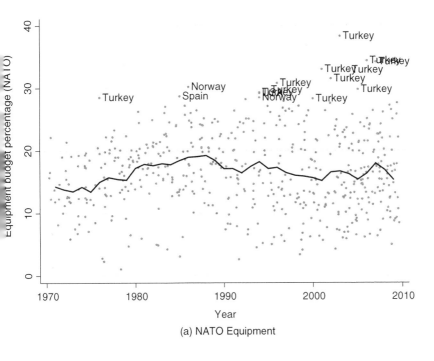

(a) NATO Equipment

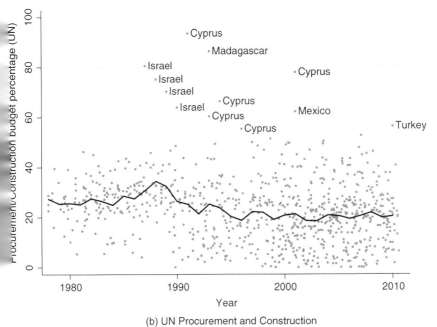

(b) UN Procurement and Construction

Figure 4.3 Capital spending (and annual mean) over time

The fact that economic inequality may correlate to capitalization appears plausible in Figure 4.4. NATO equipment percentage seems to increase monotonically as inequality rises, but the larger number and broader range of countries in the UN data set show a more complicated picture, similar to the public opinion data shown in Figure 3.3. Highly unequal democracies appear to spend relatively little of their defense budget on procurement and construction. Although this complicates the theory presented earlier in the book, I will take this relationship into account for the remainder of the chapter.

4.1.1 *Explanatory and control variables*

My first explanatory variable remains the state's *Inequality*. As in the previous section, I use the SWIID Gini coefficient (which factors in other governmental redistribution programs).[7] Because the previous section suggested that the relationship between inequality and preferences for capitalization may not be linear, I have chosen to incorporate, as before, the Gini coefficient's square term. This modeling choice has important consequences that, in the interest of transparency, will be highlighted later in this section.

To operationalize the need for security, I use involvement in a recent *Conflict* (again from the UCDP data set) and the *Threat* posed by rivals' military capability. For *Threat* in the UN data I use the combined capability of a state's potential enemies from the Strategic Rivals data set (Colaresi et al., 2007).[8] Colaresi et al. identify few rivals for

---

[7] SWIID covers the years 1960 to the present. Insufficient LIS observations exist to be used for time series analysis.

[8] The CINC score combines six measures (military spending, military personnel, iron and steel production, energy consumption and total and urban population) expressed as a percentage of the total in the international system for that year. Very few states in the data set are coded as having strategic rivals. However, since this data set looks at countries over relatively long periods of time, there is sufficient variation in Threat to justify its inclusion. For the country-years found in the ISSP data sets used in the analysis of public opinion, Threat takes on a non-zero value 6 times, which severely limits its usefulness. Note that for similar reasons, a strong ally may reduce the state's insecurity as well as allow it to specialize in its abundant factor (analogous to the predictions of international trade theories of comparative advantage) rather than overweight capital in the state's military portfolio; given this my theory would suggest that strong allies will result in a *decrease* in military capitalization and its inclusion produces an additional test of the theory. In analyses not reported here, but to be included in an online appendix, I

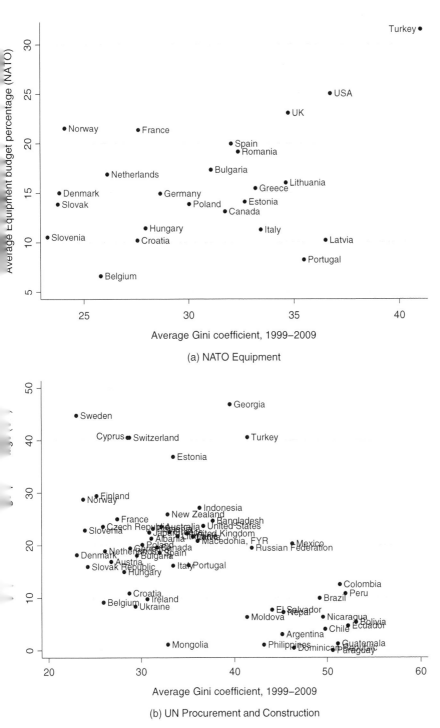

(a) NATO Equipment

(b) UN Procurement and Construction

Figure 4.4 Inequality and military capital spending in democracies

NATO countries, so I employed an alternate measure of threat in the NATO data set, the natural log of Soviet (Russian) military spending, interacted with a "Cold War" dummy for all years up through 1991.[9] My final explanatory variable, whether a military is conscripted or all-volunteer, is operationalized as the dichotomous *Volunteer* from a data set compiled by Nathan Toronto (2005).[10]

The most important control variable stemming from the theory is the price of military labor relative to that of military capital, which should reflect the underlying factor endowments of the state and thereby control for wealth as well. This is particularly essential since democracy, wealth, and even inequality are correlated with each other. I again chose *logged GDP per capita* from the UN to represent these important influences on the allocation of military resources.[11] An aging population will require a more capitalized military due to a smaller labor pool; as before I therefore include the *Population Percentage over 65*, taken from the World Bank (2006).

4.1.2 Results

Time series, cross-sectional (TSCS) data, especially across states, tend to exhibit a number of pathologies that render a simple ordinary least

incorporated *Defensive Allies' Capabilities*, based on the CINC scores taken from the COW alliance data set (Gibler and Sarkees, 2004). I assume that the public goods value of defense spending has no effect on that of allies, an obvious simplification (Sandler and Hartley, 1995). It must be noted that because information on alliance capabilities only reaches 2001, this greatly limits the number of observations.

[9] I also used the CINC score with little difference in outcomes, and thus do not report the results.

[10] Unlike the Gifford (2006) conscription data used in Chapter 3, this variable does not contain information on the percentage of the armed forces that are conscripts, but the broader coverage for the Toronto data set outweighs this consideration. Using the more fine-grained data had little effect on the regressions besides reducing the number of observations and therefore increasing the standard errors.

[11] Alternative measurements include the industrial wage rate (Rama and Artecona, 2002) and *per* capita capital *stock* (Heston et al., 2006). The three measurements correlate quite closely (the lowest correlation between the three is 0.85). While the wage rate most closely conforms to the theoretical price of military labor, I have chosen to use GDP per capita due to the larger number of available observations and its increased consistency across time and space. The direction and in most cases the significance of the explanatory variables do not change if I use these alternate measures in the regressions.

Table 4.1 *Effect of threat and inequality on capitalization (UN)*

	(37)	(38)	(39)	(40)
Gini	1.574+	1.932**	1.710*	2.136**
	(0.854)	(0.652)	(0.841)	(0.692)
Gini^2	−0.0299*	−0.0332***	−0.0317*	−0.0362***
	(0.0138)	(0.00977)	(0.0134)	(0.0105)
Conflict	0.168	0.861		
	(0.628)	(0.783)		
Rivals' capab.			37.03***	29.97*
			(8.666)	(15.17)
Volunteer	−0.988	−0.387	−1.751+	−0.821
	(1.060)	(0.992)	(1.042)	(1.125)
Pop. % > 65	−0.455**	−0.0906	−0.610***	−0.277
	(0.151)	(0.252)	(0.143)	(0.276)
ln(GDPpc)	0.847	6.703*	2.514+	7.834*
	(1.443)	(2.968)	(1.288)	(3.145)
DV$_{t-1}$	0.519***	0.493***	0.509***	0.488***
	(0.0772)	(0.0393)	(0.0877)	(0.0434)
Constant	−6.107	−69.44*	−25.10	−80.70**
	(19.90)	(28.55)	(19.42)	(30.43)
Country f.e.	Yes	Yes	Yes	Yes
Year f.e.	No	Yes	No	Yes
N	596	596	554	554
overall R^2	0.8035	0.5136	0.8135	0.5063

State, year fixed effects not reported. Panel-corrected (37 and 39) or robust (38 and 40) errors in parentheses. + $p < 0.10$, *$p < 0.05$, **$p < 0.01$, ***$p < 0.001$.

squares (OLS) regression inappropriate. The great number of steps I take to mitigate these effects are described in the chapter's appendix. This comes at a cost; fixed effects and lagged dependent variables likely mask the effect of slow moving variables such as the presence of conscription.

The statistical results for both the UN and NATO data sets are shown in Tables 4.1 and 4.2 respectively. Before analyzing the tables' results, I reiterate that including the squared Gini term is a highly consequential decision. Repeating the analysis in Table 4.2 produces, in the models with country fixed effects, beta coefficients for Gini are *negative and mostly significant*. Once the squared term is introduced,

Table 4.2 *Effect of threat and inequality on capitalization (NATO)*

	(41)	(42)	(43)	(44)	(45)	(46)
Gini	0.309	0.628+	0.666*	0.718*	0.292	0.777*
	(0.234)	(0.369)	(0.270)	(0.327)	(0.227)	(0.355)
Gini²	−0.00410	−0.0112*	−0.00988*	−0.0123**	−0.00409	−0.0136*
	(0.00383)	(0.00562)	(0.00402)	(0.00471)	(0.00365)	(0.00551)
Conflict	1.024***	0.278	0.739+	0.264		
	(0.300)	(0.340)	(0.416)	(0.445)		
Cold War	0.330	0.518			−25.60*	−27.64*
	(0.319)	(0.455)			(11.72)	(11.31)
Russia spending					−0.495	−0.137
					(0.482)	(0.419)
Russia × Cold War					1.373*	1.477*
					(0.636)	(0.607)
Volunteer	−0.674*	−0.709	−0.644	−0.720	−0.197	−0.518
	(0.329)	(0.499)	(0.409)	(0.473)	(0.238)	(0.459)
Pop. % > 65	−0.148*	−0.0808	−0.199*	−0.0753	−0.161**	−0.190
	(0.0647)	(0.120)	(0.0942)	(0.138)	(0.0596)	(0.124)

Table 4.2 *(cont.)*

	(41)	(42)	(43)	(44)	(45)	(46)
ln(GDPpc)	0.957**	2.045	0.991*	1.484	0.508*	2.329+
	(0.298)	(1.320)	(0.408)	(2.413)	(0.242)	(1.237)
DV_{t-1}	0.691***	0.691***	0.678***	0.714***	0.714***	0.699***
	(0.0321)	(0.0414)	(0.0339)	(0.0313)	(0.0418)	(0.0329)
Constant	−10.37*	−20.51	−13.21*	−18.53	3.302	−22.16
	(4.195)	(13.66)	(5.946)	(23.85)	(10.20)	(16.60)
Country f.e.	No	Yes	No	Yes	No	Yes
Year f.e.	No	No	Yes	Yes	No	No
N	503	503	503	503	458	458
pseudo R^2	0.8234	0.8434	.8331	0.7703	0.8455	0.8703

State, year fixed effects not reported. Panel-corrected (41, 42, 45, and 46) or robust (43 and 44) standard errors in parentheses. + p < 0.10, * p < 0.05, ** p < 0.01, *** p < 0.001.

the results depict a curvilinear relationship. F-tests show that the joint effects of Gini and Gini squared in all but one of the models are unlikely to be zero, and so I present the results of the more complicated model.

Figure 4.5 graphically depicts the predicted value for the dependent variable in representative models from the UN and NATO data sets, as a function of the Gini coefficient. The figure includes a histogram for the observed values of the Gini coefficient to provide a sense of how the predicted curve fits the distribution of states' inequality in the data. As can be seen from the curve, the positive effect of inequality begins to drop off at approximately the mean level of inequality. While the shape of the curve conforms to the theorized model, two caveats must be added. First, as the previous paragraph makes clear, one's choice of model has a large effect on the conclusions one can make. Second, even the models depicted in Figure 4.5 show that after a certain, relatively modest level of inequality, capitalization decreases dramatically as inequality rises.

The results in Tables 4.1 and 4.2 provide stronger support that democracies respond to threat and conflict by increasing the capital investment relative to personnel. Involvement in a *conflict* does increase the CPR in all of the models, although not always at conventionally significant levels when fixed effects are included.[12] In the two NATO models without country fixed effects, a recent conflict produces a relatively large (0.7–1.0%) increase in equipment percentage. On the other hand, *threat* more clearly appears to have the theoretically predicted effect. An increase in strategic rivals' capability produces a significant increase in capital procurement in the UN data set. Likewise, increased Soviet military spending results in increased capitalization in the NATO data, but only during the Cold War.

For similar reasons, the use of fixed effects and the lagged dependent variable are likely to mask the effect of having a volunteer military. Nonetheless, the coefficients for having a volunteer military are all negative, although at conventional levels of significance in a minority of models. Wealthier states not surprisingly spend a larger percent

---

[12] Again, the aggressive use of fixed effects (while frankly unavoidable) may inflate the standard errors to such a degree that one cannot test this aspect of the theory.

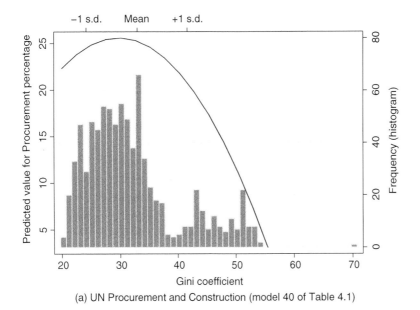

(a) UN Procurement and Construction (model 40 of Table 4.1)

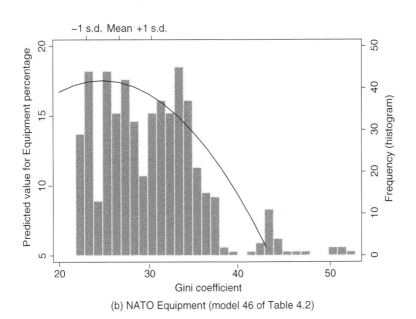

(b) NATO Equipment (model 46 of Table 4.2)

Figure 4.5 Inequality and predicted capitalization levels

of their budgets on capital. Democracies with older populations rely significantly less on military capitalization.

4.2 Military aggression

Two major challenges arise when testing the empirical implications of a strategic theory such as the one presented in Chapter 2's appendix, which focuses on the ability of states to coerce each other. First, many factors and implications are simply not observable. One cannot determine directly an actor's valuation of the "prize" at stake, and this is compounded by the incentive to bluff, yet another unobservable implication. It is equally hard to determine when deterrence takes place, as many successful instances of deterrence are not identified in the literature on crises precisely because the deterrence was successful.

The second major problem arises from the strategic nature of the interactions. While the occurrence of war is an important concern of the MTM model, its relationship to the explanatory variables is not straightforward. For example Todd Sechser (2007) shows how overwhelming power can lead to an *increased* likelihood of failed compellence, i.e. war. The relationships between power, resolve, and redistribution to the outbreak of fighting are not monotonic.

To test the role of redistribution in the coercive use of the military, I will therefore focus on one important component of a militarized grand strategy: the decision to change the status quo through the use of military force ("aggression" for simplicity). "Aggression" does not entail war exclusively; from the formal model of Chapter 2, in many cases the Compeller will find it worthwhile to mobilize sufficiently to guarantee obtaining the prize without bloodshed. While war is a difficult dependent variable to test due to its non-monotonic relationship to the explanatory variables, cost distribution theory suggests that the number of compellence attempts (from Chapter 2's appendix, a compellence attempt is the equivalent of choosing $m_C > 0$) has a strictly positive relationship to redistribution, whether or not it results in war.

The formal theory of Chapter 2 focused on the redistribution parameter θ, the degree to which the costs of arming and war are shifted away from the median voter (in a democracy). Two factors affect this redistribution parameter: economic inequality and military capitalization. I therefore test the following relationships:

H_{11} *The more capitalized a democracy's military, the more attempts at compellence it will make.*

H_{12} *The more economically unequal a democratic state, the more attempts at compellence it will make.*

As in the previous section, my principal focus remains on democracies. Again, while I would expect the redistribution effect to be reversed among plutocracies, I cannot assume that all non-democracies work that way (Peceny et al., 2003). However, while public opinion and military capitalization data for non-democracies are scarce, sufficient information on inequality and militarized disputes exists to test a regime-based version of H_{11} and H_{12}.

H_{13} *Military capitalization has a greater effect on compellence attempts in democracies than in non-democracies.*

H_{14} *Economic inequality has a greater effect on compellence attempts in democracies than in non-democracies.*

The unit of analysis is the directed-dyad-year, where state "A" is the potential aggressor against state "B." The time periods for each of the nine models tested here (using three versions of the explanatory variable and dependent variables) range across the years 1960 through 2005. No measure perfectly captures the theorized variable of *military aggression* and so I analyze three different operationalized versions.

I first identify whether a given state successfully revises the status quo in its favor over the course of a "militarized interstate dispute" (MID, taken from the Correlates of War dataset), a *revisionist MID*.[13] The result is 2,943 positive outcomes from 1960–2001. As a second pass at the theorized variable, I use Todd Sechser's *militarized compellent threat*, defined as "an explicit demand by one state (the challenger) that another state (the target) alter the status quo in some material

---

[13] A revisionist MID occurs when it ends with either a "victory for A," "B yields," a "compromise," or with fighting (a COW "hostility level" of 4 or 5, equivalent to State B resisting the compellence attempt in Chapter 2). I do not use the MID's coding of "initiator" since deciding who initiated a conflict is a difficult empirical task and is not essential to the theory.

Table 4.3 *Correlations of four military aggression measures*

	MID	Revision	Compellence	Intervention
MID	1.00			
Revision (MID)	0.81	1.00		
Compellence (Sechser)	0.13	0.13	1.00	
Intervention (Kisangani & Pickering)	0.17	0.19	0.12	1.00

way, backed by a threat of military force if the target does not comply" (Sechser, 2011, 380). Sechser's data meet the precise definition of the dependent variable, but there are relatively few observations (100 positive outcomes from 1960–2001).[14] My final operationalization is *intervention*, "the movement of regular troops or forces (airborne, seaborne, shelling, etc.) of one country inside another, in the context of some political issue or dispute," taken from the latest International Military Intervention (IMI) data set (Kisangani and Pickering, 2008). This is a less precise fit to the theorized dependent variable, but does capture some of the behavior I seek to explain. The 674 positive outcomes in the intervention data also extend to 2005, unlike the Sechser and MID data sets. Table 4.3 shows the (relatively slight) correlations between them and the broader MID data and to each other.

4.2.1 Explanatory and control variables

In a democracy, building a heavily capitalized military shifts the cost of the provision of defense onto the relatively wealthy since they pay the bulk of the state's tax bill. Similarly, while many other factors might contribute to a democracy *building* a capital intensive military (high per capita wealth, aging populace, etc.) this should not be confused with the effect this capitalized military has on conflict propensity. The percentage of the budget devoted to equipment deployed in the previous section is a less appropriate operationalization here (nor does it allow for testing based on regime type, i.e. H_{13} and H_{14}). What alters the likely outcome of war as well as the costs of war for the median

---

[14] Sechser uses these data to test theories about outcomes within the set of compellence attempts, not the attempt itself.

voter is the amount of materiel on hand at the time of conflict. As Donald Rumsfeld famously observed, one goes to war with the army one has.

Simply counting the number of pieces of equipment in a state's arsenal gives no sense of quality. On the other hand, exclusive focus on defense budgets gives little sense of where these dollars are spent (let alone the problems inherent in inevitable differences in purchasing power). I therefore employ several different operationalizations. I consider two different types of capitalization sources – armored ground vehicles and combat aircraft – not only in the interest of robustness, but because these two platforms can have plausibly different effects. This *ground mechanization* (GM) variable is taken from an updated version of Sechser and Saunders (2010), using data from the *Military Balance* series of publications (IISS 2013).[15] The *ground mechanization* variable is calculated by dividing an army's number of motorized vehicles (including main battle tanks, light tanks, and armored fighting vehicles) by the number of ground soldiers. Tanks, armored combat vehicles, and infantry transport vehicles belonging to marine or naval infantry units are also counted.[16]

For the *combat aircraft ratio* (CAR), I tallied the number of combat aircraft for each country-year (IISS, 2005). Among fixed wing aircraft I included fighters, bombers, and command and control planes. I also included helicopters of any description. I chose not to include transport or refueling planes, mostly because there are very few of these. While there is likely to be wide variation in the quality of these aircraft, I suspect it is less pronounced compared to ground vehicles.[17]

The final measure does not directly measure capital to personnel, but has a larger number of observations and can mitigate the quality concerns inherent in the other two measurements, the natural log

[15] Sechser and Saunders (2010) provided mechanization for all odd-numbered years from 1979–2001; I supplemented these data by collecting mechanization data for even-numbered years during this period.

[16] Sechser and Saunders (2010) also exclude strategic nuclear forces, paramilitary forces, domestic police forces, and reserves, since these forces are not consistently tracked across issues of *The Military Balance*.

[17] Both of these measurements are likely to be biased if, as one might suspect, democracies' individual aircraft and vehicles are much more sophisticated and capable compared to those of non-democracies. But if this is the case, the bias makes finding a regime-based difference less likely, making this a tougher test.

Table 4.4 *Descriptive statistics of three military capitalization measures (non-zero observations)*

Variable	Years	N	Mean	Std. Dev.	Min	Max
Aircraft	1962–2005	3564	0.0027	0.0041	0.000017	0.1125
Armor	1979–2002	3084	0.023	0.027	0.000047	0.20
Spending	1960–2005	6550	22,303.83	53,728.57	2.24	2,251,307

Table 4.5 *Correlations of three military capitalization measures*

	Aircraft	Armor	Spending
Aircraft	1.0000		
Armor	0.5442	1.0000	
Spending	0.2770	0.1774	1.0000

of *military spending per personnel* (MSPP). This also factors in wage rates, and so I use the broader measurement of "military personnel" from the COW data set. Table 4.4 shows some descriptive statistics of each measurement, and Table 4.5 the correlations between these three variables. Armor- and aircraft-to-soldier ratios covary considerably, while spending per personnel has little correlation with the others.

Inequality data again come from SWIID. The previous section analyzed the role that inequality plays in producing military capitalization. Including it as an explanatory variable allows us to explore conflict's redistributive nature independent of military capitalization. As before, I include the squared Gini term. I again include the dichotomous *Volunteer* military variable (Toronto, 2005), since conscription, according to cost distribution theory, lowers the expected value of conflict. This also allows me to test the widely held belief that volunteer militaries are more likely to be employed.

I take advantage of data availability to test the strong and weak versions of cost distribution theory by examining the role of regime type. To simplify the comparison and the number of interaction terms required to test the theory, I employ a dummy variable to split states by regime type, acknowledging that this lacks nuance. I code all states with a Polity IV score of 6 or higher as a *democracy*.

I interact democracy with capitalization, inequality, and type of military (conscripted or volunteer) to test whether any regime-specific difference exists in these theoretically derived variables.

Because distance is likely to contribute to the capital intensity of any given conflict as well as the conflict's likelihood I include a *distance* variable (COW), the logged great circle route between capitals. The *wealth* of a state (logged GDP per capita) obviously will have an impact on its ability to capitalize its military, but it is unclear that it also causes conflict, and therefore may not have a confounding effect.

4.2.2 Results

A battery of tests on all three dependent variables show striking differences between democracies and non-democracies (results in the appendix), and provide encouraging evidence for the theory's validity by showing that military capitalization increases the likelihood of democratic aggression. Inequality appears to play an important role, even after controlling for the potential mediating effect of capitalization. Finally, democratic volunteer militaries are more likely to be used aggressively as well.

Figure 4.6 depicts the marginal effect of a small change in all three of the capitalization measures for each of the three dependent variables. An increase in any measure of capitalization is associated with a positive increase in the probability of aggression, regardless of how the dependent variable is operationalized.[18] Seven of the nine changes in predicted probability are at conventional levels of statistical significance. On the other hand, capitalization does not appear to shift the prospect of aggression in non-democracies. Whereas a higher number of aircraft or vehicles per soldier correlate to a lower probability of aggression in non-democracies (but almost never to the point of statistical significance), higher spending per personnel appears to have a positive effect on aggression, even in non-democracies (albeit one significantly smaller than in democracies).

Because the marginal effect of inequality is a function of inequality itself (due to the square term), I depict the effects of the Gini

---

[18] The use of this measure is useful because it allows us to intuitively compare the effects of models across all nine combinations of the three capitalization measures and three dependent variables.

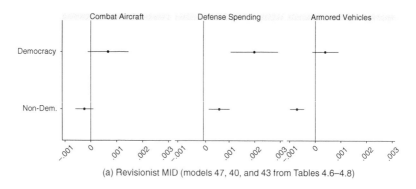

(a) Revisionist MID (models 47, 40, and 43 from Tables 4.6–4.8)

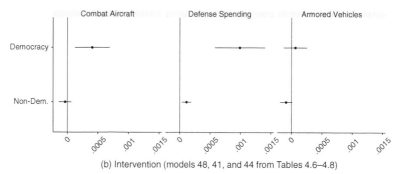

(b) Intervention (models 48, 41, and 44 from Tables 4.6–4.8)

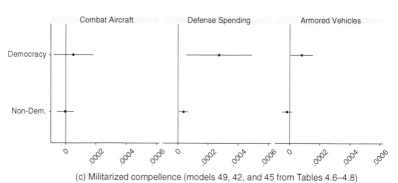

(c) Militarized compellence (models 49, 42, and 45 from Tables 4.6–4.8)

Values depict the average marginal effect of a one unit increase in the logged
explanatory variable averaged across all other values of the control variables, by
regime, with 95% confidence intervals.

Figure 4.6 Capitalization's marginal effects on aggression by regime type

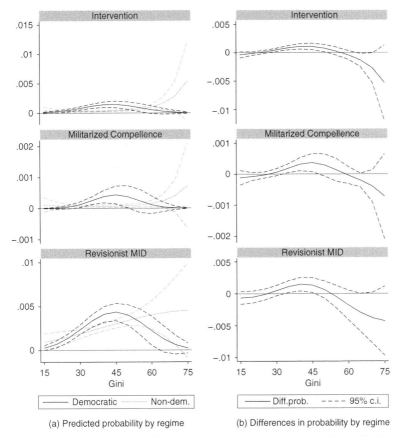

(a) Predicted probability by regime   (b) Differences in probability by regime

Values depict predicted probabilities of aggression across the range of inequality, by regime, with 95% confidence intervals.

Figure 4.7 Inequality's marginal effects on aggression by regime type

coefficient in a different manner. Figure 4.7a plots the role of inequality on the predicted probability for one version of aggression for both democracies and non-democracies (the same graph for either the other two dependent variables is quite similar and therefore not presented). The darker line, for democracies, shows the familiar curvilinear relationship. However, the peak of the curve occurs at a considerably higher level of inequality than that of Figure 4.5. Unlike in the analysis of military capitalization, the probability of initiating an act of aggression continues to rise with growing inequality well beyond the mean. Moreover, for most of the range of values of the Gini coefficient, the model predicts that democracies are *more likely* to initiate a revisionist MID. Figure 4.7b maps out which points along the range of inequality the differences between democracies and non-democracies are statistically significant (both graphs shows 95 percent intervals using dashed lines).

Finally, Figure 4.8 shows the first differences in predicted probability for a shift from a conscripted to a volunteer military for all nine combinations of dependent variables and measures of capitalization. The effect of a volunteer military is less pronounced than that of capitalization but nonetheless positive in all models (and significant in four). On the other hand, the effect of a volunteer military is always negative and rarely significant in non-democracies. Interestingly, a volunteer military never obtains significance at 95 percent levels (although it comes close) when the dependent variable is Sechser's compellence attempt, which does not necessarily entail violence. On the other hand, in the other two dependent variables – which entail some element of active, militarized hostility – the effect of a volunteer military significantly increases the probability in two of the three models.

On balance, there appears to be a great deal of evidence that shifting the costs of conflict through capitalization, economic inequality, and volunteer militaries leads to increased aggressiveness in democracies.

4.3 Summarizing the findings

In this chapter, and the one preceding it, I have submitted cost distribution theory to a battery of tests. To establish the robustness of the empirical findings, I employ multiple measurements of important variables such as military capitalization, drawing on several different data sources. I aggressively control for biases inherent in TSCS analysis, even at the risk of failing to find support for an actually existing relationship (i.e. Type II error). The implications for the dependent variables over substantively interesting values of the explanatory variables are explored and portrayed graphically. The strong and consistent support for my theory of defense redistribution and the sources of military aggression is therefore both robust and transparent.

From the micro-level analysis of Chapter 3, individuals' relative income appears to play a role in their assessment of defense spending, and this average attitude towards defense spending is exacerbated

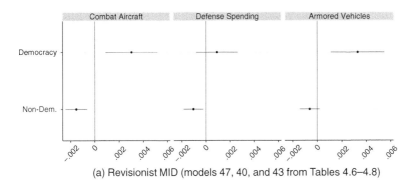

(a) Revisionist MID (models 47, 40, and 43 from Tables 4.6–4.8)

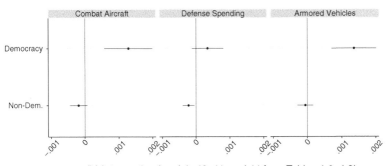

(b) Intervention (models 48, 41, and 44 from Tables 4.6–4.8)

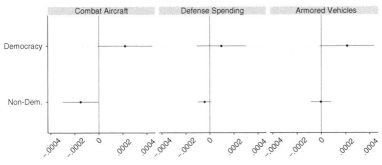

(c) Militarized compellence (models 49, 42, and 45 from Tables 4.6–4.8)

Values depict the average marginal effect of a shift from conscripted to volunteer military averaged across all other values of the control variables, by regime, with 95% confidence intervals.

Figure 4.8 Voluntary military's marginal effects on aggression by regime type

by state-level inequality, threat, and the capitalization of the military. Democracies respond to a strategic threat by increasing the percentage of their defense budget devoted to the purchase of equipment, a novel finding. On the other hand, the relationship between inequality and capitalization appears more complicated than predicted by the theory. Highly unequal democracies devote very little of their military budget to buy military capital. Many factors encourage democracies to invest in a heavily capitalized military. To show that inequality plays a role, even a small one, in its creation gives us a sense of its redistributive potential.

Indeed, once we accept that capitalization shifts the costs of arming and conflict then the underlying causes of a heavily capitalized military are less important than the effects that military's existence has on the grand strategy. The effects of inequality and military capitalization differ strikingly between democracy and non-democracies. Moreover, there appears to be a large difference between conscripted and volunteer militaries. Volunteer militaries appear more aggressive in democracies, but this effect reverses for non-democracies. These models of military aggressiveness provide excellent evidence that the explanatory variables play very different roles in democracies relative to other regime types.

Regardless of whether inequality affects the structure of the military, the link between heavily capitalized militaries and increasingly aggressive behavior appears to be on much firmer ground empirically. When costs are shifted away from the median voter (through inequality, capitalization, and the related volunteer military) democracies become more likely to pursue attempts at militarized revisionism (successful or not). My measurements probably understate the degree of capitalization in a democratic military; Biddle and Long (2004) have shown that democracies tend to have more highly educated militaries. Democracies may indeed be exceptional, but not necessarily in the ways envisioned by classical liberals and their contemporary social science successors.

4.3.1 Is militarism a luxury good?

The analyses in these two chapters reveal an important caveat to the link between inequality and my dependent variables. Democracies at the extreme end of the inequality scale appear to be less capitalized and less aggressive than those at the more moderate part of the Gini coefficient's range. This finding suggests that the effect of cost distribution on militarism is highest among the world's wealthiest and most mature democracies, the "easy cases" for democratic exceptionalism (Mansfield and Snyder, 2005).

Several plausible, if ad hoc, modifications to cost distribution theory could explain this non-linear relationship between inequality and democratic militarism. The first is that when differences between rich and poor are very large and per capita income is modest, even the median voter is likely to be extremely poor. The marginal benefit of a reduction in the tax burden will likely outweigh the benefits of a larger military effort or of a more aggressive, riskier grand strategy. Alternatively, democracies with extreme economic inequality (well beyond the United States' level) may also be relatively new democracies and thus be unsure of the extent of civilian supremacy over the military. One can imagine that, given the atrocities committed by the military, the average Argentinian would hesitate before giving it more resources after the fall of the junta in the early 1980s.

The third possible explanation for the curvilinear relationship between inequality and militarism is perhaps the most plausible and the most interesting: highly unequal democracies may not be all that democratic; the wealthy enjoy an oversized amount of political power not captured in the factors used by social scientists to code the level of a state's democracy. This conviction motivates the recent "Occupy Wall Street" movement, and some recent scholarship has begun to address the political effects of extreme distributions of wealth in democracies. However, were this third causal mechanism to be true, the negative coefficients of the squared term suggest that increased political power for the wealthy leads to a *moderating* effect on democratic militarism.[19] Such a conception is also supported by the effect of income quintile on one's attitude towards defense spending and foreign policy; wealthy (and more educated) respondents tend to provide more dovish responses to questions on defense spending, grand strategy, and the use of the military. It is appropriate then that the next chapter examines an important case in which the dramatic shift of political power within a state from an oligarchy to a more democratic form coincided with one of the most aggressive examples of empire-building in world history.

---

[19] This would appear plausible given the argument of Winters and Page (2009) that oligarchs are motivated by wealth defense, and that large crises like a major war will actually weaken the very wealthy's political power.

4.A Appendix: statistical results

Tables 4.6–4.8 depict the full results of the statistical models used to generate Figures 4.6–4.8. The remainder of this appendix discusses the choices of models and robustness checks associated with the tables.

State-level fixed effects will help correct for unit heterogeneity and thus omitted variable bias, but this comes at a cost of efficiency. There are almost certainly biases in how (and whether) data on military spending are reported. On the other hand, state fixed effects will mask the influence of stable variables such as conscription, and undermine that of slow-moving variables such as household inequality. Nonetheless, F-tests reject resoundingly the null of no unit heterogeneity in the data, and the conservative approach is to employ fixed effects, again at the risk of Type II errors.[20]

The need to use fixed effects for the NATO data (and its fewer observations) is less clear cut. The loss of power may not justify fixed effects use given the homogeneity of NATO states in terms of region, allies, rivals, wealth, and equipment (much of it bought from each other). F-tests reject the null that country fixed effects are jointly zero ($p = 0.03$). However, since it is more plausible that NATO members have more in common than the more diverse group in the UN data, I analyze the models with and without country fixed effects to explore the roles of slow-moving variables. There is also a high likelihood that time-based shocks to the system (global economic crises, end of the Cold War, the war on terror) will result in biases. In one set of models, I therefore introduce year fixed effects in addition to the unit level ones (analyzed with robust "Huber-White" standard errors), even if this results in additional costs in efficiency and inflated standard errors.

Not surprisingly, both the Gartzke and the NATO data exhibit strong serial correlation, as evidenced by autoregressions of the dependent variables. Solid theoretical reasons exist to expect autocorrelation as capital investment is likely to be a long-term, multi-year investment plan given the amount of time it takes to build advanced weapons platforms and their lengthy depreciations. Lagged dependent variables (LDVs) are the simplest means of controlling for this, although debate

---

[20] In cases of "marginal rejection," Beck and Katz (2001) suggest that the costs of fixed effects outweigh the benefits (but see also Wilson and Butler, 2007). The use of random effects models is more efficient than fixed, but Hausmann tests convincingly reject their appropriateness.

Table 4.6 *Effect of military spending to personnel ratio on military aggression*

	Revision attempt (47)		Intervention (48)		Compellence attempt (49)	
	Constituent variable	Democracy interaction	Constituent variable	Democracy interaction	Constituent variable	Democracy interaction
Democracy	-1.391		-6.302*		-6.185	
	(2.485)		(2.629)		(9.634)	
ln(Spending/Personnel)	-0.264***	0.425***	-0.213+	0.286+	-0.323	0.964*
	(0.0517)	(0.111)	(0.120)	(0.172)	(0.267)	(0.384)
Gini	0.126+	0.158+	0.185	-0.201*	0.430**	-0.0268
	(0.0895)	(0.124)	(0.0990)	(0.143)	(0.352)	(0.476)
Gini^2	-0.00117	-0.00266+	0.00288**	-0.00563**	0.000803	-0.00569
	(0.00104)	(0.00150)	(0.00111)	(0.00176)	(0.00390)	(0.00548)
Volunteer	-0.218	1.129***	-0.161	1.496***	-0.0759	1.540
	(0.179)	(0.283)	(0.297)	(0.395)	(0.809)	(1.025)
Joint democracy	-0.655***		-2.314***		-0.554	
	(0.176)		(0.349)		(0.566)	
Distance	-0.000648***		-0.000545***		-0.000347**	
	(0.0000676)		(0.0000559)		(0.000106)	
ln(GDPpc)	0.244***		0.329***		0.463*	
	(0.0698)		(0.0788)		(0.227)	

Table 4.6 (*cont.*)

	Revision attempt (47)		Intervention (48)		Compellence attempt (49)	
	Constituent variable	Democracy interaction	Constituent variable	Democracy interaction	Constituent variable	Democracy interaction
Cap. ratio	-0.203		1.282***		2.292**	
	(0.195)		(0.338)		(0.767)	
Constant	-8.400***		-5.456**		-11.71	
	(2.030)		(2.086)		(7.862)	
N	303827		303827		303827	
pseudo R^2	0.373		0.170		0.425	

Robust standard errors clustered on dyad in parentheses. $+ p < 0.10$, $* p < 0.05$, $** p < 0.01$, $*** p < 0.001$.
Peace years (squared and cubed) not reported.

Table 4.7 *Effect of combat aircraft to soldier ratio on military aggression*

	Revision attempt (50)		Intervention (51)		Compellence attempt (52)	
	Constituent variable	Democracy interaction	Constituent variable	Democracy interaction	Constituent variable	Democracy interaction
Democracy	-4.726*		-5.492**		-8.845	
	(2.134)		(2.052)		(6.433)	
ln(Aircraft/Soldier)	-0.105+	0.333**	-0.0657	0.433**	-0.0245	0.341
	(0.0613)	(0.122)	(0.0955)	(0.162)	(0.187)	(0.465)
Gini	0.0142	0.384***	-0.148*	0.464***	-0.11	0.527+
	(-0.0702)	(0.109)	(0.0748)	(0.121)	(0.124)	(0.310)
Gini^2	0.000419	-0.00512***	0.00218**	-0.00592***	0.00171	-0.00631
	(0.000811)	(0.00133)	(0.000842)	(0.00149)	(0.00132)	(0.00401)
Volunteer	-0.643**	1.240***	-0.364	1.341***	-1.497	2.679*
	(0.201)	(0.291)	(0.273)	(0.352)	(1.019)	(1.129)
Joint democracy	-0.644***		-2.066***		-0.512	
	(0.176)		(0.303)		(0.537)	
Distance	-0.000530***		-0.000543***		-0.000385***	
	(0.0000627)		(0.0000560)		(0.000107)	

Table 4.7 (cont.)

	Revision attempt (50)		Intervention (51)		Compellence attempt (52)	
	Constituent variable	Democracy interaction	Constituent variable	Democracy interaction	Constituent variable	Democracy interaction
ln(GDPpc)	0.144*		0.143+		0.479*	
	(0.0656)		(0.0810)		(0.225)	
Cap. ratio	−0.538**		1.101***		1.756**	
	(0.202)		(0.327)		(0.627)	
Constant	−3.798*		−4.245*		−7.966+	
	(1.575)		(1.805)		(4.217)	
N	271477		271477		271477	
pseudo R^2	0.373		0.154		0.329	

Robust standard errors clustered on dyad in parentheses, $+ \ p < 0.10$, $* \ p < 0.05$, $** \ p < 0.01$, $*** \ p < 0.001$.
Peace years (squared and cubed) not reported.

Table 4.8 *Effect of armored vehicle to soldier ratio on military aggression*

	Revision attempt (53)		Intervention (54)		Compellence attempt (55)	
	Constituent variable	Democracy interaction	Constituent variable	Democracy interaction	Constituent variable	Democracy interaction
Democracy	−5.380*		−9.290***		−14.91**	
	(2.101)		(2.537)		(5.537)	
ln(Vehicle/Soldier)	0.258***	0.492***	0.294**	0.745***	0.546**	0.735*
	(0.0732)	(0.134)	(0.0936)	(0.173)	(0.209)	(0.323)
Gini	0.126+	0.229*	−0.0842	0.427***	−0.0876	0.680**
	(0.0659)	(0.0981)	(0.0679)	(0.118)	(0.117)	(0.252)
Gini^2	−0.000988	−0.00296*	0.00143+	−0.00540***	0.00141	−0.00809**
	(0.000754)	(0.00118)	(0.000749)	(0.00144)	(0.00128)	(0.00303)
Volunteer	−0.475**	0.669*	−0.625*	0.969**	−0.719	1.150
	(0.176)	(0.305)	(0.260)	(0.340)	(0.543)	(0.703)
Joint democracy	−0.789***		−2.115***		−0.820+	
	(0.171)		(0.296)		(0.480)	
Distance	−0.000581***		−0.000550***		−0.000431***	
	(0.0000619)		(0.0000574)		(0.0000994)	

Table 4.8 (cont.)

	Revision attempt (53)		Intervention (54)		Compellence attempt (55)	
	Constituent variable	Democracy interaction	Constituent variable	Democracy interaction	Constituent variable	Democracy interaction
ln(GDPpc)	−0.127		−0.271*		−0.325	
	(0.0851)		(0.106)		(0.245)	
Cap. ratio	−0.429*		1.184***		1.460**	
	(0.178)		(0.261)		(0.482)	
Constant	−4.028**		−2.904		−3.767	
	(1.417)		(1.809)		(3.159)	
N	441767		441767		441767	
pseudo R^2	0.368		0.177		0.348	

Robust standard errors clustered on dyad in parentheses, + $p < 0.10$, * $p < 0.05$, ** $p < 0.01$, *** $p < 0.001$.
Peace years (squared and cubed) not reported.

continues over their advisability due to their tendency to reduce the significance of the other independent variables. While often cited in order to avoid their use, Achen (2000) does not reject LDVs but simply exhorts scholars to consider whether they are theoretically appropriate and required to correct for autocorrelation. An LDV is clearly appropriate on both counts, even if this results in some explanatory variables' coefficients losing significance.

When combined with country fixed effects, models with LDVs will always be biased, but multiple Monte Carlo simulations suggest that even with a small amount of residual serial correlation (less than 0.1) the bias is modest relative to the gains (Beck and Katz, 2004). Lagrange multiplier tests of the dependent variables reveal little or no remaining serial correlation following the introduction of an LDV.[21] The conservative tack is to include LDVs.

The data are likely to exhibit groupwise heteroskedasticity. Particularly in the UN data set, the quality and consistency of the data correlate with wealth and regime type. Panel-corrected standard errors (PCSE) control for this as well as for the cross-sectional correlation of errors (Beck and Katz, 1995). Their use has become standard in quantitative analysis of political science data; I therefore employ them in one set of models that do not include year fixed effects.

There also exists the potential for integration, that is, the dependent variable may contain one or more processes exhibiting a trend (OLS regression assumes a long-run equilibrium level for the dependent variable). Even if the data are stationary but highly persistent OLS is likely to produce spurious results.[22] Tests for stationarity in panel data tend to have low power, but a useful rule of thumb is to see whether the autoregressive coefficient, i.e. that of the LDV, is very

---

[21] I tested other specifications of the model, such as an autoregressive distributed lag and error correction (to diagnose co-integration) model. However, because the independent variables are obviously highly collinear (confirmed by VIF test), an ADL model, in the words of Beck and Katz (2004) "may be asking too much of the data."

[22] De Boef and Granato (1997). Lin and Ali (2009) also analyzed inequality and per capita military expenditure (rather than defense burden or capitalization) and found only the former to be non-stationary. Using an error correction model I did not find convincing evidence of co-integration, thus leaving me with a first differences model as my only option (the LDV's coefficient, while significant, was always less than -0.01). Since my explanatory variables are likely to have long-term rather than immediate effects, I reject this approach.

close to one (Beck and Katz, 2004). The autoregressive coefficient for the UN data was 0.87 and standard error of 0.02; 0.90 and 0.019 respectively for NATO). I therefore reject, albeit cautiously, the presence of non-stationarity in capitalization (something that cannot be said for budgets).

Turning to military aggression, many studies of conflict propensity use the Correlates of War's "militarized interstate dispute" (MID) as their dependent variable. The use of MIDs is inappropriate for a number of reasons.[23] Most importantly, the formal model makes monotonic predictions about the likelihood that one country would fail to deter an aggressive compeller.

The formal model incorporates State B's *military effort.* In regressions not reported here, I used three different measurements of this explanatory variable, all from the COW: military spending, CINC scores, and capability ratio (State A's CINC score divided by the combined score for A and B). The effects of my explanatory variables were not disturbed by any of these measures, and so I choose to report *capability ratio* due to its common use in previous work and its additional ability to control for the informational element of the balance of power (important strands of the rationalist study of conflict suggest that the miscalculations leading to war are more likely when power is evenly distributed within a dyad).[24]

I introduce other variables based only on the likelihood that they may have a confounding effect, serving as an antecedent cause of both military capitalization and the dependent variable of conflict initiation. Omitting such variables would create a spurious relationship between my explanatory and dependent variables. I do not include variables from alternative explanations for arming and war or those that may help determine military capitalization but are unlikely to play a role in the dependent variable (Ray, 2003, 2005).

Testing a binary dependent variable arising from a strategic relationship using TSCS data poses a number of potential complications,

---

[23] I also ran the models using all MIDs as the dependent variable, and got very similar results to those presented in the chapter. I report these results in the online appendix.

[24] Much of the data set was assembled using the EUGENE software (Bennett and Stam, 2000).

some of which have been addressed in the previous section. As in the previous data sets, groupwise heteroskedasticity is assured. Beck and Katz (2004) find that Huber-White standard errors clustered around the group (in this case the dyad) work effectively to mitigate these effects. The time between compellence attempts within a dyad likely plays a role and I control for it using a dyadic *peace years* term (that is the number of years since the last MID between any given pair of countries), as well as peace years' square and cube for smoothing purposes (Carter and Signorino, 2010). Country- or dyad-specific effects are not appropriate for analysis of dichotomous dependent variables (Beck and Katz, 2001).

5 | British electoral reform and imperial overstretch

When Robert Cecil, the future Lord Salisbury and Conservative prime minister, infamously referred to India in 1867 as an "English Barrack in the Oriental seas" he was not suggesting this arrangement's desirability.[1] The less well-known portion of his speech proved as pessimistic as it was prophetic, "it is always bad for us not to have a check upon the temptation to engage in little wars which can only be controlled by the necessity of paying for them."[2] Cost distribution theory ties together two historical developments that cannot be explained by existing explanations in IR and historiography: the expansion of the British franchise deep into the middle class in 1867 and into the working class in 1884, and the explosion of imperial military campaigns (often against the better judgment of the government) over the same period of time. The two Reform Acts' large and sudden reductions in the wealth requirements for voting represent clear and discrete changes in the value of my key explanatory variable, the relative income of the median voter. It is therefore a natural case for establishing both the plausibility of the book's causal mechanism and the theory's usefulness in explaining important cases of democratic militarism, among which the late Victorian British Empire surely belongs.

More specifically, cost distribution theory sheds light on the links between a number of important developments occurring during this period, including:

(i) Massive increases in suffrage and corresponding decreases in the wealth of the average voter in Britain.

(ii) The growing obsession with the defense of India even as it developed into a strategic liability.

---

[1] The full quotation begins, "I do not like India to be looked upon as an English barrack..."

[2] *Hansard*, 1867, col. 406.

(iii) The lack of conscription in Britain, unique among European great powers.

(iv) Increased great power competition on the European continent.

(v) The simultaneous reduced defense commitments by Britain to the White Dominions and increased territorial expansion in Africa and Asia.[3]

These can be explained neither by democratic exceptionalism nor by the historiographical argument that British imperialism in the nineteenth century amounted to a "subsidy" for the Victorian upper class. One cannot explain change with a constant; Britain's elites remained the same, while the median wealth of the voter changed in discrete ways correlating with expansion. While the increase in "wins" by the British in Africa and Asia over this time period would seem to validate the "selection effects" argument of democratic exceptionalism, deliberations in the press and government evinced considerable skepticism about the benefits provided by these costly expeditions.

As the British public became more aware of the growing threat of great power war on the European continent, the Empire was viewed not only as a source of economic resources, prestige, and territory, but also as a means of reducing the risk of conscription within the United Kingdom itself. In a time when warfare required massive amounts of labor, the British middle-class voter looked abroad – particularly to India – to obtain the bodies necessary for a small, conscription-free island to engage in aggressive international politics and European great power competition. The use of Native troops to achieve British strategic objectives, while often considered unwise by elites in terms of grand strategy, was popular among voters.[4] Britain pursued a capital-intensive form of empire-building, parlaying taxes on the relatively wealthy to maintain the necessary military labor required

---

[3] The term "Britain" will refer to the metropole United Kingdom as opposed to the imperial possessions. The "White Dominions" was the term to describe the largely self-governing components of the Empire in Canada, Australia, New Zealand, and South Africa.

[4] To avoid confusion I will take my cues from the records of the time and refer to white soldiers originating from the British Isles as "European," white soldiers originating from the Dominions as "colonial," and non-white soldiers originating from imperial territories as "Natives." The Indian Army consisted of European and Native soldiers; however, when I use the term "Indian troops," I am referring to Natives only.

for balance of power politics, security of the homeland, and maintenance of great power status. Even as the cost of defending India grew in terms of British expenditure, the reduction in the likelihood of conscription justified its expense to the average person. Only upon India's Commander-in-Chief Herbert Kitchener's 1904 estimate that it would take over 100,000 *British* soldiers to defend the approaches to India via Afghanistan did the British government finally seek to appease Russia (Friedberg, 1988; Gooch, 1981). Thus ended one of the simultaneously most aggressive and unprofitable bursts of territorial conquest in history.

5.1 Why conquer Somaliland?

I have already argued that the average voter prefers a capital-intensive military. However, the median voter's ability to substitute materiel for labor is limited, but not prevented, by technology. In periods when labor-intensive warfare dominates, such as the nineteenth century, we are thus likely to see relatively small democratic militaries, *unless the wealthy's tax money can be used to fund alternate sources of labor.* A military can be "capitalized" even in a labor-intensive environment by hiring mercenaries or acquiring new sources of labor through imperialism. Additionally, the state can spend money to make each individual soldier more effective, as well as choose military operations that will cost more in terms of treasure than lives. When alternate sources of labor are available, the average voter will be more willing to employ military force as a tool for international politics. As the median voter becomes poorer and/or the threat to the state rises, the state will expend more resources to secure these sources of military labor. The easier it is to turn warmaking into a problem of tax collection rather than domestic labor mobilization, the more attractive military coercion becomes for the average voter. The average voter will demand more campaigns of lower expected value for the state, and thus the preferences of the government leadership and those of public opinion will diverge.

5.1.1 Elite capture: imperial subsidy theory

Explanations abound for the puzzling explosion of British imperialism in the late nineteenth century, but the dominant one argues that the Second Empire served as a subsidy paid by the middle class in taxes to cover the defense and administration costs necessary for the elite to achieve high investment returns abroad. In terms of economic gains, Davis and Huttenback (1988, 279) claim that while "The elites and the colonies with responsible government were clear winners; the middle class certainly, and the dependent empire, probably, were losers." This is not a new claim; thinkers such as Hobson, Herbert Spencer, Joseph Schumpeter, and Vladimir Lenin drew similar conclusions around the turn of the twentieth century (Cain, 2007). Yet the metastasizing Empire was very popular; indeed "the majority of English people cheerfully and even proudly shouldered a tax bill for an empire from which they derived very little in the form of tangible pecuniary gains" (O'Brien, 1988, 195). That the newly empowered electorate did little to stop this elite-driven expansionism has been chalked up to ignorance on the part of the public or explained away by painting the newly enfranchised as passive recipients of elite-concocted imperial propaganda.

The late Victorian empire is particularly relevant for democratic exceptionalist explanations that privilege the marketplace of ideas and competitive politics as means of avoiding imperial overstretch. Jack Snyder focuses on the earlier Palmerston era of British imperialism, in which the British Empire retrenched after a brief flurry of imperialism in the first half of the nineteenth century. However, charges of British imperial overstretch are much more appropriate for the final third of the century. Whereas British imperialism in the first half of the century was quite moderate relative to other countries (Snyder, 1991, 207), the same cannot be said for the latter half. By Snyder's logic, the addition of more voters through the second and third Reform Acts should have led to increased moderation by making logrolling coalitions of special interests more difficult. Snyder (1991, 209) describes the "natural antipathy to imperial overextension when it grew too costly" of the "median voters" of the Second Reform Act. Yet Empire metastasized.

5.1.2 Expanding suffrage, expanding Empire

For much of the nineteenth century, voting in Great Britain was sharply restricted to the very wealthy. Even the so-called Great Reform Act of 1832 only expanded the franchise from 15 to 18 percent of the male population. The act ushered in the "Age of Equipoise" (Burn, 1964; Hewitt, 2000), where the interests of aristocratic landowners were in balance with those of the wealthy manufacturing and financial elite newly empowered by the Great Reform Bill.

Whereas the 1832 Act changed the type of wealth represented in the electorate, its successors drastically altered the range of wealth, putting in place the conditions for increased redistribution by the government. The Second Reform Act of 1867 doubled the electorate to about 1.5 million men, including most urban male householders or lodgers paying more than ten pounds in annual rent, bringing the middle economic classes firmly into the electorate in large numbers. The 1867 Act made the median voter fairly representative of the population. The 1884 Act, while less dramatic in its reduction of median voter wealth, essentially introduced universal household suffrage; roughly 60 percent of the adult male population, about 5.5 million men, formed the electorate by then.

Multiple votes for the wealthy, the importance of the House of Lords, and the Crown's continued foreign policy power mitigated the influence of the relatively poor voter. Nonetheless, the change in the median voter was sufficiently large to shift domestic policies: public education; aid for the aged, sick, and unemployed; strengthened trade unions' legal standing; and an increasingly progressive tax code (Justman and Gradstein, 1999). Imperialism was yet another public good whose provision was increased in this overall redistributive effort.

Theories of cost internalization, elite capture, and cost distribution produce starkly contrasting predictions for the results following an increase in suffrage. The imperial subsidy argument would expect some reduction in imperialism as the economic distance between the elite and the masses grew. Both cost internalization and imperial subsidy theories would expect a more measured and conservative foreign policy in order to maximize individual consumption. Cost distribution theory predicts relatively less concern with controlling military spending and relatively more concern with the source of military labor. Finally, in contrast to the other theories, as long as the median voter pays little of the costs, cost distribution theory claims that a more democratic state will act increasingly aggressively.

5.1.3 What constitutes evidence?

The most important piece of evidence for the theory should be an increase in military aggression in pursuit of trivial stakes as a function of increased suffrage. Were there no change in the threat environment this would provide excellent support for my theory. Clearly, however, the threats from other powers such as Russia and Germany began to increase at the same time as the franchise, making increased provision of security overdetermined. I therefore focus on how the security was provided (in the imperial periphery as opposed to at home or in Europe), as well as the means by which it was provided (increased reliance on Native soldiers). The form of expansion was inefficient in that, at least in the opinions of the government leadership, the gains did not outweigh the costs for the state.

I focus on government elites, the "transmission belt" linking the voter to international politics, finding that increased suffrage changed the attitude of British governments, regardless of political party, towards expansion. Leaders issued public statements supportive of aggression, but their private deliberations often conveyed their personal belief that such expansion was unnecessary and even counterproductive. While the probabilistic nature and lack of information on stakes makes quantitative analysis of ill-advised wars extremely difficult, this case study can show that important actors *believed* the state was fighting in a less-than-efficient way, but plowed on regardless. Finally, the support for increased aggression should be consistent across political parties, since the two major parties can be expected to fight over the pivotal support of the new median voter.

5.2 A different kind of imperialism

With few exceptions (Robinson and Gallagher, 1968; Rodgers, 1984), most scholars describe the brand of imperialism practiced by the late Victorians as a remarkable shift.[5] Turn of the century observers agreed. John Hobson (1902, 19) identifies the "beginning of a conscious policy of Imperialism" in 1870; the process accelerated greatly

---

[5] Even defenders of the continuity of elite-driven British imperialism in the face of public apathy acknowledge the "burst of jingoism in the last quarter of the nineteenth century" if only to dismiss it as "aberrant" (MacKenzie, 1984, 1).

beginning in 1884. During the first half of the nineteenth century, "no sensible politician cared to stake his future upon the issue of overseas expansion" nor did any statesman attempt "to convince the small and privileged electorate that theirs must be an imperial future" (Morris, 1974). On the eve of reform, the Empire remained a "haphazard array of local treaties and a scattering of British Consuls" (Porter, 1999, 15). The Tory Prime Minister Benjamin Disraeli, now known as an arch-imperialist, suggested divesting Britain of its West African colonies in 1865, which were costing the Treasury £300,000 annually (McIntyre, 1967). That same year, a Parliamentary Select Committee not only commented that "all further extension of territory or assumption of government, or new treaties offering protection to native tribes would be inexpedient," it recommended an almost complete withdrawal from Africa (Davis and Huttenback, 1988, 9). To be sure, the British Empire increased in the earlier part of the century, but with the exception of large-scale territorial acquisition by the quasi-private East India Company, the focus was on small strategically located islands and ports such as Singapore (1819), the Falklands (1833), and Hong Kong (1842). Informal empire, which guaranteed access to British merchants through an occasional bout of "gunboat diplomacy" was, for both economic and ideological reasons, sufficient to satisfy Britain's politically powerful.

By the 1870s this had changed. David McIntyre (1967) describes three small "experiments": the establishment of a Crown Colony along the Gold Coast of West Africa, the appointment of British residents in the Malay States, and the annexation of Fiji in the South Pacific. Lord Carnavon, the Conservative Secretary of State for the Colonies, implemented these novel foreign policies, but they were conceived by the previous Liberal government. These experiments were to be replicated many more times. Governments expended enormous resources to acquire and administer small colonies. Where much of the expansion prior to 1867 appeared instigated by "men on the spot," this form of "absent-minded imperialism" (Porter, 2004) is an unconvincing explanation once metropolitan control increased with the mid-century advent of steamships and telegraphs (Blyth, 2003, 4).

The new imperialism differed in character as well as rate. By the final third of the century the so-called "White Dominions" – Canada, Australia, and New Zealand – which had the strongest economic ties to the metropole, were gradually encouraged, even forced, to fend for themselves militarily. In contrast, Britain scrambled to acquire increasingly peripheral territories – what Robinson and Gallagher (1968, 27) describe as "scraping the bottom of the barrel" – favoring direct rule with little chance of self-governance even in the "White" South African states (see also Hobson, 1902, 25). John Darwin (1997, 631) summarizes the puzzle for economic determinists: "Tropical Africa, where traders were few and settlers almost non-existent, was swallowed while juicier morsels (like Persia or Siam), economically or strategically more desirable, were turned away or their annexation deferred."

Simultaneously, the British Empire grew more politically and culturally salient.[6] Popular entertainment with imperial themes increased at an enormous rate over this period. The Great Exhibitions (akin to World's Fairs) only took on an explicitly imperial tone from the 1880s on. Patriotic music hall shows, which famously produced the term "jingoism," were popular with working and middle class alike (MacKenzie, 1999). The emergence in 1896 of the famously pro-Empire, "down-market" newspaper *The Daily Mail*, "written by office boys for office boys," served more as a "conduit of public opinion" than a shaper of it (Eldridge, 1984, 96).

Politicians recognized this shift. One junior minister noted in 1873 that "Whatever may be the policy of this or any government *Public Opinion* will not permit the withdrawal of British authority from the W. Coast of Africa" (McIntyre, 1967, 120).[7] Salisbury told his Chancellor in 1886 that while "a pacific and commercial policy is up to a point very wise...there is a point beyond which it is not wise either in a patriotic or a party sense" (Mahajan, 2002, 202). The Conservative secretary of the India Office Lord Randolph Churchill would later claim that his only regret over the decision to invade and annex Burma was that the news of the successful campaign arrived in Britain too late to influence the 1885 election (Foster, 1981, 206). When the party of Gladstone pursued their own policy of imperialism, horrified liberals outside of government accused the party of fleeing from "the truest test of Liberalism in their generation." By leading the country into the Boer War, the Liberal Party was "gladly abandoning themselves to whatever

---

[6] The word "imperialism" only entered the language around 1870.
[7] Contemporary observers' penchant for using "Public Opinion" as a proper noun indicates its role as a novel and independent force in politics.

shallow and ignoble defences a bleary-eyed, raucous 'patriotism' was ready to devise for their excuse" (Hobson, 1902, 152).

Despite the fierceness of partisan politics, a strong foreign policy consensus emerged as both parties fought to win over this newly empowered, and pro-empire middle class (Thompson, 2005). While the two great political parties of the time, the Liberals (led by William Gladstone) and the Conservatives (led by Benjamin Disraeli and later Lord Salisbury), often took fiercely different stances on empire rhetorically, British foreign policy changed little regardless of who held power. A Gladstone cabinet initiated and its Conservative successor executed the annexation of Fiji and the establishment of the Gold Coast protectorate in 1874 (McIntyre, 1967). While Gladstone's famous set of 1879 speeches known as the Midlothian campaign contained much anti-imperialist language – lambasting fighting in Afghanistan as "a war as frivolous as ever was waged in the history of man" – his Liberal colleagues generally supported the maintenance and even extension of the British Empire (Durrans, 1982).[8] Any party wishing to remain in power could not stray far from the public's desire for imperial success.

Hobson does not connect the new imperialism to the Reform Act, and this oversight has largely gone uncorrected by historians. The absence of the Reform Acts in any consideration of nineteenth-century imperialism is striking. Despite its 774 pages, the *Oxford History* volume on the subject (Porter, 2001) makes no mention of "public opinion," "democracy," "elections," or "Reform" in the index; the only elections discussed at length are those in the White Dominions. Freda Harcourt (1980) does link the Abyssinian campaign and the 1868 Reform Act as simultaneous Conservative attempts at reaching out to the middle class (see also Swartz, 1985; Thompson,

[8] Parsing out the different platforms of the Conservative and Liberal parties is not easy, given that they often switched given the winds of politics. For example, while the extension of the vote is associated with Liberalism, the Conservative Disraeli pushed through the 1867 Reform Act. In general, the first steps towards a welfare state were taken by Liberal governments. Liberals tended to be more enthusiastic than Conservatives about free trade and personal liberty, with less attachment to the Crown and Church of England. Gladstone in particular was dedicated to balanced budgets and low taxes, but Conservative prime ministers such as Lord Salisbury largely followed suit. There were tremendous divisions within the parties as well, each of which contained a "radical" element.

2000, 2005). Others focusing on the Empire as instigated by elites acknowledge that the state's "freedom abroad had its conditions," which changed as the result of increased suffrage (Robinson and Gallagher, 1968, 23).

In short, British imperial logic – once personified by Canning and Palmerston and concerned with national prosperity as the means to international political power – shifted in focus to territory, lines of communication, the preservation of India, and above all military manpower in the final third of the century. Often the ministers overseeing this expansion knew and acknowledged that the operations had little strategic and less economic value. Most of these acquisitions were considered of limited strategic value by senior military officers, who focused on Europe rather than the Empire (Adams, 1998). If they possessed any worth at all, it was to provide marginal improvements for the security of India (Robinson and Gallagher, 1968).

5.2.1 The importance of India

Elite, peripherally oriented groups such as the East India Company may have initially provoked the expansion into and conquest of India, but by mid-century, with control of the territory largely consolidated, British rule of India had evolved. Trade and prestige remained an important component of the relationship, but the discourse about India grew increasingly strategic over the century's course. Without it, Britain was, according to one contemporary observer, a "third class military power" (Williams, 1991, 7). India made up 85 percent of the Empire's territory and 78 percent of its population (Mahajan, 2002, 5). Nonetheless, while acknowledging India to be "the key to the problem of Britain's late nineteenth-century expansion east and south of Suez, a code which reveals the meaning of so many inexplicable acquisitions," John Darwin (1997, 624) points out that this logic begs the question: "India's astonishing rise to become the second pole of British world power is part of the puzzle of mid-Victorian imperialism, not an explanation of it."

Britain went to remarkable lengths to defend the Raj. The occupations of Cyprus, Egypt, Sudan, and South African Transvaal were all justified by the defense of India. Sneh Mahajan (2002, 201) observes that "when any threat was perceived to the Indian Empire, irrespective of remoteness, triviality or irrationality, the reaction in favour of retaining the Indian Empire was instantaneous and vociferous." Aaron Friedberg (1988, 221) is even more blunt: "The British attachment to India seems to have transcended reason and to have become an article of faith that most concerned citizens shared." Keith Jeffrey (1982) sums up the puzzle of apparent irrationality, and not coincidentally employs the language of moral hazard: "It might be possible to regard India and Indian resources generally as an 'insurance policy' undersetting the British position and prestige throughout the East, but it is a fine sort of policy where the premium cost more than the value of the property itself."

This puzzle becomes comprehensible when we consider that the costs and benefits of security were not distributed evenly within Great Britain. Contrary to the classical liberals of the time and historians in the present, it was not the rich that benefited most but the newly enfranchised voter. India's first and most important perceived virtue was as the essential link to Britain remaining a great power in an increasingly competitive Europe. Given the large financial outlays required to paint the map pink, expansion may not have been a "good deal" for the state as a whole, but by finding alternate sources of military labor the median voter was better off. As Britain became increasingly successful at employing these Native soldiers, the temptation for the median voter to initiate conflicts grew, just as Salisbury had predicted in 1867. The public was aware of the rising threat of Russia, France, and Germany. The Crimean War and in particular the American Civil War made it clear that prevailing military technologies required massive amounts of labor in uniform. Tax money underwrote expeditions to remote corners of the earth by Native soldiers as a means of balancing against the European powers, and most importantly to keep the English barrack of India safe. It was a rather neat trick (or, from another perspective, Ponzi scheme), using Indian soldiers to conquer territory in an effort to protect the source of Indian soldiers for a future war.[9]

The prestige of possessing India, a public if ineffable good, also exhibited this self-justifying feedback loop. The Raj conferred upon

---

[9] Note that the Indian Army was used to expand and secure the Raj's frontier, and this cannot be considered outside of a European context. Nonetheless I will set that aside for the purposes of this chapter.

the tiny island nation a great deal of international standing. British prestige was also believed essential to order and rule within India, allowing a tiny number of British soldiers and civil servants to hold sway over such a massive landmass and population (Harrison, 1995). Thus the spread of empire in a continual effort to reify the British Army's (or public's, or race's) prestige was a means of protecting India as well, and was accordingly invoked routinely by politicians and writers.

5.2.2 *The end of the mid-century liberal consensus*

The expansion of empire represented a remarkable contradiction of the liberal ideology – variously referred to as the Manchester School, Radicalism, and political economy – almost universally accepted by the leadership of both the mid-century Conservative and Liberal parties (Harling, 2003). Tenets of the school focused on the absolute necessity for balanced budgets and good credit as well as the moral, economic, and political imperative to leave people alone. In short "government should permit industrious Britons to get on with the business of living" (Harling, 2003, 904).

This liberalism included an outright hostility to the military, particularly the army. Defense spending was not only unproductive but also invited tyranny: "Taxes would soar, the labour supply would shrink, military habits would spread, and the people would be living perpetually under the shadows of the garrisons" (B. Porter, 1987, 19). Charles Trevelyan, a highly influential assistant secretary to the Treasury, observed in 1850 that "Should events require a British Army to take the field, a body of well-trained commissariat officers, animated by the best spirit, would be ready to perform all the necessary services and to keep in check the lavish expenditure which has generally been incurred at the commencement of a campaign" (quoted in Strachan, 1980, 797).

For liberals, taxation, particularly the income tax, was an abomination. While Gladstone was its most implacable opponent, the Conservative Lord Salisbury quite clearly loathed the accompanying increases in direct taxation that accompanied foreign adventures (A. N. Porter, 1987). With the possible exception of Disraeli, no prime minister of either party believed that the income tax was a sound fiscal policy.

Accordingly, in the middle of the century "Most [Members of Parliament] probably spent more time complaining about the costs of empire than they did on any other imperial subject" (Harling, 2003, 917). Free trade, rather than conquest, was regarded as the way to ensure British power and prosperity, lower defense expenditures, and increase British capital and credit (MacDonagh, 1962). One important Radical, Richard Cobden, lumped the colonies, the army, and navy in with trade protectionism as "merely accessories to our aristocratic government," sarcastically writing in 1867 "Where is the *enemy* (?) that would be so good as to steal such *property*?" (Cobden, 1903, 29, emphasis in original). Even Disraeli referred in 1852 to the (White Dominion) colonies as being "a millstone around our necks," and proposed in 1866 to "Leave the Canadians to defend themselves; recall the African Squadron; give up the settlements on the West Coast of Africa, and we shall make a saving which will, at the same time, enable us to build ships and have a good budget" (Blake, 2010, 760, 455).

Given this logic, liberal thinkers argued that a rational electorate would not support an exercise so contrary to their self-interest. Writing in 1835 Richard Cobden argued that

If it could be made manifest to the trading and industrious portions of this nation, who have no honors or interested ambition of any kind at stake in the matter, that, whilst our dependencies are supported at an expense to them, in direct taxation, of more than five millions annually, they serve but as gorgeous and ponderous appendages. (Cobden, 1903, 1:51)

John Hobson (1902, 104–107) agrees that "Where any real forms of popular control existed, militarism and wars would be impossible if every citizen was made to realise their cost by payments of hard cash." Hobson's logic may explain why he fails to connect expansionism to the 1867 Reform Act, although he comes tantalizingly close when he states that the funding of British imperialism through "progressive income-tax and death duties, must be regarded, then, as an exceptional policy, due mainly to a combination of two causes – the difficulty of reverting suddenly to the abandoned practice of [trade] Protection, and the desire to conciliate the favour of the new unknown democracy."

At the time of the Second Reform Act, however, many observers did not agree, seeing enfranchisement as a threat to sound fiscal policies and anti-militarism. Many contemporary journals made the link between empire, Reform, and the income tax. Referring to the highly popular invasion of Abyssinia, one Liberal observer bemoaned Disraeli's "throwing all extraordinary outlay on the payer of Income-tax," even as he "just before handed over the control of policy and finance to a class which pays not a shilling of Income-tax. Mr. Gladstone's benevolent desire to prevent war by making it dis-agreeable will but rarely attain its object if taxation and representation are permanently dissevered" (*Saturday Review*, March 20, 1869, 370). The concern was not limited to Liberal publications; one Tory maga-zine noted that "The landowner, the capitalist, the manufacturer, and, to some extent, the professional man, will be made to feel themselves a class apart from the real electors. They will be the smallest fraction of a minority hovering on the skirts of the electoral circle, but not at too great distance for a democratic Government to put its hand in their pockets when a war-tax is needed" (*Blackwood*, 1884, 808). W. R. Greg, a well-known Radical essayist, also anticipated the effects of "wholesale enfranchisement" because "Those classes – with all their excellences, with all their capabilities of good – are yet undeniably the least informed, the least competent to anticipate the future, the most excitable, and probably also, with the exception of the upper ten thousand, the most likely under excitement to give their votes for war" (Greg, 1878, 405). Greg posits an unholy alliance in which "the higher classes might find their surest supporters in the lowest classes, whom we have thoughtlessly relieved from the sensible pressure of those fiscal burdens which could once be calculated upon for restraining them from so suicidal an alliance."

The electorate seemed to conform to these predictions, demon-strating a newfound willingness to spend public money in pursuit of empire. The once-hated income tax (previously an emergency measure only used in wartime) inexorably rose even during times of ostensible peace, from twopence on the pound (or 0.83 percent) in 1867 to eight (3.3 percent) by the mid-1880s (Swartz, 1985, 11). While some of the increase went towards more domestic spending, the majority of the revenue went towards defense and servicing the national debt (from previous wars). The admittedly partisan Conservative Lord Hamil-ton (1917, 220) links Reform and military expenditure in his memoirs: "the great additions made to the electorate by the Reform Bill of 1884 had, to a large extent, swamped the old niggardly and skinflint policy of the Manchester School," due in no small part to the fact that "the mass of the recently enfranchised escape direct taxation out of which new burdens of expenditure were mainly defrayed."[10] Indeed some of the most aggressive Radical politicians such as Joseph Chamberlain and Charles Dilke, dedicated to reaching out and bettering the lives of workers, were among the most enthusiastic imperialists; Chamberlain advised Dilke in 1892 to "be as radical as you like...but be a little Jingo if you can."[11]

5.2.3 The renewed fortunes of the Army

I focus on British ground forces due to the overdetermined nature of naval spending in Britain. Cost distribution theory predicts middle-class enthusiasm for the capital-intensive Royal Navy over a labor-intensive Army. The turn towards navalism in the late nineteenth century is unsurprising, since Britain was a wealthy island with a massive trading economy with a centuries-old policy of naval superiority.[12] Increased use of the Army represents a more profound change in British grand strategy. The link between additional expense and a ground war is more direct; the costs of sending a gunboat or even a fleet of them were already sunk in the annual naval budget, which funded building, crewing, and coaling these ships. Deploying significant numbers of soldiers to distant places required taking on large expenses on top of a peacetime Army budget. The increased reliance in this period on the use of ground forces as the tool of choice for foreign policy is striking and, from most perspectives, puzzling.

The heightened interest in Empire was accompanied by a celebration of the average British soldier, once dismissed by Wellington as "the scum of the earth", accelerating to unprecedented heights in the

---

[10] He goes on to note that "independently of this personal consideration, the wage-earning classes are very proud of the Navy, and they have an instinctive belief that without such adequate naval insurance the supplies of food and raw material from over the seas upon which they depend would in time of emergency be seriously imperilled, in which case they would, to a large extent, become wageless and foodless."

[11] Joseph Chamberlain to John Dilke, 20 January 1883, Dilke Papers, cited in Crosby (2011, 114).

[12] For the new voters' willingness to flood the Admiralty with resources, see Paul Smith (1996). Offer (1985) argues that increased naval expenditure was a large subsidy designed to keep food cheap for the newly empowered masses, compared to the tariffs against foreign grain that kept prices high and landowners wealthy.

last three decades of the nineteenth century (Peck, 1998; Spiers, 1992, 180). Soldiers' welfare, from the Crimean War on, became increasingly important to the public. This newfound concern for "Tommy" was coupled with increased attention to the support structure that underpinned his well-being.[13] Popular assessment of a successful campaign rested on more than simple victory; as Sidney Herbert wrote to Lord Elgin, the leader of the British expedition in the Third China War of 1863, "a first rate general, a capital staff, an excellent commissariat, and a good medical department are four things the English public are especially pleased to see" (Bond, 1967, 103).

The logistics underpinning expeditions such as the Mahdist War were quite awesome. The Maxim gun was a very economical killing machine in terms of both capital and labor, but required tremendous resources to get it to a desolate place like Omdurman – in which an Anglo-Egyptian Army slaughtered 11,000 of the enemy, while itself suffering 48 fatalities – famously described by Winston Churchill (2004, 161) as "the most signal triumph ever gained by the arms of science over barbarians." The 1885 Suakin expedition alone required ten desalinization ships, which burned 353 tons of coal a week (Robson, 1991). Five hundred miles of new railroad track were laid in the Sudan in 1898; as Churchill (2004, 87) describes it, "fighting the Dervishes was primarily a matter of transport."

The increased use of ground forces is all the more remarkable given that conscription was never a possibility in Great Britain despite the growing concern over the mass armies of Europe. By 1871, Britain was the only major power without some sort of universal service (Barnett, 1970; Friedberg, 1988). So unpopular was the idea of a draft that Britain did not institute one until two years into the First World War (Adams and Poirier, 1987). As one Army reformer and Liberal, Charles Dilke (1888, 62) wrote, "There can be no doubt that the majority of the people in this country prefer to pay the extra millions which the absence of a conscription costs." Salisbury observed in 1878 that "to ask us to pursue a bold policy towards the military powers of Europe, when we have no conscription, is to ask us to make bricks without straw. Diplomacy which does not rest on force is the

---

[13] Not coincidentally, the simultaneous, growing discourse of imperial difference based on race, culture, and ethnicity – particularly for Indians – represented a striking shift from mid-century imperial ideologies (Metcalf, 1994).

most feeble and futile of weapons, and except for bare self defence we have not the force" (Steele, 1999, 108). Salisbury went elsewhere for his straw.

5.3 "Leave it to the mild Hindoo": empire as labor source

The solution to Salisbury's conundrum was quite clear to voter and minister alike; many of the soldiers fighting for British interests did not come from Britain. The use of indigenous forces to fight colonial wars was certainly not new, but the scale and the aim changed dramatically. In turn this ready availability of Native labor lowered the costs of military coercion by a previously impossible degree. As the government hesitated over the purchase of Dutch outposts on the Gold Coast of Africa in 1872, J. T. Delane, the editor of *The Times*, counseled Lord Carnarvon that "the British Public will not excuse you from the task of civilizing the Ashantis and will point out that in Houssas and other tribes you have the means of raising an army of natives sufficient with a few European Officers for all contingencies" (Swartz, 1985, 13–14).

All parts of the "dependent" Empire were potential sources of labor.[14] The African Wars required drafting large numbers of indigenous peoples to not only fight but to transport the massive amounts of materiel necessary for a successful Victorian military campaign. The rivalry between Britain and France (not coincidentally another democracy with an even greater tendency to use non-European soldiers) in West Africa was based in part over concerns that one side would gain an advantage in military recruiting (Killingray, 1979, 422).[15] The British employed an enormous Egyptian Army with European officers to informally control Egypt from 1883 onwards.

Of all the sources of Native labor, India was by far the most important. In 1880 the standing Indian Army consisted of 66,000 British soldiers, 130,000 Natives, and 350,000 soldiers in the so-called "princely armies" (Robinson and Gallagher, 1968). It would see action in at least 27 conflicts outside of its home territory from 1867–1904 (India Office, 1900, 1905). Figure 5.1 shows the increase

---

[14] The White Dominions such as Canada and Australia, where military labor could not be used with impunity, were gradually left to fend for themselves militarily at the same time.

[15] For an in-depth description of the French use of Native soldiers as a tool for great power politics, see Echenberg (1991).

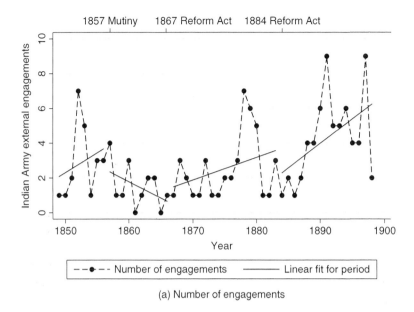

(a) Number of engagements

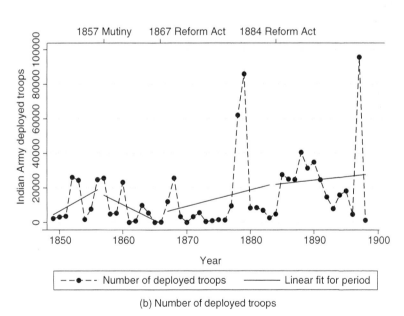

(b) Number of deployed troops

Figure 5.1 Use of Indian forces outside of India (1849–1898)

in the number of deployments and the number of Indian soldiers sent outside of British India from the beginning of direct British rule in 1857 to the end of the century, with the average levels for the period before, between, and after the Second and Third Reform Acts. The average number of annual engagements doubled from 2.1 to 4.2 over the course of these two suffrage increases, while the annual average number of Indian soldiers deployed abroad rose from 9,400 to 14,000 to 25,000 after 1884. Following the 1857 Rebellion (also known as the Sepoy Mutiny) and its drastic cut in the Native component of the Indian Army, deployments and engagements decline. The trend reverses with the arrival of the middle-class electorate. The contrast becomes even more striking when one considers that many of the earlier operations were devoted to conquest of new territory that became part of the Raj, a process largely complete by 1867.

Instances exist where Native soldiers were used to explicitly preserve lives of British soldiers in battle. For example, the deputy adjutant general for South Africa directed in 1878 that, "When a body of Natives is attached it should invariably be employed in examining bush or rugged ground offering concealment to an enemy, before any European body is ordered to advance in the country to be passed over" (Bailes, 1980, 96). However, while in some operations such as Abyssinia, Indian soldiers bore the brunt of the casualties, this was far from the rule. European soldiers did much of the fighting, mostly because the commanders on the spot, more concerned with victory than with the political consequences of casualties at home, considered them to be vastly superior fighters. Native labor helped make the European soldier a much more effective fighting force. As one observer noted of the 1883 Egyptian campaign, "When employed under the Indian Government every effort is made to render [the British soldier] a mere fighting machine, by relieving him as far as possible of the cares and routine duties generally incident on camp life" (Goodrich, 1885, 302). It is important to acknowledge, as many accounts of imperial warfighting fail to do, the amount of labor that was required to get a single soldier, European or Native, into the fight. The relatively small Zulu War of 1879 required 6,639 European and colonial soldiers, 9,300 local Native soldiers, and about 30,000 laborers (Featherstone, 1973; Killingray, 1989).[16] While conscription of British subjects was out

---

[16] The extensive use of contractors (many non-American) in support roles in Iraq and Afghanistan has a precedent.

of the question, impressment into service was standard practice for Bantu and Basuto drivers in the Zulu Wars (Bailes, 1980). Death tolls from disease always swamped the more glamorous losses from combat, and thus employing native support personnel reduced the number of European deaths for an expedition precipitously. Natives were considered most appropriate for garrison duties in the tropics specifically because they were more resistant to disease rather than because their lives were considered intrinsically less valuable than a European soldier's.

The use of tax revenue to fund non-British fighters was quite explicit and the lengths the government would go to buy Native and colonial labor striking. The British government would pay lavish sums to have colonials and Natives fight in a European's stead. During the Zulu War of 1879, basic pay for a British soldier was a shilling a day, while a South African volunteer received twelve times that amount (Killingray, 1989).

While the 1858 Act for the Better Government of India suppos-edly prevented using India as an English barrack, by 1887 Charles Dilke (1888, 102), an important Member of Parliament on Army matters, observed the British imperial policy in place: "Our little wars should be conducted by the Indian army supplementing local forces." India served primarily as a source of labor rather than revenue. To be sure, taxation of Indians supported in large part the garrisoning of both white and Native troops in India but this had been a long-standing policy; what changed over the century was the increased aggressiveness of the use of these Native troops even as the cost of their employment abroad was shifted to the metropole.[17]

A Parliamentary Select Committee convened in 1867 (the eve of Reform) to consider the use of Native troops outside their home states, and its lengthy report – considering everything from cost–benefit an-alysis to the role of caste to the strictures of racial sensitivities ("in purely English Colonies [natives] would be wholly out of place") – pro-vides fascinating insight into official thinking about the pros and cons of Native military labor. The overall consensus of the Commission was of the extreme value of the sepoy in "these days of rapid concentration

---

[17] This did not stop the Treasury from trying to force the Indian government to pay for at least part of many of the deployments (Metcalf, 2007, 71, 85).

and movement of troops in the event of war." Deploying Indian soldiers abroad would:

Improve the discipline of the [Indian] army, strengthening our military hold in India. It would also be a great assistance to the British Army, and would relieve it of many of its duties in time of peace; while in time of war we should have a system in working order which could be expanded to meet any exigency of requirement. (House of Commons Papers (HCP) 1867–68 (197) VI.768, vii)

This positive assessment had little to do with financial consideration: "the superior cheapness of the native soldier disappears in a great degree when he is employed out of India," once one factored the cost of their transport as well as their perceived fighting ability relative to a white soldier.[18]

The Committee report's most compelling piece of evidence for the potential of Native soldiers as substitutes for British labor is the British military's testimony *against* the deployment of sepoys. The generals, apparently in bureaucratic self-defense, objected because "partially relieving the British Army of some of its colonial duties, would tempt the House of Commons to reduce the European force of the British Army" (HCP 1867–68 (197) VI.789, viii).

The following sections trace over time the development of a doctrine substituting Indian for European military labor, its connection to great power politics, and its popularity with voters. Figure 5.1 shows that these three cases are not the only examples. They are chosen because they span the length of time under consideration, involved leadership from both the major political parties, show the increasingly aggressive use of Indian (and other Native) personnel over time, and reveal the reaction of the public.

5.3.1 Abyssinian campaign (1867–68)

Rarely has so much been done for so few than in the 1867 rescue of seven European hostages from the Abyssinian emperor Theodore.

---

[18] Indeed British tax money was useful for overcoming other obstacles. One of the Committee's principal concerns was the role of caste in restricting overseas service; it was determined not to be a problem, "if sufficient pecuniary advantages were held out to them as an inducement" (HCP (1867–68) (197) VI.789).

The nine-month expedition cost the rough equivalent of 2 percent of Britain's GNP.[19] It necessitated the construction of an artificial harbor replete with floating lighthouses, 12 miles of rail track for the two locomotives brought over from England, and eight bridges linking 110 miles of new road to the mountain fortress of Magdala. Carrying this materiel required the importation of 22,000 horses and mules as well as 44 elephants. The campaign involved 13,000 troops and roughly 40,000 support personnel, but only 4,000 of these were British (or Irish), the vast majority of soldiers and attendants being taken from India. Indians suffered the brunt of the admittedly light casualties, 30 out of 37 (Stanley, 1874; Ashcroft, 2001).

The campaign was an unqualified (if fiscally prodigal) success. After the long march inland from the coast, the army quickly overran the Emperor's fortress, rescued the hostages, and found Theodore, dead by his own hand. In a celebratory speech to the House of Commons, Disraeli made no reference to the role of the Indian Army, instead noting that "The manly qualities of the Abyssinians sank before the resources of our warlike science" (*Hansard* 1868, 513). Britain's aggressive entry into large-scale land warfare represented a definitive break from Britain's previous gunboat diplomacy.

Significantly, the event that supposedly triggered this punitive expedition, Emperor Theodore's detention of the British consul, occurred four years before the expedition was initiated. Sound strategic reasons existed for this reluctance by British defense and foreign policy elites. To invade a landlocked country in the middle of a very inhospitable continent was an extraordinarily risky undertaking, and it was hard to justify the effort for the sake of British honor and seven hostages. Freda Harcourt (1980, 101) argues that only the imminence of the Second Reform Act forced the government's hand. Harcourt

---

[19] Based on the estimated cost by Monypenny and Buckle (1920a) and the GNP estimate from Kennedy (1989). Some of the capital requirements were quite literal. Preparations for the campaign included an order of 500,000 1780 Maria Theresa dollars from the Austrian mint, as this was apparently the only acceptable currency in Abyssinia. See Hozier (1869, 58–61) for a somewhat over-the-top description of the means used, including "ships fitted with every appliance which science could suggest or experience dictate for the restoration of the sick," "vast stores of coal," the "electric fluid" in the form of a telegraph, and "the discoveries of chemists...combined with the skills of the mechanician" to create long-distance signaling lamps.

still views the invasion as an elite-driven phenomenon, a search for a "national" cause to keep the Tories in power by creating a "vicarious release from tension for the classes to whom honor and prestige mattered." Nini Rodgers (1984, 147) disagrees, and sees the confluence of domestic and international forces as "coincidental." Noting the profound unease of elected Cabinet officials regarding the task, Rodgers chalks up the campaign to the influence of the Civil Service under-secretaries.

By reversing Harcourt's top-down story, cost distribution theory reconciles these two views. Most government ministers never wanted to invade Abyssinia, but popular pressure from a newly empowered electorate made it an imperative, so long as the Indian Army did the fighting. Rodgers herself acknowledges the important new roles of the "Ottoman and Bombay lobbies" and the press in forcing a change in policy, which surely cannot be the result of an aggressive foreign civil service going off the reservation.

Money was no object. Despite the fact that the £8.6 million price tag raised the income tax from fourpence on the pound to five, the operation was wildly popular.[20] Disraeli viewed not only the use of Indian troops abroad but also the expenditure to be an important precedent: "It certainly cost double what was contemplated, and that is likely to be the case in all wars for wh. [sic] I may be responsible. Money is not to be considered in such matters: success alone is to be thought of" (Monypenny and Buckle, 1920a, 45).

For this investment, the average voter got a relatively costless war in return, while sending a message to other powers that "Britain was no longer timid about everything but India" (Harcourt, 1980, 102). As one chronicler of the campaign stated, "England acquired from it no territorial aggrandizement. Yet it did not pass unrewarded for its result was greatly to raise the British army in European estimation" (Hozier, 1869, 1). Despite his previously stated misgivings about the English barrack, in 1874 the future Lord Salisbury, then Disraeli's Secretary of the India Office, took a more direct hand in managing the Raj in order to "counter the Indian government's unwillingness to adopt a more forward stance" in the region (Blyth, 2003, 23).

---

[20] "Public opinion was still sufficiently alive to the honour of England to approve the addition of a penny to the income-tax to maintain it" (Markham, 1868, 296).

Observers, such as the liberal Conservative (not a contradiction) *Saturday Review*, noted the implications for the future: "In former times demagogues contended for the taxation of the wealthier classes on the imaginary ground that they were in the habit of waging unnecessary wars for the purpose of providing their sons and brothers with promotion. It can hardly be alleged that such motives had anything to do with the Abyssinian enterprise, or with the extravagant outlay which it involved."[21]

5.3.2 *The Eastern Question (1878)*

The power of Native troops to restore the popular acceptability of military aggressiveness is perhaps best illustrated by Disraeli's so-called *"coup de théâtre"* in the 1878 flare-up of the Eastern Question, the perennial debate on how to manage the Ottoman Empire's gradual collapse and the territorial ambition of a rising Russia. Following the revelation of Turkish atrocities in Bulgaria in 1876 the public generally supported, if not a pro-Russia policy, then certainly an anti-Turkish policy. This shifted notably in the face of Russian military successes against the Ottoman Empire in January 1878, and very nearly resulted in Britain fighting Russia in defense of Turkey. The enormous public enthusiasm for a war against Russia epitomized the new phenomenon of "jingoism," the often violent disturbances of peace protests by middle- and working-class mobs (Cunningham, 1971). The rapidity of this reversal of opinion coincides with the shifting of 7,000 Indian Native soldiers to the island of Malta, the first introduction of Indian soldiers into a European theater. Disraeli (by then Lord Beaconsfield) and his Foreign Minister returned home from Berlin to celebratory crowds delivering, in Disraeli's words, "peace with honor," a partial rollback of Russian conquest, and the island of Cyprus in British hands (Monypenny and Buckle, 1920b, 346).[22]

The personal correspondence of the government ministers gives a clear indication of the popular pressure they felt to do something

---

[21] *Saturday Review*, March 20, 1869, 370, and May 9, 1868.
[22] Neville Chamberlain referred to this diplomatic success on his own return from a more infamous conference in Germany (Beck, 1989, 170).

against their better judgment. A letter from the decidedly dovish Foreign Secretary Lord Derby reveals Disraeli's political logic:

The Premier sincerely & really believes that it will be better for us to risk a great war, & to spend £10,000,000 upon it, than not to appear to have had a large share in the decision to come to when peace is made. Most continental statesmen would agree with him, & a considerable section of the English public. (Swartz, 1985, 66)

Indeed many of the ministers thought Disraeli's course of action so unwise that two resigned and several others threatened to do so (Robinson and Gallagher, 1968, 66).

One liberal MP remarked that "the bringing of the Indian troops upon the stage produced a movement of surprise and admiration among all classes" (Durrans, 1982, 281).[23] The fact that Disraeli called the troops up without consulting Parliament represented a significant constitutional crisis, but this disturbed its members far more than the public, for whom the "technical discussions on the Bill of Rights seem to nineteen Englishmen out of twenty as idle as subtle pleas for this or that view of the Thirty-Nine Articles" (Thompson, 1886, 444).

The liberal *Daily News* wrote despondently that the operation could not be blamed simply on the traditional instigators of imperialism – financial interests and ambitions politicians – but that, "Undoubtedly, too, there is a strong and senseless impulse in favour of war stirring among many classes in this country, who are as far out of the range of political ambition as they are innocent of financial enterprise." The more conservative *Times*, while expressing reservations about the policy's wisdom, also noted that, "It has been abundantly shown that the Government are, on the whole, acting with the support of the country" (Thompson, 1886, 421). A popular parody of a patriotic song emerged:

We don't want to fight
But by Jingo if we do
We'll stay at home and sing our songs
And leave it to the mild Hindoo.[24]

---

[23] Except "the section of the liberals who own the leadership of [Gladstone]."

[24] Like Salisbury's English barrack remark, some version of these lines makes perennial appearances in work on the British Empire (cf. Ferguson, 2003); a

Disraeli and Salisbury returned from the Congress of Berlin to immense popular acclaim, and could report to their Queen that, "After all the sneers of not having any great military force, the imagination of the Continent will be much affected by the first appearance of what they will believe to be an inexhaustible supply of men" (Durrans, 1982, 281).

The implications of establishing the precedent of sending Native troops to Europe were recognized immediately both at home and abroad. Firstly, many acknowledged the enormous consequences for European power politics. One British commenter noted that "the principal advantage would undoubtedly be the almost limitless power of expansion of military resources we should thus gain," going so far as to suggest that "Even in time of peace native troops would furnish cheap garrisons for the Mediterranean fortresses." Consequently, "the nations of Europe too would see that we could draw soldiers from a wider field than that of these little isles and the theory of English impotence if it exists would be exploded" (Chapman, 1878, 580–581). Others noted the outsized impression this made on the public. Acknowledging that "England's European influence has been increased, and her military positions strengthened, by the dramatic disclosure of her unforeseen Indian resources," a Conservative writer attributed to "popular fancy" and the "unlearned" the more grandiose notion that "there seemed no limit to the reinforcement which we might draw from this source, except such as we might impose upon ourselves from considerations of financial prudence" (Clerke, 1878, 233).

Secondly, the incentives this created for British adventurism were equally clear. From the Opposition benches in the House of Commons, William Forster acknowledged the revolutionary nature of the deployment, "Is it no change to rely not upon the patriotism and spirit of our own people, but upon the power of our money bags, to get the Ghoorkas and Sikhs and Mussulmen to fight for us?" (Lucas, 1921, 54). The editors of *The Spectator* (1878, 556) critically noted that "there would be no difficulty except money in landing 60,000 native troops officered drilled and provided like Europeans in any part of the Mediterranean. We could conquer the Turkish Empire in Asia from

contemporary journalist notes that it was circulating Parliament during the debate over the movement of Indian forces to Malta (Lucy, 1885, 418).

the European side and never expend an Englishman," and worried that the English people could "dispose of other races than their own, that they have a recruiting-ground in Asia which costs them nothing but money, and which cannot be exhausted," and which by design precludes the conscription or universal military training "which every statesman among them of both parties would if it were politically safe to speak out tell them was directly for their good." Disraeli's prediction about the foreign policy implications proved prophetic; one American intelligence officer would later refer to the Maltese deployment as an event "whose complete meaning was only made clear four years later" in Egypt (Goodrich, 1885, 333).

5.3.3 *The Egypt campaign*

The Liberal landslide victory on a largely anti-imperialist campaign in 1880 would challenge my arguments about the median voter's preferences and influence were it not for the consistency of British foreign policy by the new Gladstone cabinet.[25] Within two years, under considerable public pressure, Britain mounted an expensive campaign with Indian soldiers in Egypt. The irony was not lost on Conservatives; "Poor Lord Beaconsfield!" wrote Salisbury, "If he could have lived to see Gladstone suing the Turk for assistance in maintaining British interests – sending for Indian troops – & using Cyprus as a place of arms" (Swartz, 1985, 208).[26]

The invasion served as a watershed for British imperialism: "after Egypt there was no turning back: both parties, in their different ways, had become imperialists" (Hopkins, 1986, 387). As such, its complicated causes have been scrutinized closely. Party leaders on both sides evinced deep ambivalence over involvement in Egyptian affairs (Robinson and Gallagher, 1968). The Admiralty did not assess the Suez Canal as being in any danger (Galbraith and al Sayyid-Marsot, 1978), and the sea lane around the Horn of Africa was the main supply route to India anyway. Many scholars subscribe to variations of the "bondholder thesis," in which the invasion was done at the behest

---

[25] The economic depression, an unemployment rate of 11.4 percent, and the use of the army to put down worker unrest in Lancashire probably did more damage to the Conservative cause than Gladstone's Midlothian campaign (Swartz, 1985).

[26] Disraeli (Lord Beaconsfield) had died in April 1881.

of influential investors who had bought a great deal of debt from the local Egyptian government.

Others note the public's role. A. G. Hopkins (1986) argues that because the economic benefits were more diffuse (Egypt was a major supplier of cotton and purchaser of British services), "a strong foreign policy, selectively applied to areas where success seemed likely, had a popular appeal, not least among the relatively affluent voters and small investors of the south-east, where the headquarters of the burgeoning service sector were located." Gladstone's party had been "coming under pressure at a time when new social forces, represented by the rise of trades unions and by the slowly spreading stain of democracy, were causing influential segments of Liberal support to turn towards the Conservative party" (Hopkins, 1986, 387). Not coincidentally, famous Radical imperialists such as Joseph Chamberlain and Charles Dilke rose to prominence at this time.

Gladstone, an outlier even among his party colleagues in his virulent anti-imperialism, would feel compelled to reverse his Midlothian platform upon entering office in 1880.[27] Determined to hand Cyprus to Greece, transfer Heligoland to Germany, and quickly resolve Egypt's outstanding Suez Canal debt, he found himself stymied by public opinion and Parliament (Knaplund, 1935, 23).

Since 1876, the government of Egypt (a largely autonomous province of the Ottoman Empire) was under heavy French and British financial supervision to ensure the payment of the large amounts of debt held by Europeans. Popular unrest against the Egyptian government accordingly grew and became increasingly influential and occasionally violent. British and French ships responded by sailing to the region in early 1882. The campaign that resulted in the occupation of Egypt commenced with a naval bombardment of Alexandria in response to rioting, which "like all butchery is popular" according to one unhappy Liberal minister. "At last," the Home Secretary William

---

[27] Gladstone's reluctance to use force is overstated. Gladstone disagreed regarding whom the British military should be used against, not whether it should be used. His Midlothian speeches lambasted operations in Afghanistan, but criticized the Tories for allowing other European powers to spearhead the liberation of European Christians from the Turk: "a great work of emancipation has been going on in the world, and you have been prevented by your Government from any share in it whatever." Gladstone actually chastises the Conservative government for taking three years before "coercing the Turk" by sailing a fleet through the Dardanelles (Gladstone, 1879, 53).

Harcourt noted sardonically, "we have done something popular" (Shannon, 1982, 303).[28]

A parliamentary vote of credit and the shifting of Native (Indian) troops to Egypt quickly followed this attack. The income tax, which Gladstone had tried to abolish in 1874, rose by 30 percent to 6 pence on the pound (Swartz, 1985). While only 15 percent of the expedition's costs came from Indian revenues, the 10,300 Native soldiers made up almost a third of the expeditionary force (Swartz, 1985, 142). The Egyptian Army was defeated at the Battle of Tel el-Kebir in September of the same year.

A Tory publication crowed,

Not only was there a war, but the very thing was done by Mr. Gladstone which Lord Beaconsfield was all but impeached for doing – the 'dusky warriors from Hindostan,' as one Liberal writer put it, were brought over the sea to fight our battles." Indeed, "the more completely he has turned his back upon the Midlothian doctrines, the more closely has he found himself acting in accord with the national wishes and sentiment. (Jennings, 1882, 543–548)

The policy implications appeared clear: "A small garrison of Indian troops in Egypt would be of far greater service to England than could be estimated by its numbers alone; the effect which it would produce in India and Europe alike would be such as every English statesman ought to desire" (Jennings, 1882, 553). Foreign observers also took notice. According to one American analyst:

These oriental soldiers of the British Empire can be brought on any field of action by the scores of thousands (there were about 17,000 cavalry and 100,000 infantry habitually under arms); indeed, the number has hardly any limit. That the practice, once begun, of drawing upon this reserve will ever be abandoned, should future complications require a sudden reinforcement of her military strength, cannot be hoped for by any possible enemy of England. (Goodrich, 1885, 333)

Significantly, the Indian garrison only stood down when an Egyptian army officered by Europeans stood up, solidifying Britain's "temporary" occupation of Egypt.

---

[28] "The news of the bombardment certainly called up a little excitement and enthusiasm at home. It was gratifying to find that our untried ironclad and huge guns could do their work after all, and for a day or two there was a general disposition to sing 'Rule Britannia' " (Lane-Poole, 1882, 389).

Given Gladstone's anti-imperialist instincts, his reluctant support for increased annexations is powerful evidence of the source of imperialist pressure. But the same can be said for the Conservative Lord Salisbury, who described himself as a "reluctant imperialist" and complained of "constant wars at distant points which bring us such large bills and such little credit" (Taylor, 1975, 13).[29] Nonetheless, in 1886 he wrote to Randolph Churchill in response to renewed Russian threats against Constantinople:

My belief is that the main strength of the Tory party both in the richer and poorer classes lies in its association with the honour of the country. It is quite true that in order to save that honour, we have to run into expense. We shall suffer for it as a party – that is human nature. But what I contend is that we shall suffer as a party more – much more – if the loss of Constantinople stands on our record. (Churchill, 1906, 161–162)

5.3.4 Rising great power competition and Native military use

These three crises culminating in the Egyptian campaign firmly established the use of Native troops to conduct operations against the better judgment of the governing elite absent concern for public opinion and election results. Indian soldiers were deployed outside of British India 78 times from 1867 through 1898 (India Office, 1900). By 1888, Charles Dilke was advocating "Frank acceptance of the principle that in any great struggle which may come upon the country we shall have to form and officer levies, and perhaps even officer existing armies of certain minor states in the East" (Dilke, 1888, 317).

While since 1857 the ratio of Native to British troops in India had been maintained at two-to-one to prevent another Mutiny, the British circumvented the requirement in 1887 by creating the "Imperial Service Troops," controlled by the leaders of the Independent Indian States, autonomous entities within the Raj, but equipped to modern standards and available for deployment on imperial service. Lord Roberts, the Indian Army's Commander-in-Chief, admitted that in "holding India under the circumstances we do [i.e. through the threat of force], some risk is inevitable" by creating more Native troops, but this was outweighed by their contribution to internal order and

---

[29] For an excellent take on the role of public opinion forcing Salisbury into the Fashoda crisis, see Peterson (1995).

defense, the fragmenting of the Indian Army into autonomous groups, and their potential for use abroad (Stern, 1988, 211).

Although Native troops were specifically excluded from directly fighting in the South African theater due to racial tension concerns, the Indian Army nonetheless played an essential role in the Boer War. For the first time, the Indian Army became permanently garrisoned abroad; 14,000 Native soldiers put down the Boxer Rebellion in China and others were deployed to Somaliland and East Africa. Moreover, the British Treasury assumed these deployments' costs entirely, to the tune of £3 million from 1899 through 1904 (India Office, 1905). In the Boer War itself, General Kitchener armed about 30,000 Africans to fight directly in South Africa and approximately 100,000 Africans were involved in fighting or logistics across Southern Africa (Saunders and Smith, 1999, 619).

Over the subsequent decades, the use of Native troops accelerated even as the concern for the safety of India from Russian invasion grew. British Treasury funds were thrown at the defense of India; in 1904 Prime Minister Arthur Balfour noted, "were India successfully invaded, the moral loss would be incalculable, the material loss would be important – but the burden of British taxation would undergo a most notable diminution!" (Friedberg, 1988, 248). As early as 1890, influential military officers such as Lord Roberts made the case that India was Britain's strategic center of gravity, and envisioned "converting the British Army and the Colonial Militias into one gigantic reserve for the Indian Army" (Preston, 1978, 273). Unsurprisingly, such a policy reversal failed to gain purchase among civilian leaders in London (Beckett, 2005). It was much later, when the realization became unavoidable that defending the English barrack in an oriental sea would have to be calculated in terms of British soldiers rather than British sterling, that accommodation with Russia became an imperative (Friedberg, 1988, 265). Accord with Russia allowed the continued use of the now safe imperial reserve for great power politics against a rising Germany, and this paid off amply in the Great War, in which 1.3 million Indians fought (Porter, 1996).

Following World War I, 185,000 Indian Army troops remained deployed outside of India in Iraq, Egypt, around the Black Sea, and elsewhere (Tinker, 1988, 220). As Indian political restiveness grew, Britain looked elsewhere for substitutions. Indian soldiers were deployed to Africa to form the initial nuclei of other Native military

units such as the King's African Rifles and the West African Frontier Force, which were then filled with indigenous forces recruited as
voluntary, long-term recruits with a contractual "obligation to serve
abroad" (Gutteridge, 1970, 289).[30] In 1920 Winston Churchill, then
Secretary of War, mooted a plan to use East African troops as garrison forces in the Middle East and even India so that "by a process
of evolution" akin to the development of a deployable Indian Army,
these troops could become a "truly Imperial East Africa Force." One
War Office official observed that, "It must be expected in a few years
that Indian troops would no longer be available for service outside
India. It was necessary, therefore, to contemplate that in, say, ten years
we should need a force of, say, 500,000 African troops available for
service outside Africa" (Killingray, 1979, 428).

In addition, technology had developed to the point that machines,
particularly those of the Royal Air Force (RAF), could be used as a
labor substitute. In June 1918, the Chief of the Air Staff proposed an
Imperial Air Force not only to police imperial territory cheaply, but
also to free up "black troops" for service overseas (Killingray, 1984).
Facing another outbreak of rebellion in Somaliland, the Secretary of
State for the Colonies responded to the original proposed plan requiring a thousand British soldiers by going to the Chief of Air Staff. The
Chief replied "Why not leave the whole thing to us? This is exactly
the type of operation which the R.A.F. can tackle on its own." In
1920 the British finally put down the 20-year-old rebellion, led by the
man known in Britain as the "Mad Mullah," using 200 RAF personnel and 12 De Havilland bombers (Killingray, 1984, 434). A lecture
from that same year on the subject, entitled "Substitution," described
bombing colonial rebellions as "both economical and humane since it
inflicts neither great nor permanent suffering upong [sic] the people
against whom it is used nor heavy casualties among those who have
to wield it" (Killingray, 1984, 440). The book's theory suggests that it
is no coincidence that as technology developed – allowing for efficient
military capitalization – the age of European imperialism declined.

---

[30] David Killingray (1979, 426) argues that, due to population sparseness and
theories about "martial races," Africa was not seen principally as a source of
manpower until Indian troops were tapped out in the middle of World War I.
Significantly, efforts at recruiting black Africans for the war were made by a
reluctant Colonial Office only "in response to the clamour from press,
parliament and the War Office."

5.4 Sources of democratic overstretch

Scholars of Great Britain's arming at the turn of the twentieth century describe it as a great logrolling exercise: "those who wished to see spending on arms progressively increased would have to pay for the privilege through an augmented income tax...Militarists and social collectivists discovered, as a consequence, that their interests, far from being diametrically opposed, were actually complementary" (Holland, 1991, 45–46). More accurately, and consistent with this book's argument, these actors were one and the same. While not the only cause of British expansion – developments such as the Suez Canal's constrcution transformed the strategic picture – public approval became a necessary condition, and this expansion often proceeded in spite of liberal government officials' skepticism within both parties. In the words of Winfried Baumgart (1982, 185), the formal Empire was the product of a "small bundle of factors" of which the newly empowered middle and lower class was an important component.

This chapter flips the classical liberalism of Hobson on its head by showing that the extension of the British Empire through military conquest and of the British franchise through the Second and Third Reform Acts are intimately connected in a way left unremarked by conventional political science theories and many historiographical explanations. Mainstream democratic exceptionalism would also suggest that the extension of suffrage would produce a far different policy than that of late nineteenth-century Britain. The rather dubious logic that giving the middle class the vote could lead to its subsidizing the British elite's imperial adventure also finds little empirical support, especially given the shift of defense resources from the economically productive White Dominions to colonial conquest of Africa and Asia. Victorian military campaigns were lavishly expensive, logistically demanding affairs, costly to the Exchequer and to the local populations from which labor was drawn (often through coercion), and required little sacrifice from newly empowered middle- and working-class voters. When the world seems more dangerous but war seems less costly to a majority of its voters (if not to the state), a democracy will act very aggressively indeed, even if the gains are likely to be small or uncertain.

I am in good company making this argument. The fiercely anti-imperialist Hobson wrote in 1902 about what he termed the "new

Imperialism," asking, "Why should Englishmen fight the defensive or offensive wars of this Empire when cheaper, more numerous, and better-assimilated fighting material can be raised upon the spot, or transferred from one tropical dominion to another?" The danger was clear to him that "through reducing the strain of militarism upon the population at home, it enhances the risks of wars, which become more frequent and more barbarous in proportion as they involve to a less degree the lives of Englishmen." Hobson went on to observe that, "A regular provision for compulsory foreign service will never be adopted when the alternative of mercenary native armies remains" (Hobson, 1902, 143–145). One popular magazine at the turn of the twentieth century saw the implications clearly, and its words echo many similar statements about the distribution of war costs in the contemporary United States:

There are indeed families scattered through the land which have felt the dread that comes with every post and telegram from the seat of war. But only a very small per-centage of our populace is even wounded by the casualty lists. The mentality of the remainder (at least of the majority) rather resembles at this moment that of a crowd which has been let in free to watch a great football match. In this case they went in to see the match on a representation that there would be little or nothing to pay. (*The Speaker*, November 1900, 169)

5.4.1 Extended implications

While primarily seeking to add a crucial middle-class credit to the historiographical "balance sheet of empire" (Porter, 1988), the case provokes several extensions for future research. First, the use of British capital and Indian labor suggests an interesting twist on the "arms versus allies" tradeoff (Morrow, 1993). Whereas Britain developed into a parliamentary democracy where the relatively poor possessed a great deal of political power, India remained a partially autonomous autocracy where the wealthy possessed all political power. India combined the cost-reducing virtues of an ally with the low-risk elements of internal balancing for the labor-intensive requirements of late nineteenth-century war. Even such enthusiastic a celebrant of "Imperial co-operation in war time" as the official historian of the Royal Colonial Institute admits that "the Parliament of the United Kingdom represents primarily the taxpayers of the United Kingdom, and India in the past necessarily stood in a less advantageous position as a contributing unity of the Empire than the self-governing Dominions, free to contribute or not at their own will" (Lucas, 1921, 57). Even were the peripheral autocracy autonomous from the metropole, my theory predicts that democracies should seek out such allies that can deliver regime-based gains from trade, providing cash in return for soldiers in pursuit of mutual interests.

A second implication of this comparative advantage argument suggests a reexamination of the classical liberal assumption that imperialism inevitably leads to tyranny at home. Hobson wrote that it is the "nemesis of Imperialism that the arts and crafts of tyranny, acquired and exercised in our unfree Empire, should be turned against our liberties at home."[31] More recently, some scholars have suggested that Britain's imperialism abroad may have contributed to a steady, measured increase of liberalism at home either from exposure to progressive examples in the White Dominions (Thompson, 2005, 149) or by providing "an outlet for the vicarious adventures for an otherwise well-ordered society" (McIntyre, 1967, 4). Other scholars take a more constructivist or post-modern approach, arguing that a process of "othering" the colonial races was an essential prerequisite for more British men to secure the vote over the course of the nineteenth century. For example José Harris (1993, 6) argues that:

Imperial visions injected a powerful strain of hierarchy, militarism, 'frontier mentality', administrative rationality and masculine civic virtue into British culture, at a time when domestic political forces were running in quite the opposite direction towards egalitarianism, 'progressivism', consumerism, popular democracy, feminism, and women's rights.

Cost distribution theory suggests a complementary approach that contradicts the claims of classical liberals as well as democratic exceptionalists. The militarized expansion of the Empire using Native soldiers may have helped *preserve* important liberal aspects of political life in Britain. The imperial system until the beginning of the twentieth century was fundamental to maintaining a conscription-free Britain. An important effect of Empire becomes clear upon comparison to the other contemporary European states' movement along a liberal-authoritarian axis in response to increased security competition. One

---

[31] Also see Taylor (1991).

Conservative leader claimed that Britain would "sooner throw over imperialism than accept the military system of foreign countries [i.e. conscription]" (Williams, 1991, 7), but perhaps the two phenomena are related differently. While France, Italy, Germany, and other states created large standing armies, maintained universal military service, extended conscription terms, strengthened the autonomy of the executive, and generally centralized political power; the average voter in Britain may have well avoided the development of such a garrison state by using the wealthy's capital and the Empire's labor to engage in international politics for him.

Reducing the median voter's relative wealth will have an effect on democratic aggressiveness regardless of how labor-intensive an era's prevailing military technology may be. Substitution technology is not determinative; given enough political power, the middle class can still get the wealthy to pay for enhanced security (and potential overstretch) in such an environment. The effect becomes more acute as technology allows easier substitution of capital for labor. The shrinking British Empire in the twentieth century was accompanied by a growing consideration of materiel to compensate for the smaller (and politically powerful) military labor pool. The consequences of the increasing ability to send a bullet instead of a man will become readily apparent in the United States experience during the Vietnam War.

6 | *Vietnam and the American way of small war*

Maxwell Taylor, an architect of US Cold War grand strategy in general and the Vietnam War in particular, observed in that war's aftermath that "When one considers the vast resources committed to carrying out our Vietnam policy, the effective power generated therefrom seems to have been relatively small" (Taylor, 1972, 402). What would cause a democracy to spend such vast resources to conduct a flawed counterinsurgency campaign? Why would leaders choose war despite intending to fight in a manner making failure more likely? This book's theory, illustrated in Figure 2.1, argues that civilian leaders, anticipating voter preferences, will deploy an inefficient strategy against an unconventional opponent in pursuit of moderate aims because the reduction in costs outweighs the sacrifice in expected value.

The case is an important one. Like the British Empire, Vietnam represents an "anomalous case," for democratic exceptionalism (Downes, 2009). Many consider it as a paradigmatic example of capture of a state's grand strategy by an elite, in this case a myopic military obsessed with technology and firepower. Finally, interpretations of Vietnam continue to influence contemporary American strategic debates.

This chapter examines the development of American counterinsurgency strategy before and during the Vietnam War to competitively test my theory of moral hazard against other explanations for aggression from IR, historical, and policy-oriented research.[1] This case complements the previous chapter; whereas Britain expanded its Empire by fighting many trivial wars well, the United States fought an important

---

[1] While space precludes expanding beyond military doctrine, many aspects of the war conform to cost distribution theory, such as Congress's remarkable "willingness to continue approving appropriations for a war that most opposed" (Johns, 2010, 4). Caverley (2010a) draws on public opinion evidence to make this case. John Dumbrell (2012) provides a spirited, efficient, and informative tour of current Vietnam War scholarship and the debates therein.

small war poorly. Whereas the key factor in Chapter 5 is the median voter's relative wealth, this chapter takes on the role of military doctrine. Vietnam, as John Lewis Gaddis (1982, 237) observes, provided the perfect "test case" for new, flexible, and relatively uncostly capabilities.

In contrast to the British case, this chapter covers a time period without large swings in the franchise or economic inequality in the United States.[2] The strategic threat environment also stayed largely stable; if anything tensions between the United States and the Soviet Union had been declining since the Cuban Missile Crisis ended and the brinksmanship over Berlin dissipated. While these other explanatory variables remained roughly unchanged, from the Eisenhower administration onward, military doctrine slowly but steadily evolved in an increasingly capital-intensive direction. Partially as a consequence, American foreign policy under multiple administrations grew both increasingly ambitious and militarized.

Given the pace of change in this explanatory variable, I do not claim that my theory explains why the Vietnam conflict escalated into the American-dominated war when it did. Few IR theories are capable of making such point predictions. Rather my theory predicts that as military technology shifts the cost of conflict away from the average voter by making war a matter of fiscal rather than social mobilization, initiation and escalation of a crisis such as Vietnam becomes increasingly likely. This chapter uses cost distribution theory to link earlier findings of mainstream Vietnam War scholarship in a novel and consistent way.

Previous work has judged the strategic logic underpinning American intervention as a highly aggressive form of containment, and an attempt to send a costly signal to potential aggressors. Most members of the administration were at least skeptical of the domino theory and realized that prospects for success were low. The principals understood that they were adapting "ends to fit preferred means" (Gaddis, 1982, 253) in the conduct of the war. Prior work has faulted the firepower- and airpower-intensive nature of American warfighting, the lack of a systematic COIN doctrine, the avoidance of casualties, and even the deliberate substitution of capital for labor. As John Mueller (1980, 505) observes, "The American military machine

---

[2] The successes of the Civil Rights movement and the twenty-seventh amendment had only modest effects in this sense.

was specifically designed to maximize enemy losses while minimizing American losses, even if the imbalance could be achieved only at enormous monetary cost." The war enjoyed many years of strong public support through the Tet Offensive of 1968. Multiple administrations' refusal to mobilize society is well known, as is Johnson's simultaneous efforts to preserve his Great Society domestic legislation. To the military's dismay, civilian leadership played an intimate role in nearly all elements of the war's conduct. The chapter ties these previous findings into a coherent and parsimonious explanation as well as to draw in additional, hitherto overlooked elements drawn from primary source materials.

6.1 Why did the United States fight poorly . . . or at all?

Most previous analysis agrees with Robert Komer, an important Vietnam War policy-maker, that allowing the military to "do its thing" during wartime is a mistake (Komer, 1973). Work specifically addressing US conduct of small wars frequently locates blame within its military culture (Krepinevich, 1986; Nagl, 2005). Eliot Cohen (1984, 165) argues that "The most substantial constraints on America's ability to conduct small wars result from the resistance of the American defense establishment to the very notion of engaging in such conflicts, and from the unsuitability of that establishment for fighting such wars."[3] This cultural explanation for poor war performance begs the question. Why does culture not adapt in response to repeated failure, or why do civilian planners not adapt to the stubborn culture?

Andrew Krepinevich (1986, 196) calls this culture ingrained in the US military (particularly the Army) the "Army Concept." The Concept emphasizes a firepower-intensive strategy of attrition that is "nothing more than the natural outgrowth of its organizational recipe for success – playing to America's strong suits, material abundance and technological superiority, and the nation's profound abhorrence of US casualties." Krepinevich (1986, 5–6) recognizes that much of this

---

[3] H. R. McMaster (2008, 28) widens the blame to encompass "the 'iron triangle' of defense contractors, military establishments and governments which can undermine the ability to think about future conflicts."

stems from "the substitution of material costs at every available opportunity to avoid payment in blood," and notes that this effect is likely to be more pronounced during limited wars, when the United States has more discretion over the employment of its resources.[4]

The case for the military's independent and unconstructive role rests on three major pieces of evidence. The most important is that the person most epitomizing the "Army Concept" – Military Assistance Command Vietnam (MACV) commander, William Westmoreland – chose a foolish ground strategy.[5] Westmoreland, according to his critics, "displayed an utter obliviousness to the political nature of the war" (Record, 2007, 121), and resolutely rejected an alternate strategy that was simultaneously more effective and less casualty-intensive, one exemplified by the Marine Corps' "Combined Action Platoons" (Krepinevich, 1986, 21).

Advocates of the military myopia thesis employ two other pieces of evidence. First is the resistance of the military to the COIN focus of the Kennedy administration; "In the early 1960s," writes Jeffrey Record (2007, 129), "the army essentially blew off President Kennedy's demand that it take counterinsurgency seriously." These scholars argue that John F. Kennedy developed an enlightened enthusiasm for a military designed to fight COIN in the developing world, only to be resisted by the Army leadership (Gallucci, 1975; Halberstam, 2001, 91). The final component to the myopia argument relies on the apparently abrupt change in both strategy and success upon the relief of Westmoreland by General Creighton Abrams, the exception that proves the Army Concept rule (Sorley, 1999).

---

[4] Krepinevich challenges Harry Summers (2007), who had provided the dominant explanation for the loss in Vietnam among American military circles since its original publication in 1981 (Nagl, 2005). This chapter incorporates elements from both of these important works. I agree that civilians set most of the ground strategy in an effort to control the costs of war, but disagree that these civilians pushed the Army to devote too many resources towards COIN. While I focus on COIN in this chapter, it should be noted that Krepinevich and Summers are wrong in arguing, respectively, that Vietnam was primarily a counterinsurgency or a conventional war; it was both.

[5] For additional evidence from the Johnson administration on this subject, see Caverley (2010a) as well as the subsequent exchange between McAllister (2010) and Caverley (2010b).

6.1.1 Competitive testing

The interpretation of the war's conduct presented here challenges the military myopia thesis without rejecting it entirely. Evidence that the military favored capital over labor is overwhelming. However, military myopia is a confounding, rather than a causal variable. Even counter-productive practices seemingly internal to the military, such as rotating individuals rather than units through the conflict, were designed for the approval of civilian leaders and ultimately the public. If Army leadership was devoted to firepower, it was because their civilian leaders promoted them. Thus, even if the military was indeed myopic, the distortion of their collective lens is ultimately traced back to the civilian leadership and the voters that elected them. No disintegration between grand strategy and military doctrine existed in Vietnam.

Figure 6.1 depicts the relationship of cost distribution and military myopia theories to the dependent variable of flawed counterinsurgency. Military myopia explanations fixate on the causal relationship depicted by "Path 1," where the military's predilection for conventional and firepower-heavy warfare (MM) is a sufficient cause of poor, capital-intensive operations (CO) to fight the insurgency. Cost distribution theory offers a causally prior independent variable labeled, for simplicity's sake, "civilian preferences" (CP), and argues that this is a necessary condition for MM, "Path 2." Although MM is not necessary for CO, CP is. Were the military simply a transmission belt for civilian preferences, democracies would still engage in CO, or causal "Path 3."

Evidence of a military preference for capital-intensive warfare, Figure 6.1's Path 1 does not favor one theory over the other. In equilibrium, the military and civilians should be of the same mind (Avant, 1998). If, as cost distribution theory assumes, civilians are the dominant force in grand strategy, it would be unlikely that President

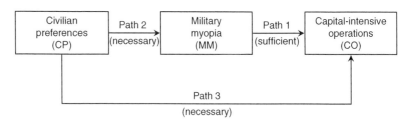

Figure 6.1 Competing causal pathways leading to poor counterinsurgency

Johnson appointed a commander in Vietnam (MACV) who did not share his views. Indeed, H. R. McMaster (1997) locates the Vietnam-era military at the Cold War nadir in terms of policy influence. The Kennedy and Johnson administrations ensured their principal military advisers were handpicked "team men, not gladiators" (Herring, 1994, 29–30). Beyond appointments, civilian leaders can shape their uniformed subordinates' actions in many indirect ways. The Joint Chiefs of Staff anticipated the Johnson administration's preferences in developing and presenting their campaign plans (McMaster, 1997, 329–334). Statements to the American public also influenced and constrained the military; a 1965 Air Force Policy Letter for Commanders and a 1968 Air University Review article cite Defense Secretary Robert McNamara's televised statement that "what the U.S. sought in South Vietnam was a limited objective, and it would be accomplished with the lowest possible loss of lives and not necessarily with the lowest expenditure of money."[6]

Showing CP to be a superior explanation for MM requires focusing on Paths 2 and 3. The evidence for these relationships may not be plentiful given that cost distribution theory predicts civil – military harmony in equilibrium. On the other hand, any finding of instances where civilians helped direct, shape, and reinforce the military's capital-intensive campaign (i.e. Path 2) should be given great weight. Evidence that civilian leaders pushed for a capital-intensive counterinsurgency effort in the absence of the military (Path 3) would also support cost distribution theory. Linking civilian preferences to counterinsurgency strategy absent a role for military myopia (Path 3) is not entirely counterfactual, given the Johnson administration's dealings with more COIN-oriented civilians such as Ambassador Henry Cabot Lodge (who by definition did not suffer from military myopia).

A competing explanation might assign causal priority to MM, but make CP necessary as well. Deborah Avant (1994) argues that the "electoral circumstances" of civilians prevented them from forcing the US Army to change its conventional bias. In this case we would need to find evidence of Path 2's arrow going in the opposite direction.

---

[6] Robert McNamara interview, February 8, 1965 quoted in "Air Force Policy Letter for Commanders," February 15, 1965. References to both are in Kipp (1968).

Sustaining my argument over that of military myopia therefore requires establishing three propositions. First, the public must support a capital-intensive approach to limited war as well as an aggressive employment of such a doctrine. Second, government officials must act upon these views, preferably in ways they would not have pursued otherwise. Finally, contra military myopia's implications, these officials must direct the military to fight accordingly. Step one and three are relatively easy to establish.

Showing that officials set strategy in response to public demands is harder to pin down empirically. The historiography of the war is both extensive and controversial, containing a wealth of primary and secondary sources that allows the exploration of complex interactions among decision-makers who regularly contradicted each other and even themselves. Given policy-makers' "great pressure to keep one's mouth shut, to think and speak of foreign affairs as if they are something above mere politics, something sacred" (Gelb and Betts, 1979, 221), the fact that the president's closest national security advisers spoke and wrote quite frequently about domestic politics is especially powerful evidence. Finally, "eyes-only" messages within the military distinguish between uniformed leaders' professional beliefs and their responses to the president's wishes. I also look for deliberations in which important actors including the president acknowledged their actions to be suboptimal, but ordered them anyway. These actions should persist over time despite continued feedback that the strategy was not working. When Johnson did something he suspected would meet with voter approval, he made sure to tell them; public statements by him and his subordinates emphasizing capitalized warfare over labor-intensive COIN are therefore good sources of support for the theory.

An important component of military myopia theory is the claim that General Westmoreland chose a foolish ground strategy with minimal civilian interference. Showing that civilians overruled military pacification plans due to labor constraints contradicts the military myopia thesis, as well as the more subtle one in which the military provides the civilian with preferences (Path 2 reversed, Avant 1994). Finally, the military myopia explanation requires a counterfactual alternative strategy that was simultaneously less labor-intensive and more effective. The chapter examines civilian assessments of the war's most successful COIN program, the Marines' "Combined Action Platoons" (CAP). In doing so, this chapter also helps answer one of the great puzzles of the Vietnam War – one even Westmoreland's fiercest critic describes as "baffling" (Sorley, 2011, 93) – the lack of administration interference in the ground strategy given its involvement in every other aspect of the war.[7]

While evidence is presented from three administrations in chronological order, the chapter focuses on the Johnson administration, since during this period almost all of the major escalation and warfighting decisions were made. The Kennedy administration merits attention because it contains the seeds of the military doctrine employed by Johnson. I briefly cover warfighting during the Nixon administration to show the essential continuity of the American way of war. Including evidence from the Kennedy and Nixon administrations also demonstrates that the war's conduct did not rest on the contingent existence of a man like Johnson (Logevall, 1999).

6.2 What made Flexible Response flexible?

Krepinevich (1986, 72) describes the Kennedy administration as attempting a doctrinal "revolution from above," which ultimately foundered on a resistant Army. However, Kennedy's devotion to counterinsurgency is only remarkable if it is considered out of context with the rest of his defense reforms (and with a heavy dose of hindsight). Indisputably, he pushed for innovation in the conduct of guerrilla warfare and counterinsurgency, and was troubled by the Soviet predilection for small wars (Gelb and Betts, 1979, 71), but this occurred in the context of a larger military buildup, one that conforms comfortably with cost distribution theory. Kennedy's rhetoric about small wars and his fascination with the Green Berets notwithstanding, the most important pieces of evidence of his or any president's priorities are the programs he tries to fund and the officials he places in positions of influence. Judging by Kennedy's budget requests and his appointments, Krepinevich's military myopia appears less convincing. Flexible Response distinguishes itself from Eisenhower's New Look in its intention to make more types of war politically acceptable, which required copious amounts of new spending. The resulting forces and doctrine enabled Johnson to escalate in Vietnam.

---

[7] I am hardly the first to argue that the Johnson administration rejected a more intensive pacification strategy. See Buzzanco (1996, 252), Hunt (1995), and Saunders (2011, 5).

6.2.1 Kennedy's funding priorities

John Lewis Gaddis (2009, 254) argues that "budgetary concerns carried little weight during the Kennedy and Johnson administrations. The theory of 'flexible response' implied unlimited means and hence, little incentive to make hard choices among distasteful alternatives." While Kennedy did increase spending on irregular warfare capabilities, there was no part of the military he did not fund with enthusiasm. His first defense-oriented address as president (Kennedy, 1961a) makes this clear.

While research and development spending on nuclear deterrence and defense totaled 226 million dollars, Kennedy proposed a mere one million dollars to "limited warfare research," a broad category that includes "entirely new types of non-nuclear weapons and equipment – with increased fire-power, mobility and communications, and more suited to the kind of tasks our limited war forces will most likely be required to perform. I include here anti-submarine warfare as well as land and air operations." Of 725 million dollars of spending unrelated to nuclear weapons, half of it is devoted to platforms such as tactical fighters, airlift, amphibious assault craft, and Navy modernization. Even the materiel spending not devoted to such platforms has little to do with counterinsurgency; the president asked for 230 million dollars for helicopters, ordnance, and small arms, observing that "Some important new advances in ammunition and bombs can make a sizable qualitative jump in our limited war capabilities." Special operations forces are only one of the categories of personnel for which Kennedy asked a scant 39 million. The money was to fund "increases in Army personnel strength to expand guerrilla warfare units and round out other existing units, and an increase in the Marine Corps to bring it up closer to authorized strength levels. (In addition, personnel are being added to the Navy for Polaris crews, and to the Air Force for the ground alert expansion)." As for training existing personnel, counterinsurgency was not mentioned.[8]

Kennedy reemphasized these priorities (Kennedy, 1961b) in an extraordinary address to a joint session of Congress on "Urgent

---

[8] The money instead would be used to "provide for additional field training and mobility exercises for the Army and test exercises for the composite air strike forces and MATS [Military Air Transport Service] unit."

National Needs." The speech declared the need for "further reinforce-ment of our own capacity to deter or resist non-nuclear aggression," which for Kennedy included the entire spectrum "of non-nuclear war, paramilitary operations and sub-limited or unconventional wars."

While Kennedy did advocate an increase in special forces and that a "new emphasis must be placed on the special skills and languages which are required to work with local populations," Kennedy empha-sizes that "I find no present need for large new levies of men" but rather "still further increases in flexibility." This flexibility required modernizing the Army:

to increase its non-nuclear firepower, to improve its tactical mobility in any environment, to insure its flexibility to meet any direct or indirect threat, to facilitate its coordination with our major allies, and to provide more modern mechanized divisions in Europe and bring their equipment up to date, and new airborne brigades in both the Pacific and Europe. And secondly, I am asking the Congress for an additional 100 million dollars to begin the procurement task necessary to re-equip this new Army structure with the most modern material. New helicopters, new armored personnel carriers, and new howitzers, for example, must be obtained now.

Much of the confusion over Kennedy's priorities might rest on the fact that his term "limited war" referred to any conflict that did not involve nuclear weapons, whereas a counterinsurgency would be a "sub-limited or unconventional war." Clearly, Kennedy aimed sim-ply at fighting all kinds of conventional war (Saunders, 2011, 103), albeit with the same number of bodies in a manner acceptable to the American people.

6.2.2 *Kennedy's advisers*

Presidential appointments also provide concrete evidence of an admin-istration's inclinations. Krepinevich credits Kennedy for pursuing COIN capabilities, and then evinces puzzlement over the people appointed to oversee the process, such as national security adviser Walt Rostow, who were enthusiastic in their pursuit of capital-intensive warfare, above all strategic bombing (Krepinevich, 1986, 33). This chapter advances a simpler explanation; the appointees favored the type of counterinsurgency wanted by the political leadership.

General Maxwell Taylor, whose 1960 book *The Uncertain Trumpet* lambasted Eisenhower's "New Look" strategy, became Kennedy's principal military adviser, then chair of the Joint Chiefs of Staff (JCS), and finally Ambassador to South Vietnam. Taylor was no advocate of counterinsurgency; he objected to New Look reliance on massive retaliation because it precluded the use of American conventional military power for any kind of war. Taylor, and Kennedy, instead sought to develop American military power that could be used in small (i.e. non-nuclear) wars. One historian of counterinsurgency acidly remarks that "Taylor might as well have donned an air force uniform" (Asprey, 1994, 724). Taylor also chaired Kennedy's Special Group for Counter-Insurgency (SGCI), established in January 1962 to "assure unity of effort and the use of all available resources with maximum effectiveness in preventing and resisting subversive insurgency and related forms of indirect aggression in friendly countries."[9]

Taylor was far from an isolated appointment in the administration. Like Taylor, the other SGCI members had little counterinsurgency expertise; potential members who did, such as Roger Hilsman (Burma in World War II) and Edward Lansdale (Philippines and Vietnam), were not included. McGeorge Bundy considered sustained air reprisals against the North to be the United States' preferred means of fighting guerrilla wars.[10] Kennedy eventually purged the military's leadership of less manageable war heroes such as Curtis LeMay for more pliable officers. McNamara exerted tremendous influence over the uniformed services, particularly in his first years there, yet had little interest in counterinsurgency. Nonetheless, as one of his first acts as president, Kennedy transferred responsibility for paramilitary actions from the CIA to the Pentagon.

---

[9] *Foreign Relations of the United States 1961–1963* (FRUS), Kennedy Administration, Vol. 8, Doc. 68.

[10] *Foreign Relations of the United States, 1964–1968* (FRUS), Johnson Administration, Vol. 2, Doc. 84. When the document is found in both the "Gravel edition" of the *Pentagon Papers* (PP) and *Foreign Relations of the United States, 1964–1968* (FRUS), I cite the FRUS due to its availability online at www.state.gov/r/pa/ho/frus/johnsonlb/. The number for FRUS citations refers to the volume and document, rather than page.

6.2.3 *Kennedy's Vietnam*

Wading into the debate over whether Kennedy would have pulled out of Vietnam is beyond the scope of this book. What is not in question is that Kennedy (like Johnson) believed he would be unelectable if he did so. He tells the dovish Senator Mansfield "I can't do it until 1965 – after I'm re-elected" (Asprey, 1994, 761–762).[11] In an April 16, 1961 memo to the president on "gearing up the whole Viet-Nam operation," Walt Rostow advocated "The sending to Viet-Nam of a research and development and military hardware team which would explore with General McGarr which of the various techniques and gadgets now available or being explored might be relevant and useful in the Viet-Nam operation" as well as "finding a way of introducing into the Viet-Nam operation a substantial number of Special Forces types" (PP 2:35). Rostow and Taylor prepared an August 4, 1961 memo for the president in anticipation of an upcoming mission to South Vietnam:

As we understand your position: you would wish to see every avenue of diplomacy exhausted before we accept the necessity for either positioning US forces on the Southeast Asian mainland or fighting there . . . you would wish to see indigenous forces used to the maximum if fighting should occur; and that, should we have to fight, we should use air and sea power to the maximum and engage minimum US forces on the Southeast Asian mainland. (Rostow, 1972, 271)

Kennedy's task force on Vietnam recommended that if American forces were used, they should take the form of two US battle groups and an engineer battalion, to be "located in the 'high plateau' region, remote from the major population center of Saigon-Cholon." These forces would "provide maximum psychological impact in deterrence of further Communist aggression from North Vietnam, China, or the Soviet Union," and "release Vietnamese forces from advanced and static defense positions to permit their fuller commitment to counterinsurgency actions; provide maximum training to approved Vietnamese forces; and provide significant military resistance to potential North Vietnam Communist and/or Chinese Communist action" (PP 2:49).

---

[11] For much of the next administration, Mansfield agreed, and would give similar advice to Johnson.

The report contained a personal "eyes-only" assessment from Taylor suggesting the "extreme vulnerability of North Vietnam to conventional bombing." Acknowledging that American combat forces may be necessary, a contingency plan for these troops should be "designed to take over the responsibility for the security of certain relatively quiet areas, if the battle remained at the guerrilla level, or to fight the Communists if open war were attempted." Taylor made clear the administration's general concept of how to deal with Krushchev's "para-wars of guerrilla aggression," which was a "new and dangerous Communist technique which bypasses our traditional political and military responses." Taylor suggests that "the time may come in our relations to Southeast Asia when we must declare our intention to attack the source of guerrilla aggression in North Vietnam and impose on the Hanoi Government a price for participating in the current war which is commensurate with the damage being inflicted on its neighbors to the south" (PP 2:107–108).

Kennedy rejected the Mission's proposal to send 8,000 US combat personnel under the cover of "flood relief provision," but authorized nearly every other part of the Report's recommendations (including airlift, helicopters, small water craft, and "additional equipment" for "air reconnaissance, photography, instruction in and execution of air-ground support techniques, and for special intelligence"). The rejection was quickly leaked; the *Pentagon Papers* describes the "unattributed but obviously authoritative stories that Kennedy was opposed to sending troops and Taylor was not recommending them" (PP 2:99). While the decision to deploy troops in Vietnam had been postponed, the American conception of how to fight an insurgency appears to have been already in place for Kennedy's successor.

6.3 The Johnson administration in Vietnam

Recently sworn in after Kennedy's assassination and already preparing for the 1964 election, President Johnson convened an ad hoc committee on Vietnam chaired by diplomat William Sullivan, who was told in advance that the policy would be a "slow, very slow, escalation" of bombing pressures against North Vietnam. Sullivan briefed the JCS that a military "presence" without "heavy forces" would maintain public support indefinitely (McMaster, 1997, 68). One contemporary analysis based on anonymous State Department interviews assessed that Johnson was "more inclined to listen" to advocates of "selective bombing of North Vietnamese targets and clandestine naval raids along the coast" because "1964 was an election year" and Johnson realized he had to "take some action soon to show that his administration was on top of the situation" (Stempel, 1966, 221). Perhaps the most telling evidence of the election's influence comes from McGeorge Bundy's observation that of all the political forces in the 1964 election, the "Goldwater crowd" was "more numerous, more powerful and more dangerous than the fleabite professors" (Herring, 1986, 140).[12]

Towards the end of 1966, Secretary of Defense McNamara told General Westmoreland that "he would approve whatever related requirements were developed to ensure that RVN [Republic of Vietnam, also referred to in primary documents as GVN and SVN] manpower and U.S. money substitute for U.S. blood" (Gibbons, 1994, Vol. 4, 106–107). This set the tone for the rest of the war. Despite obvious evidence of a failing strategy, the *Pentagon Papers* (the Defense Department analysis of the war's conduct) describe further attempts to de-emphasize labor, "certain 'oblique alternatives,' *those which were not directly substitutable options* appeared during this time – all of them designed to relieve pressure on US resources, especially manpower" (PP 4:385; emphasis added).

The Johnson administration and its uniformed subordinates highlighted this substitution for the public. Robert Komer, Johnson's principal counterinsurgency adviser, recalled the political exchange rate in 1982: "What it costs you in blood is much more politically visible than what it costs you in treasures" (Lorell and Kelley, 1985, 80). JCS Chairman Gen. Earle Wheeler told a Rotary Club, "the United States policy is to expend money and firepower, not manpower, in accomplishing the purpose of the nation" (quoted in Krepinevich 1986, 198). Asked by a journalist "How large a commitment of men is the United States prepared to make at the end of 1965?" McNamara refused to answer directly, instead replying that "the thing we prize most deeply is not money but men. We have multiplied the capability

---

[12] The North Vietnamese understood the direction of public pressure; the NVN foreign minister (Pham Van Dong) told an unofficial Canadian intermediary that "Johnson worries also of course about the coming electoral battle in which it is necessary to outbid the Republican candidate" (Logevall, 1999, 209).

of our men. It's expensive in dollars, but cheap in life" (Graff, 1970, 81–82). Responding in a televised congressional hearing to a question on the economic costs of strategic bombing, McNamara stated that financial comparisons do not "have great value in affecting the decisions as to whether to bomb or not bomb specific facilities." Rather "one of the standards I use in recommending targets for attack on the North [is comparing] the value of facilities destroyed in the North with the number of U.S. lives lost in the process of destroying them."[13]

6.3.1 Airpower as counterinsurgency strategy

The Johnson administration designed both the strategic bombing of North Vietnam and the more tactically oriented air operations in the South with the insurgency in mind (Thompson, 1969, 135). A pivotal memo on "sustained reprisal," written by National Security Adviser Bundy in February 1965, argued that strategic bombing was a "new norm in counter-insurgency" because "to stop it [the bombing] the Communists would have to stop enough of their activity in the South to permit the probable success of a determined pacification effort" (FRUS 2:84). Later that year, Bundy noted the importance of population security and "the civil side of the war," but then describes how it should be conducted: "It is less than a full-scale war and more than a guerrilla war. It is being fought in the shelter of sea and air power." Bundy continues with a remarkable perversion of COIN, "All of South Vietnam is an enclave; the populated area is all accessible from the sea" (Graff, 1970, 94).[14] Walt Rostow, Bundy's successor as national security adviser in 1966, agreed, describing airpower as "the equivalent of guerrilla warfare."[15]

The administration understood that bombing was unlikely to be effective, even as it ordered its use. In a late 1964 memo to Maxwell

---

[13] Preparedness Investigating Subcommittee, Air War against North Vietnam, p. 283.

[14] The "enclave strategy" was advocated by retired General James Gavin, who had recently written an article for *Harper's* defending the current limited deployment in Vietnam and noting that "we are stretching these resources beyond reason in our endeavors to secure the entire country of South Vietnam from the Vietcong penetration" (Gavin, 1966, 18).

[15] Walt Rostow to Averell Harriman, January 28, 1966, Box 13, Papers of Walt Rostow, Lyndon Baines Johnson (LBJ) Library, quoted in Milne (2006).

Taylor, then US Ambassador to Vietnam, Johnson observed, "I have never felt that this war will be won from the air" (FRUS 1:477) making the point more colorfully in a March 1965 phone conversation with Senator Richard Russell, "Airplanes ain't worth a *damn* Dick!" (Beschloss, 2001, 212, emphasis in original).

The United States nonetheless embarked on a massive air campaign and continued it long after sufficient evidence existed that it had little, if any, effect on the insurgency (or the war in general). Indeed the ratio of airpower to ground forces rose over the course of war. The near one-to-one ratio of combat sorties in the theater to personnel in Vietnam is shown in Figure 6.2. In 1966 the number of sorties overtook the number of personnel, rose more steeply to the peak deployment of 1968, and then declined less sharply. Before the ratio increased by an order of magnitude in 1972, the largest sorties-to-personnel ratio occurred during 1969, when the US military had supposedly shifted to a less firepower-intensive pacification strategy. McNamara clearly instructed the reluctant Joint Chiefs that the South had priority over the North when determining how to use airpower assets (Van Staaveren, 1966, FRUS 3:183). Administration officials

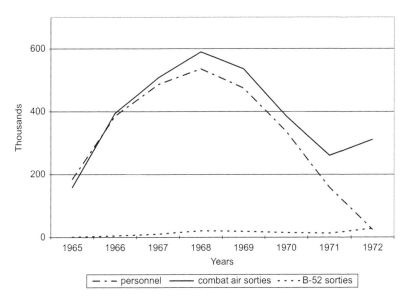

Figure 6.2 Numbers of US personnel/aircraft sorties in Vietnam, 1965–72 (Thayer, 1985, 32)

set daily requirements for ordnance expenditure and air strikes, causing Westmoreland to complain in an eyes-only cable to Pacific Forces
commander Adm. Ulysses Sharp that McNamara "manifested uncom-
mon interest" about reports that these quotas were not being met.
According to Westmoreland, McNamara "voiced concern that 'policy'
concerning use of in-country and carrier based air in support of operations in SVN [was] not being adhered to," stressing the "relative ease"
of obtaining "additional carriers if needed."[16]

President Johnson was much less worried about revealing the extent
of the bombing campaign than he was the ground escalation (Schandler, 1977, 18). National Security Action Memorandum (NSAM)
328, authorizing escalation on the ground and air campaign in April
1965, infamously concludes with the president's desire to "minimize
any appearance of sudden changes in policy," but this admonish-
ment applied specifically only to the additional personnel deployments
and the "more active use" of Marines in Vietnam. Other actions, in
particular "the present slowly ascending tempo of ROLLING THUN-
DER operations [i.e. strategic bombing of North Vietnam]," were not
subject to this restriction (FRUS 2:242).

In an October 1965 memo, Assistant Secretary of State for Far Eastern Affairs William Bundy linked strategic bombing, US casualties, and
public opinion: "We are faced with the pressures from various quar-
ters...to hit the North substantially harder. The degree to which this
will rise during the next 3–6 months will depend heavily on actual
casualty experience." Bundy tied support for increased bombing to the
"Phase II" ground force deployment anticipated for 1966 in light of
"US domestic reaction." Bundy cautioned, "There would be a lot of
rumbling below decks and among the harder-action school of critics,"
and "pressures would be enormous thereafter [a bombing pause] to
'really clobber' [North Vietnam]."[17] Deliberating in November 1967
over McNamara's proposal to level off ROLLING THUNDER sorties, Rostow again advised the president that doing so would push
the president off his "middle ground at home," and cited a Gallup

---

[16] Westmoreland to Sharp, July 17, 1965, Eyes Only Message File (EOMF), Box
    34, LBJ Library. McNamara pushed Wheeler and Westmoreland to improve
    the close air support provided to army ground forces. Wheeler to Sharp,
    December 22, 1965, EOMF, Box 30.

[17] FRUS 3:181. For similar sentiments from Rostow and McNamara, see FRUS
    4:232, which refers to the November elections.

poll showing 67 percent approval for continued bombing. "Acknowledging my limitations as a judge of domestic politics, I am extremely skeptical of any change in strategy that would take you away from your present middle position," Rostow argued, "If we shift unilaterally to de-escalation, the Republicans will move in and crystallize a majority toward a stronger policy" (FRUS 5:381). Taylor attached a note to Rostow's analysis concurring that the curtailment of American bombing would mobilize "the large majority of our citizens who believe in the bombing but who thus far have been silent" (Berman, 1989, 104-107).

The popularity of airpower, its linkage to troop levels and casualties in the minds of the American public and policy-makers, and the limits of military influence on the administration are well illustrated by a rare instance of successful military subversion of presidential policy. Given the opportunity in the summer of 1967 to testify publicly before John Stennis's hawkish Military Preparedness Subcommittee, the JCS pushed to expand strategic bombing even as the defense secretary, convinced by then of ROLLING THUNDER's futility, resisted. McNamara gave a masterful brief on bombing's limitations, but was contradicted by both the generals and the senators, who suggested that "we probably would have suffered fewer casualties in the south if the air campaign against the north had not been burdened with restrictions and prohibited targets."[18]

Generals appearing before the subcommittee were treated to leading questions such as Strom Thurmond's, "It is important for us to continue this bombing. Otherwise, we will lose thousands more American men. That is correct, is it not?" Senator Stuart Symington's comments reveal the public's awareness of the ineffective nature of bombing – "Why is it that we are putting out this gigantic effort, but getting so little, so terribly little results? It is what everybody wants to talk about when I go back to Missouri" – and an unwillingness to consider another strategy – "The people are now beginning to realize that we have shackled our seapower and shackled our airpower."[19] Despite being incensed by the insubordination of the JCS, the hearings helped

---

[18] Preparedness Investigating Subcommittee, Air War against North Vietnam, p. 208.

[19] Preparedness Investigating Subcommittee, Air War against North Vietnam, p. 420.

convince Johnson to abandon his civilian advisers' recommendations
of restraint in favor of the military's more politically palatable ones
(Schandler, 1977, 61).

6.3.2 Counterinsurgency by barrier

Even when the air war's shortcomings became clear, the Johnson
administration chose neither to increase the number of ground forces
nor reconsider US involvement in Vietnam. Instead it attempted to
build one of the *Pentagon Papers'* "oblique strategies": a collection
of electronic surveillance equipment, mines, and physical barriers to
prevent infiltration into the South. Variously named "Practice Nine,"
"Muscle Shoals" and "Igloo White," its colloquial name became the
"McNamara Line," reflecting the defense secretary's enthusiastic support. Paul N. Edwards (1996, 5) describes it as "a microcosmic version
of the whole United States approach to the Vietnam War" in which
the operations of the entire US military were centralized under civilian
control.

Designed partly to head off an army request for four more divisions
to block incursions from the North, its development was champi-
oned by McNamara and other politically oriented officials in the
face of objections from military experts. Expectations for its effectiveness were minimal; William Sullivan, Ambassador to Laos and an
important player in the counterinsurgency effort, recalled that "Neither [General Maxwell] Taylor nor I thought very much of it" (Rego,
2000, 1). The Joint Chiefs generally agreed with Admiral Sharp's
assessment: "an inefficient use of resources with small likelihood of
achieving US objectives in Vietnam" (PP 4:114).

Despite these objections, McNamara approved the plan in September 1966, including it in a presidential memo the next month as one
of the five principal means of reversing the war's course (FRUS 4:233
and 268). In early 1967, NSAM 358 assigned the "highest national
priority category" to the program.[20] The system cost a striking $3–5
billion in total (Mahnken, 2013, 111).[21]

---

[20] Walt Rostow, "NSAM 358: Assignment of Highest National Priority to the
Mk 84, Mod 1 2000 lb. Bomb and to Project PRACTICE NINE," LBJ Library,
www.lbjlib.utexas.edu/johnson/ archives.hom/NSAMs/nsam358.asp.

[21] Mahnken (2013) provides a fascinating survey of the immense American
technological effort in Vietnam, including an attempt to create a mechanical
elephant.

The classified plans were quickly leaked. A *Washington Post* column trumpeted the project as "a revolutionary new approach" that could "conceivably transform the Vietnamese war" (Evans and Novak, 1966). A subsequent column, noting that at least two of the Chiefs privately objected, observed that "the go-ahead for the wall from the White House is one instance, rare of late, in which President Johnson is following the advice of McNamara rather than the uniformed military" (Evans and Novak, 1967) since for a change the Secretary was recommending a policy that was more politically palatable than that of the JCS. Polls backed up this assessment; when respondents were asked to evaluate ways "to step up our military effort in Vietnam," the most popular option (60 percent in support vs. 18 percent opposed) was "building a military barrier across all entrance routes into South Vietnam."[22]

The barrier's public reception was in the minds of policy-makers as it developed. In a May 19, 1967 memo suggesting ways to shore up domestic support, Rostow explicitly considered the McNamara Line as a publicly acceptable substitute for bombing, noting the need to "manage" a "turn-around in policy."[23] Rostow continues:

We shall have to devise a way of presenting our total policy in Viet Nam in a manner which is consistent with diminished attacks in the Hanoi-Haiphong area; which is honest; and which is acceptable to our own people. Surfacing the concept of the barrier may be critical to that turn-around as will be other measures to tighten infiltration, an improved ARVN effort in pacification, and the provision of additional allied forces to permit Westy to get on with our limited but real role in pacification – notably, with the defense of I Corps and the hounding of provincial main force units. (FRUS 5:162)

Rostow describes this "pacification strategy," that is, "the defense of I Corps and the hounding of provincial main force units," as a component of presenting a policy "acceptable to our own people."

6.3.3 *Main force focus as counterinsurgency strategy*

The Rostow memo's conception of pacification in the above paragraph helps explain one of the Vietnam War's most puzzling aspects, and

---

[22] Harris Collection, No. 1735, May 1967.
[23] This assessment is shared by the editor of the *Pentagon Papers* (Gravel 4: 477).

an important component of the military myopia case: the leeway the Johnson administration apparently gave to the military in pursuing an ultimately unsuccessful ground strategy (Krepinevich, 1986, 165). Cost distribution theory is consistent with Richard Betts's (1991, 11) claim that

army leaders remained less alienated than those in the other services because they were less adamant than the navy and air force in their difference with administration strategy and because the President and the Office of the Secretary of Defense did not restrict or monitor ground tactics on anything approaching the scale of which they controlled the air war.

Indeed, it suggests that the two parts of Betts's explanation are closely related. Given civilian micromanagement elsewhere, it is reasonable to assume that the commander in the field was doing precisely what the president wanted him to do. This section will show that President Johnson understood what type of war would be fought, and throughout the conflict he and his advisers reinforced the pursuit of this strategy.

Administration understanding and rejection of COIN

Both civilians and the military recognized the labor-intensive principles of COIN and that firepower was a poor substitute. Few summations of effective COIN strategy improve on McNamara's memo to Johnson in March 1964, which expresses "the basic theory now fully accepted both on the Vietnamese and US sides...concentrating on the more secure areas and working out from these through military operations to provide security, followed by necessary civil and economic actions to make the presence of the government felt and to provide economic improvements" (FRUS 1:84). The administration understood the limitations of fighting an insurgency conventionally; McNamara briefed the president in July 1965 that "success against the larger, more conventional, VC/PAVN [People's Army of North Vietnam] forces could merely drive the VC back into the trees and back to their 1960–64 pattern – a pattern against which U.S. troops and aircraft would be of limited value" (FRUS 3:67). "The large-unit operations war," McNamara again told Johnson in October 1966, "is largely irrelevant to pacification as long as we do not lose it."

Yet the president rejected COIN on multiple occasions. The ground campaign was confined to using ordnance for main force attrition; the president constantly exhorted his chiefs to "kill more VC."[24] Despite information suggesting this approach was not working well, Johnson stuck with it. Johnson may have "clearly endorsed an improved pacification effort," during the famous February 1966 Honolulu conference, but he also explicitly instructed Westmoreland that attrition was "the primary operational objective" (Hennessy, 1997, 82–83).

In fact, the administration's pacification strategy *was* the main force war. During a July 1965 briefing on ground force employment, Johnson expressed concern about putting "U.S. forces in those red areas." McNamara responded, "You're right. We're placing our people with their backs to the sea – for protection. Our mission would be to seek out the VC in large-scale units" (FRUS 3:71). In a September 1965 memo to Johnson, National Security Adviser Bundy summed up the challenge facing the president: deciding "how we use our substantial ground and air strength effectively against small-scale harassment-type action, whether we should engage in pacification as opposed to patrolling actively, and whether, indeed, we should taper off our ground force build-up." Bundy reported that "we asked [Ambassador Henry Cabot] Lodge to develop a specific plan for our joint consideration which would involve the concentration of GVN forces on pacification and the reliance on U.S. forces to handle large-scale VC actions" (FRUS 3:151). This notion that more American troops should be sent only to engage in main force battles also appears in Bundy's earlier memo recommending that "we should explicitly and plainly reserve decision about further major deployments. After all, we have not yet had even a company-level engagement with Viet Cong forces which choose to stand their ground and fight" (FRUS 3:151, see also 3:67, 83, and 149).

In November 1965 deliberations over how best to pursue pacification, Ambassador Lodge forcefully argued that the "crux of the problem" in the American pacification effort "is security. To meet

---

[24] Jack Valenti (one of Johnson's most loyal aides) observed in an eyes-only memo to the president that "you are rightly judging the trends of the war from . . . numbers of VC killed" and that "the kill rate is vital to you judging the amount of punishment being meted to the enemy." Valenti to Johnson, March 24, 1966, Box 9, White House Central Files, Confidential File, LBJ Library.

this need we must make more U.S. troops available to help out in pacification operations as we move to concentrate ARVN [Army of the Republic of Vietnam] effort in this work."[25] The administration's negative reaction could not have been stronger or clearer: a joint telegram to Lodge from Rusk, McNamara, and Taylor stated that beyond Westmoreland's planned "use of limited number U.S. forces in buddy system principle to guide and motivate ARVN...there should be no thought of U.S. taking on substantial share of pacification." Rusk later emphasized to Lodge that the strategy was discussed "at highest levels [i.e. the president], who wished to emphasize that this represents a final and considered decision" (FRUS 4:304).

At this time, McNamara not only recommended troop increases without revising the ground strategy – "The principal task of U.S. military forces in SVN must be to eliminate the offensive capability of the regular units" – but gave Johnson a choice between two versions of search and destroy. The first would be "to increase friendly forces as rapidly as possible, and without limit, and employ them primarily in large-scale 'seek out and destroy' operations to destroy the main force VC/NVA North Vietnamese Army] units." The second was "a similarly aggressive strategy of 'seek out and destroy' but to build friendly forces only to that level required to neutralize the large enemy units." McNamara advocated a shift to the second option in part because "an endless escalation of U.S. deployments is not likely to be acceptable in the U.S." (FRUS 4:312).

When Westmoreland requested additional personnel in April 1967, Taylor noted that the enemy main force strength had leveled off and that half of the American maneuver battalions were already supporting pacification "by dealing with the middle war, the VC main force provincial battalions." Robert Komer, Johnson's pacification expert, warned that a "major U.S. force commitment to pacification also basically challenges the nature of our presence in Vietnam and might force U.S. to stay indefinitely in strength." Observing the political reality that "another major U.S. force increase raises so many other issues," Komer recommended more Vietnamese involvement, coupled with "a minor force increase...accelerated emphasis on a barrier, and some increased bombing" (FRUS 5:147). Undersecretary of State Nicholas

---

[25] The telegram is found in Gravel, *Pentagon Papers*, Vol. 2, pp. 602–605, and footnoted in FRUS 4:290.

Katzenbach wrote in June 1967 that the time had come to "change" the war strategy and "use the great bulk of U.S. forces for search and destroy." A "small number" of troops could be used for pacification but "targeted primarily on enemy provincial main force units." According to Katzenbach, "pacification is not the ultimate answer – we have neither the time nor the manpower" (PP 4:508). During a July 1967 meeting, Johnson agreed with McNamara's recommendation that "U.S. units will continue to destroy the enemy's main force units," while ordering his subordinates to "shave [any additional troops requests] the best we can."[26]

Again, the evidence that Westmoreland and other military leaders enthusiastically supported firepower as counterinsurgency is not in dispute. However, evidence also exists that civilians expended effort to ensure this. Asked if domestic opposition was a factor in JCS decisions, General Wheeler replied, "Not directly…[but] the Chiefs are well aware of the problems engendered for the President by the minority dissent to his course of action," citing the need not to "put a club in the hands of dissenters" (Graff, 1970, 125–126). When the JCS were deemed unlikely to support the president's strategy, they were excluded from deliberations. Many of the most important military policies – the escalation decisions of June and July 1965, the establishment of the principal war aim of "killing more VC," the emphasis on B-52 bombing of Vietcong sanctuaries – were made with little strategic input from the JCS, to the point of lying to Wheeler about the purposes of meetings to which he was not invited (McMaster, 1997, 301).

Civilians influenced the campaign through troop ceilings

Both civilian and military leaders regarded the setting of ceilings on troop numbers as sufficient to preclude a COIN approach (McMaster, 1997, 272). Facing severe constraints on personnel and none on the use of air and ordnance in South Vietnam, Westmoreland and his subordinates felt they had little choice but to pursue a strategy of attrition. Herbert Schandler (1977, 56) observes that setting force levels "in numbers far below that deemed necessary by the military to pursue their tactical concept, would necessarily force a change in the way the

---

[26] "Notes from Meeting of the President with Secretary McNamara to Review the Secretary's Findings during Vietnam Trip," July 12, 1967, Tom Johnson Papers, Box 1, LBJ Library.

war was pursued on the battlefield." An eyes-only message to General Westmoreland from a close aide observed, "the smaller the number of maneuver battalions the more B-52's we need."[27]

"Official" MACV requests for additional forces always emerged after negotiations with the Defense Secretary, resulting in far lower numbers than Westmoreland originally desired (Buzzanco, 1996). The pressure on Westmoreland from civilian leaders to reduce troop requests was intense and obvious; in a remarkably plaintive memo to McNamara in October 1966, Westmoreland made clear that he was "very sensitive" to Johnson's position and thus avoided making "exorbitant demands." In lobbying for more troops in July 1967, Westmoreland reminded Johnson that the general had made every effort to "ease [the President's] burden by my conduct and demands" (Herring, 1994, 49).

Yet the US Army adapted to the constraints in ways inconsistent with the military myopia story, deploying dismounted infantry units in 1965 rather than armored brigades and divisions, so as to field as many soldiers as possible given personnel caps.[28] Moreover, the generals understood that heavy forces were inappropriate for the terrain and the type of war being fought; Westmoreland insisted to his Pentagon-based colleagues that "Vietnam is no place for either tank or mechanized infantry units." Army Chief of Staff Gen. Harold Johnson agreed: "The presence of tank formations tends to create a psychological atmosphere of conventional combat."[29] MACV did not control the number of soldiers at its disposal but could decide which units to deploy. Westmoreland and other army leaders favored less heavily armored units because they understood that Vietnam was not a conventional war, and thought that lighter battalions would be most effective given manpower constraints. This emphasis by the military commanders is hard to square with military myopia's claims of an obsession with firepower rather than soldiers. The Army's shift to armor occurred gradually over 1966 only as the need to substitute for labor became more apparent (Starry, 1980, 55–56).

The zombielike reemergence of the attrition strategy over the war's course and its intimate link to troop deployment is epitomized in

[27] Depuy to Westmoreland, January 31, 1966, EOMF, Box 35.
[28] Westmoreland to H. Johnson, July 5, 1965, and July 7, 1965; and Westmoreland to Waters, August 11, 1965, EOMF, Box 34.
[29] H. Johnson to Westmoreland, July 3, 1965, EOMF, Box 34.

McNaughton's observation that, "Limiting the present decision to an 80,000 add-on does the very important business of postponing the issue of a Reserve call-up (and all of its horrible baggage)..." (FRUS 5:161). The redistributive logic behind sending a limited number of draftees and no reservists to Vietnam was clear to contemporary observers. Leslie Gelb (1972, 464–465), the Pentagon's Director of Policy Planning from 1967 to 1969, sums up the case against deploying the reserves:

Domestic politics imposed a dominant constraint on the size and development of the ground war in the South as well. As many US servicemen as possible could be sent to Vietnam as quickly as possible for short terms of service, subject only to a presidential prohibition against calling up the Reserves...Because the President did not want to incur this political liability, he chose to deplete and weaken US forces stationed in Europe and America and to increase draft calls. The burden fell on the young and the poor; for this and other reasons, political opposition to the war tended to congeal around these groups and their legislative allies.

Put more bluntly, "reservists and guardsmen were better connected, better educated, more affluent, and white than their peers in the active forces" (Baskir and Strauss, 1978, 50). The middle-class voter remained protected from the costs of conflict to the largest extent possible.[30]

Civilians overrode the military's (few) COIN recommendations

General Westmoreland was one of the few in 1964 to recommend continuing the advisory effort – "Option A" of the famous three-option framework that led to the ROLLING THUNDER bombings.[31] In a January 6, 1965, cable to Johnson via Ambassador Taylor, Westmoreland asserted that "if [the American advisory] effort has not succeeded there is less reason to think that U.S. combat forces would have the desired effect...Intervention with ground combat forces would at best buy time and would lead to ever increasing commitments." Westmoreland argued that instances from 1963 to 1964 where American ground

---

[30] It bears reemphasizing that my median voter approach claims that democratic foreign policy favors the relatively poor, not necessarily the poorest.

[31] For a description of this strategy's development, see PP 3:205–251. On Westmoreland's understanding of the importance and proper conduct of pacification, see Birtle, 2008.

forces would have been helpful were "few and far between...In balance, they do not seem to justify the presence of U.S. units" (FRUS
2:13). In an eyes-only message to Wheeler, Westmoreland was even
more emphatic, recommending the "present policy" until "some positive momentum in pacification" was made. "Expanded and concerted
U.S. attacks" on North Vietnam were inadvisable until justified by "a
firmer RVN base and prospects for victory."[32]

In September 1965 National Security Adviser Bundy reported to
Johnson that "Lodge and Westmoreland feel VC 'lie-low' tactics will
become increasingly a police-social action problem" and summarized
Westmoreland's strategy in the five points quoted below, three of which
are COIN-oriented:

1. Halt the VC offensive.
2. Destroy VC units where they can be found and pacify selected high
   priority areas.
3. Restore progressively the entire country to GVN control.
4. Support "rural reconstruction" with comprehensive attention to the
   pacification process.
5. Continue the air campaign against the DRV and infiltration routes into
   Laos. (FRUS 3:151)

Admiral Sharp, in an eyes-only message to Wheeler, complained that
the Department of State "is somehow hopeful pacification may be
achieved by the Vietnamese themselves while being aided by little if
any U.S. participation." Sharp continued:

We will do far better in pacification if we too press forward setting the
example in performance and results...The GVN cannot do the pacification alone, this would prolong the struggle beyond foreseeable limits.
If the Viet Cong go underground and revert to small-scale actions, we
should employ U.S. forces in coordination with the ARVN and proceed
with securing and pacifying areas as fast as we can.[33]

Notes from a July 22, 1965 presidential meeting (one of the few
to include the Joint Chiefs of Staff) provide yet another example of
administration resistance to pacification. They record Marine Com-
mandant Wallace Greene's argument, "The enclave concept will work.

---

[32] Westmoreland to Wheeler, "Future U.S. Actions in RVN," November 26,
1964, EOMF, Box 30.
[33] Sharp to Wheeler, September 22, 1965, EOMF, Box 34.

Would like to introduce enough Marines to do this." McNamara observes that Greene is asking for "men over and above the Westmoreland request." Johnson responds, "Then you will need 80,000 more Marines to carry this out." More Marines for pacification were not forthcoming.[34]

Contradicting both McNamara's recommendations and the claims of the military myopia argument, Westmoreland proposed a new concept of operations in August 1966 envisioning that "growing strength of US/Free World forces will provide the shield that will permit ARVN to shift its weight of effort" towards revolutionary development. Additionally, "a significant number of the U.S./Free World Maneuver Battalions" would perform pacification missions, which

encompass base security and at the same time support revolutionary development by spreading security radially from the bases to protect more of the population. Saturation patrolling, civic action, and close association with ARVN, regional and popular forces to bolster their combat effectiveness are among the tasks of the ground force elements.

In an accompanying memo to President Johnson, Ambassador Taylor acknowledged that Westmoreland's strategy could result in "speeding up the termination of hostilities," but cautioned that "there will be a cost to pay for this progress in a rise in the U.S. casualty rate." After noting the likely negative domestic reaction, he concluded that if pacification became the strategy, "General Westmoreland will be justified in asking for almost any figure in terms of future reinforcements." A handwritten note on a follow-up memo cites Johnson's instructions to "get something to Westy so that he will not assume that we have approved."[35]

---

[34] FRUS 3:76. The enclaves concept called for concentrating American forces in fortified population centers and increasing control of the surrounding areas gradually, a strategy closer to COIN than Westmoreland's or Johnson's (Hennessy, 1997, 74–77).

[35] Taylor's analysis in FRUS 4:221 explicitly describes and rejects every aspect of COIN recommended by Westmoreland. According to the FRUS editor, "Rostow forwarded [Taylor's] memorandum to President Johnson on August 30 under cover of a memorandum stating that the danger foreseen by Taylor must be met by 1) engaging elite ARVN units fully in fighting VC and North Vietnam main force units; and 2) 'getting the ARVN engaged effectively in pacification.' The President indicated on Rostow's memorandum that, prior to getting Defense, State, and Taylor to prepare analyses and recommendations,

Whereas Taylor considered Westmoreland's pacification plans overly aggressive, Ambassador Lodge believed that they did not go far enough. After lambasting Westmoreland's approach, Lodge continues,

MACV specifically states that what it calls offensive operations are conducted so as to create the opportunity to destroy terrorism, that is "pacification". But the phrase "offensive operations" is defined as meaning to seek out and destroy...I believe that the Vietnamese war will certainly never be won in this way; that the phrase "offensive operations" should be defined as "split up the Viet Cong and keep him off balance"; and that American participation in pacification operations should be stepped up. (FRUS 4:294)

According to the FRUS editor, Lodge sent "several similar communications" including a November 6 telegram wherein "he stated that the crux of the problem was security, not defective organization, and that the first priority was more U.S. troops allotted to pacification."[36] Clearly, Johnson favored the Westmoreland plan's emphasis on firepower and main force battles over Lodge's more labor-intensive option (FRUS 4:310).

Civilian objections to COIN-oriented military recommendations continued. In a May 1967 memo arguing that "the 'philosophy' of the war should be fought out now," John McNaughton counseled the rejection of Westmoreland's March 1967 request for 200,000 more soldiers because Westmoreland intended to use the reinforcements "to relieve the Marines to work with ARVN on pacification" and for similar missions in the Mekong Delta and Quang Ngai Province. Describing pacification as a "less essential mission," McNaughton (FRUS 5:161) suggested avoiding escalation by "making more efficient use of presently approved U.S. manpower (e.g., by removing them from the Delta, by stopping their being used for pacification work in I Corps, by transferring some combat and logistics jobs to Vietnamese or additional third-country personnel)." McNamara

---

Rostow should first 'talk over' pacification with McNamara." The series of memos on pacification in FRUS 4:20 and 220–223 are worth reading in their entirety to show the Johnson administration's conception of a GVN-driven pacification effort, as well as MACV's intent to "build...on the small unit models of Marines' Combined Action Companies."

[36] FRUS 4:294, and 290, n.2.

agreed with McNaughton's recommendation in a Draft Presidential Memorandum to Johnson that reveals the sensitivity to troop deployment and a continued main force focus: "We will soon have in Vietnam 200,000 more U.S. troops than there are in enemy main force units. We should therefore, without added deployments, be able to maintain the military initiative, especially if U.S. troops in less-essential missions (such as in the Delta and in pacification duty) are considered strategic reserves." McNamara justified the rejection in part by noting that Westmoreland intended to use the bulk of the first 100,000 troops for pacification (FRUS 5:177).[37] Westmoreland complained to Wheeler and Sharp in August 1967 that

Secretary Rusk is thinking in terms of the more conventional type warfare where our forces could launch such an all-out offensive from a reasonably secure area of departure, leaving behind a pacified rear area, and against identified enemy formations disposed along a recognizable front. Such is not the case in SVN.[38]

To show the Johnson administration's position on how American soldiers should be employed, I turn to Robert Komer, the person likeliest to recommend the most aggressive approach to pacification the president would tolerate. In an April 1967 memo "deliberately designed to plead an alternative case [to current operations]," Komer directly addresses the use of US forces in the first paragraph of his list of recommendations:

MACV's justification for these added forces needs further review... If enemy main force strength is now leveling off because of high kill ratios, etc., would the added US forces be used for pacification? General [William E.] DePuy estimates that 50% of US\ROK [Republic of Korea] maneuver battalions are already supporting RD [Revolutionary Development, i.e. pacification] by dealing with the "middle war", the VC main force provincial battalions. How good are US forces at pacification-related tasks, as compared to RVNAF [Republic of Vietnam Armed Forces]? What are the trade-offs? A major US force commitment to pacification also basically changes the nature of our presence in Vietnam and might force us to stay indefinitely in strength. (FRUS 5:147)

---

[37] See Gravel (1971, 477–489) for a discussion of both memos.
[38] Westmoreland to Wheeler and Sharp, August 26, 1967, EOMF, Box 37.

Johnson and Taylor chose Westmoreland's version of counterinsurgency over Lodge's more labor-intensive pacification approach, but Westmoreland also frequently appeared more interested in pacification than his civilian masters. I give Westmoreland's memoir (1989, 146) the last word on this subject:

> In reality, despite my policy of using American units to oppose the enemy's main forces, more American troops were usually engaged on a day-by-day basis, helping weed out local opposition and supporting the pacification process, than were engaged in the big fights.

This description of Westmoreland's ground war little resembles the civilian desires and expectations depicted in the above memos.

Civilian resistance to the Marines' Combined Action Program
Military myopia claims largely rest on the counterfactual that an extension of the Marines' innovative Combined Action Program (CAP) could have employed the same number of soldiers stationed in Vietnam while minimizing casualties and enhancing population security (Thompson, 1969, 198; Nagl, 2005). Krepinevich (1986, 176) argues that, given a 550,000 troop ceiling, enough soldiers could be used in hamlet-level security and civil action, with several infantry divisions left to counter large-scale incursions; "Casualties would have been minimized, and population security enhanced."[39] Obviously, this counterfactual argument cannot be tested, but it is also irrelevant if civilian as well as military leaders did not hold this position at the time. To make this case, I turn to the reference underpinning Krepinevich's claim that 167,000 American soldiers were sufficient to blanket South Vietnam with CAP teams: the Pentagon's Systems Analysis Office reports (the "SEA Reports").[40] These reports castigated the prevailing attrition strategy and acknowledged CAP's excellence, but they were also skeptical of CAP's wider viability.[41]

[39] A CAP team consisted of a 13-man Marine rifle squad assigned to a local 35-man Vietnamese militia platoon. The Marines would live among the people providing both security and civil assistance such as medical treatment.
[40] A more modest estimate in early 1969 suggested that given the number of troops deployed, the CAP concept could be extended to 2,500 (of 12,000) hamlets (Hanning, 1969, 18).
[41] Again, I do not claim that Westmoreland was not deeply resistant to the Marines' approach, only that civilians quite clearly shared this assessment.

According to the SEA reports, broadening CAP required 279,000 Popular Forces (PF) militia members, and consequently "the reluctance of the [South Vietnam government] to assign PF personnel to CAPS is a serious problem in considering any expansion." Between July 1967 and November 1968, the PF-to-Marine ratio had declined from 1.7 to 1.4 (Thayer, 1975, 26–27; Schulimson et al., 1997, 628). As of mid-1967, SEA assessed that a CAP Marine had a 75–80 percent chance of being wounded and a 16–18 percent chance of being killed (Peterson, 1989, 87–88). While one CAP supporter makes the case that "although casualties are high, they are only 50 per cent of the casualties of the normal infantry of marine battalions being flown around by helicopter on large scale operations" (Hanning, 1969, 18), at the time in Vietnam, only 80,000 of the deployed American soldiers were involved in active combat. This, as Krepinevich points out, is due to the very high "tooth-to-tail ratio" of the American military, a product of capital-intensive military doctrine. Thus a larger absolute number of personnel in the theater would have been put in harm's way by shifting to large-scale COIN.[42] Finally, a November 1968 SEA report observed, "in over three years of operations no evidence exists that U.S. Marines have been able to withdraw from a CAP solely because their Vietnamese counterparts were able to take over."[43]

Although Krepinevich dismisses as "lip service" Westmoreland's objection to CAP – "I simply had not enough numbers to put a squad of Americans in every village and hamlet" – this assessment was shared by an administration determined to hold down deployments and casualties for political rather than strategic reasons. Indeed, Ambassador Taylor (FRUS 4:221) found Westmoreland too receptive to "the 'oil spot' concept as the Marines have been doing in the I Corps area (and other U.S. forces elsewhere to a lesser degree)."

William Bundy's February 1965 memo entitled "Where Are We Heading?" underscored the need for "intensified pacification within South Viet-Nam," but then went on to caution that "to meet the security problem, this might include a significant increase in present

---

[42] Not to mention that it would require a drastic retooling of the US military's tooth-to-tail ratio.

[43] Many Marines disagreed with this assessment (Schulimson et al., 1997, 629). Francis "Bing" West argues that a systematic oil spot strategy may have worked (West, 2003). This may be true, but the decision-makers at the time did not think so.

US force strength" (PP 3:691). Seeking ways to trim personnel in
1967, McNaughton noted that "other ground-force requirements
could be eliminated if the US Marines ceased grass-roots pacification activities" (FRUS 5:161).[44] Interviewed in 1976, Taylor, reflecting
decision-makers' conventional wisdom, assessed that CAP demanded
"an enormous requirement for American infantry which we did not
have" (Schulimson et al., 1997, 620). Probably writing in mid-to-late
1968, the *Pentagon Papers'* editor acknowledges CAP's unquestioned
success relative to any other approach but warns that the Marine strategy "requires vast numbers of troops." The strategy therefore "must
be undertaken with full awareness by the highest levels of the [US gov-
ernment] of its potential costs in manpower and time" (PP 2:535).
A competent COIN strategy along the lines of CAP might have been
more effective and reduced casualties, but the civilian leadership was
unwilling to take that chance. William Bundy wrote to Katzenbach in
May of 1967 that pacification of the Mekong Delta region should be
avoided, as "apart from the military merits, any force increase that
reaches the 'Plimsoll Line' – calling up the Reserves –…might also
lead to pressures to go beyond what is wise in the North, specifically
mining Haiphong" (FRUS 5:154).

6.4 Did Nixon and Abrams fight a better war?

General William Westmoreland receives a great deal of blame for stub-
bornly pursuing a "search-and-destroy" strategy wholly inappropriate
for the means at hand. Indeed, some revisionists claim that once Westmoreland was replaced by Creighton Abrams in mid-1968, the war
was fought much more successfully, but that political will had been
too damaged by previous incompetence for the public to recognize this
(Sorley, 1999; Gray, 2006, 17–18; and Nagl, 2005, 168–174). However, any changes in tactics on the ground, such as Vietnamization,
were driven by the decisions of Johnson and Nixon to freeze and then
lower the level of troop deployments. This section briefly reviews this
period to emphasize the consistency of American military doctrine and
the continued firm control of the military by civilians. While it is certainly true that the drawdown forced the United States to rely on the

---

[44] For an earlier version of this argument, see William Bundy's February 1965
memo (PP 3:691).

South Vietnamese, the remaining American force did not alter their capital-intensive counterinsurgency approach.

Despite the war's unpopularity, Nixon understood there would be consequences if he "failed" in Vietnam. He writes in his 1972 diary that:

Both Haldeman [Nixon's chief of staff] and Henry [Kissinger] seem to have an idea – which I think is mistaken – that even if we fail in Vietnam we can still survive politically. I have no illusions whatever on that score, however. The U.S. will not have a credible policy if we fail, and I will have to assume responsibility for that development. (quoted in Clodfelter 2006, 147)

As there was no question of deploying more soldiers, Nixon escalated using the only means available to him. Once he no longer feared Soviet or Chinese counter-escalation he initiated the LINEBACKER air campaigns and mined Haiphong harbor (an operation ironically called POCKET MONEY). One need only look at the war's budget figures to obtain a sense of Nixon's priorities. Of the $21.5 billion dollars spent in fiscal year 1969, only 5 percent went towards pacification and civil operations. The amount of money spent for 1971 was lower, but the ratio was no different (Thayer, 1985, 23).

The reliance on airpower for counterinsurgency, first mooted by Taylor and Rostow to Kennedy and then by Bundy to Johnson continued throughout this period. Figure 6.2 shows that by 1966 the number of sorties overtook the number of personnel and rose more steeply to the peak deployment of 1968 and declining less sharply afterwards (until the jump of 1972). Despite one contemporary general's assessment that "the tactics changed within fifteen minutes of Abrams's taking command" (Sorley, 1999, 17), the gap between sorties and personnel hit its maximum in the first two years of Abrams's command. This is not to blame Abrams for the strategy; he had little control over these numbers which were ultimately set by the president and Congress. Thomas Thayer (1985, 26), in charge of the SEA reports for this time period, specifically describes the American war effort of 1969–1971 as, "first and foremost an air war although Vietnam was billed as a land war in Asia, and second, a ground attrition campaign against communist regular units. Pacification was a very poor third."

Johnson's limitation of troops drove the two most important strategic choices in the ground war: the focus on attrition long after the main force threat had subsided (Malkasian, 2004), and the shift to a Vietnamization strategy following Tet (Westmoreland, 1989, 358). According to Westmoreland, this strategy predated Abrams's arrival, "[Vietnamization] was the only strategy that I could come up with that was viable if there were no change in policy, if we were not going to widen the war, and if we were not going to call up the reserves" (Schandler, 1977, 62). Robert Komer, who clashed with Abrams repeatedly, did not believe that Abrams initiated a new strategy upon his relief of Westmoreland. "There was no change in strategy whatsoever. In fact [Abrams] said he didn't intend to make any changes unless he saw that some were necessary. The myth of a change in strategy is a figment of media imagination; it didn't really change until we began withdrawing" (Thompson and Frizzell, 1977, 79). In a 1974 conference of veteran Vietnam counterinsurgents (including Komer, Robert Thompson, and Francis "Bing" West), several criticized the strategy of attrition, but only one found much difference between the approaches of Westmoreland and Abrams (Thompson and Frizzell, 1977, 79–93).

While responsibility for fighting had to be shifted to the Vietnamese due to American personnel drawdowns, the US contribution to counterinsurgency retained its firepower-intensive emphasis. B-52 bomber sorties actually *increased* in the South. In developing his withdrawal plans Abrams instructed his staff to "save the armor units out until last, they can buy us more time." An analyst of the use of armor in Vietnam noted that:

Almost every air cavalry unit remained in Vietnam until early 1972. These armored units provided a maximum of firepower and mobility with a minimum of U.S. troops. By the end of 1970, with the withdrawal of American units in high gear, fourteen armored battalions or squadrons remained in Vietnam. In December 1971 armored units represented 54 percent of the US maneuver battalions still in Vietnam. (Starry, 1980, 164–165)

Abrams instead removed the infantry battalions first, resulting in lower casualty rates but delivering little in the way of COIN effectiveness (Thayer, 1985, 122). Indeed, the armor component of the departing divisions and brigades often remained in Vietnam. After the United States "shifted" to a pacification strategy, consumption of artillery rounds remained constant from June 1967 to June 1970, even as 200,000 troops were drawn down (Thayer, 1985, 57).

6.5 Democracies will fight more small wars ... poorly

Lyndon Johnson, as well as Kennedy and Nixon, was convinced that the American public would punish an administration that "lost" South Vietnam to communism, but was equally certain that the number of people to be deployed and lives to be lost needed to be constrained. In response he and his subordinates actively instructed the US military to fight what was widely acknowledged at the time to be an ineffective, capital- and firepower-intensive strategy to maintain the status quo. Ultimately this was a failure due not to an apolitical public, nor a dysfunctional military culture, nor a military doctrine divorced from grand strategy. Rather, it resulted from the average voter in a democracy getting what she wanted (Mencken, 1916, 19).

The previous sections show that the uniformed services rarely acted independently of their civilian leaders in the Johnson administration. Both groups had similar conceptions not only of how the Vietnam War should be fought, but of the domestic political pressures constraining them. The other two pieces of evidence for military myopia – the failure of John F. Kennedy to force the military to take counterinsurgency seriously and the uniqueness of the "One War" strategy of General Creighton Abrams and Richard Nixon – also do not hold up. American devotion to firepower-intensive counterinsurgency predated and outlasted the Johnson administration.

6.5.1 Extended implications

When military capital substitutability is low, as it is against unconventional opponents, a high degree of capitalization can result in non-strategic behavior at the state level, the initiation of wars for which the doctrine is ill-suited because the costs remain low for the pivotal voter. For this reason, democracies clearly prefer bombing to ground wars. While not examined in detail here, the case of Vietnam supports a number of the book's extended implications regarding strategic interactions between democracies, their allies and their opponents.

Chapter 5 suggested that democratic and autocratic allies may pursue gains from "comparative advantage" in pursuing a mutually beneficial, aggressive strategy. One implication of the theory not explored by this chapter is that by this logic democracies have reasons to cooperate with non-democracies in order to obtain the labor necessary for COIN. The strategy of Vietnamization, as well as the American campaigns in Kosovo and Afghanistan, illustrate that such "trade" can indeed increase effective military power. These alliances cannot work miracles; as American decision-makers constantly noted during the Vietnam War, local forces were not very reliable and Vietnamization was something of a last-ditch strategy. It seems clear that, for the median voter, the preference ordering for factors in the production of military power appears to be capitalization, then labor from alternate sources, then labor from one's own electorate.

For similar reasons, this logic also suggests that when two redistributive states meet, the results will be volatile. Notwithstanding its tremendous nationalism, the North Vietnamese regime was authoritarian with pretensions to totalitarianism. The United States substituted capital for labor, while the North Vietnamese leadership, in the words of McGeorge Bundy, "fought to the last Viet Cong," and then subsequently sacrificed its own regular forces with little apparent compunction. General Vo Nguyen Giap apparently noted: "Every minute, hundreds of thousands of people die all over the world. The life or death of a hundred, a thousand, or tens of thousands of human beings, even if they are our own compatriots, represents very little" (Thompson and Frizzell, 1977, 77). The willingness to spend lives boggled the minds of American commanders and policy-makers (Mueller, 1980). Westmoreland (1989, 251) complained accurately that "Any American commander who took the same vast losses as General Giap would have been sacked overnight." Robert Thompson recalls a discussion with Abrams in anticipation of North Vietnam's 1972 invasion:

I asked General Abrams what his estimate was of what Giap was prepared to spend in terms of lives. We both thought this out and the figure we came to was 60,000. We had been involved in that war for a very long time and we were 100 percent off. Giap spent twice that much. (Thompson and Frizzell, 1977, 85)

The result was a prolonged and costly war, fought by extremely inefficient and (for the United States) ultimately unsuccessful means. Given the implications of my theory, it is not clear the average voter would want it another way.

Finally, the median voter's effort to buy more security for herself at the least personal price undermines the costliness of any signal being sent to the international opponent. Stephen Rosen (1982) describes how, as American costs in Vietnam rose, policy-makers talked less about bringing combat to a successful resolution and more about sending of signals. American planners sought to communicate American resolve to North Vietnam, but were limited to means, such as bombing, that were of limited cost to the American public. Not only did this degrade the costly signal, it also allowed the public to support a war that dragged on for a shockingly long time. Military leaders disagreed vociferously, considering signals a waste of time and resources, but did not carry the day.[45] Rosen explains this shift in civilian thinking to be the result of higher-level and more academically inclined "limited war" theoreticians taking over the war's management. But many of the principals – Rostow, McGeorge Bundy, Taylor, Westmoreland, McNaughton, and McNamara – had been deeply involved in counterinsurgency and Vietnam policy since early in the Kennedy administration. They had a good understanding of what COIN entailed and still rejected it, largely for political reasons. The shift to a signaling strategy was the result of administration efforts to limit the costs of war for the voter; it was the only strategy available to them. As we will see in the next chapter, the puzzle of sending signals to opponents that do not cost the median voter much is not limited to Vietnam-era United States.

---

[45] As Rosen points out, their preferred strategy of massive bombing was not necessarily a better strategy.

7 | *Becoming a normal democracy: Israel*

What are the consequences for Israel's security of the many changes occurring in its society, its threat spectrum, and its military doctrine? How did these changes contribute to the flawed reconciliation of Israel's strategic ends and means in its fight against Hezbollah during the Second Lebanon War of 2006? What can we learn about the democratic way of war from Israel's recent experience?

Students of democratic grand strategy and civil–military relations often treat Israel as an exceptional case because of its sizable military, compulsory draft, reliance on reserves, strong war industry, and largely military-based national culture (Peri, 2006, 22). Israel is, however, undergoing profound and related shifts in its society, politics, and military. These shifts appear to draw it closer in line with other developed and well-established democracies due to reductions in threat levels, increases in liberalism and economic inequality among its citizens, and an increasingly professionalized military (Bar-Joseph, 2001).

Since the Cold War's end, Israel's perceived security problems have changed, even as many other democracies such as the United States have focused on threats – terrorism and missiles – that more closely resemble Israel's.[1] The traditional fear of a conventional attack on Israel's "wasp-waisted" mid-section has largely disappeared. On the other hand, Israel faces ballistic missile threats from neighboring state and non-state actors, and a potentially nuclear Iran in the future. It has experienced sporadic terrorism, rocket fire, and insurgency from the occupied Palestinian territories. The combination of conventional and unconventional elements in the 2006 fight against Hezbollah in Lebanon appears to epitomize the sort of "hybrid war" that

---

[1] The decline of these threats and the relative rise of unconventional ones probably predates the 1990s, to the Yom Kippur War and the Camp David Accord with Egypt.

many observers believe will typify international conflict in the coming years.[2]

In examining how Israel addresses these threats, this chapter synthesizes most of cost distribution theory's empirical implications, combining the virtues of the previous quantitative and case study chapters. After tracing the twin developments of economic inequality and military capitalization since the end of the Cold War, the chapter first explores the role that socio-economic status (SES, a proxy for individual income) plays in shaping attitudes towards the use of force, defense spending, and territorial concessions. If redistributive potential affects Israel Defense Force (IDF) military doctrine, the less well-off in Israeli society will be more prone to view military force as a viable option. In turn this increased willingness to use force should result in more ambitious strategic goals. The chapter turns to the Second Lebanon War as a clear example of flawed grand strategy, and uses the conflict to show the effects of this cost distribution process. Israel's civilian leaders, more sensitive to public opinion than the IDF, set ambitious war aims and yet were unwilling to employ the military in the labor-intensive manner likely to make attaining them feasible. Importantly, the civilians did so with a sound understanding of the tradeoffs involved.[3]

7.1 Changes in Israeli doctrine and society

Post-Cold War Israeli grand strategy and civil military relations have changed dramatically in response to developments both within Israeli society and the IDF itself. Cost distribution theory can help us understand these changes' implications.

---

[2] For a specific link between the Second Lebanon War and Pentagon thinking on future wars see Jaffe (2009).

[3] More practical reasons to study Israel exist as well. Much analysis of Israeli security policy is written in English. Public opinion data, readily available in English, allow me to test many hypotheses in ways not possible using the cross-sectional data of Chapter 3. The primary and secondary literature was supplemented by interviews with 24 Israeli policy-makers, retired military officers, academics, and other representatives of the country's strategic community. While Israel is quite a small county, I do not claim the interviews represent a comprehensive field research design. Rather, they serve as a valuable means of determining the plausibility of my claims, identifying biases in the English-language work of Israel analysts, and for collecting more speculative assessments of the war's "lessons."

Since the Cold War's end, Israel has focused on threats from its "second circle" (Iran, Libya, and Iraq) rather than the first (Egypt, Syria, Jordan, etc.).[4] Terrorism has grown in salience as conventional threats receded, although even this sort of activity has diminished considerably since the Second Intifada's peak in 2001–2002. These developments, coupled with the Gulf War's successful demonstration of American (and thus Israeli) weapons and tactics in conventional maneuver warfare, have led to a dramatic retooling of the IDF and its doctrine, a process of becoming, in the 1987 words of IDF Chief of the General Staff (CGS) Dan Shomron, "slimmer and smarter" (Cohen, 2008, 83). In the words of the government report on the 2006 war, commonly known as the Winograd Report, "Dramatic strategic changes...required a revision and an update in the thinking about everything related to the conceptual basis of the activation of the IDF."[5] These strategic changes, "universal issues," included the rise of new asymmetrical enemies and the development of new military technology. However, the Report also assigned a major role to "the understanding that the Israeli society is undergoing vast vicissitudes" and goes on to list:

- the relative place of private goals and national goals in the citizens' program for their life;
- the attitude toward self-sacrifice and the need for a strong army;
- the shift toward a post-heroic stage in the Western culture, as part of which civilians' readiness to fight and offer their lives unless in times of a real and unequivocal existential threat has diminished considerably;
- the role of the media, both local and international, in the strategic environment; and

---

[4] Although developments in Egypt, Syria, and elsewhere as part of the "Arab Spring" may change this.

[5] This chapter would be impossible without this document, a more than 600-page report of a remarkable government-sponsored independent commission set up to evaluate and publicly report the war's "systematic deficiencies." The Winograd Report was sufficiently impressive that even Hassan Nasrallah, leader of Hezbollah, admired it: "it is worthy of respect that the political forces and the Israeli public act quickly to save their state, entity, army and their existence in the crisis." Nasrallah added, "I find it hard to believe that such a committee would be established in any Arab country" (*Jerusalem Post*, 2007; *Haaretz*, 2007). The Winograd committee released an interim and a final report. All references to "Winograd" indicate the English translation of the final report by the CIA's Open Source group. I am deeply grateful to Ben Lambeth for introducing me to it.

- the effect of the disputes among the Israeli public view on using military force. (Winograd, 252–253, bullets added for clarity)[6]

Israel's means of fighting any enemy, conventional or otherwise, have evolved from a large, airpower-supported ground force quickly entering and capturing enemy territory into an avoidance of taking territory in favor of standoff fire, airpower, and "effects-based operations" which target not only enemy command and control systems, but also the very "will" of opposing fighters, leadership, and population. The IDF has become one of the world's foremost adopters of the doctrine, equipment, and personnel policy of the so-called Revolution in Military Affairs, i.e. the "RMA" (Bar-Joseph, 2001; Adamsky, 2010). As Figure 7.1 shows, following a spike due to sudden, large budget reductions following the Oslo Accords, the percentage of the

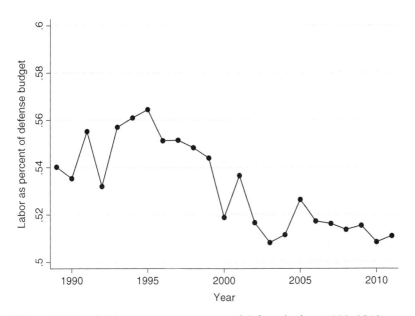

Figure 7.1 Israeli labor costs as percentage of defense budget, 1989–2010
Source: Central Bureau of Statistics.

---

[6] The other "facts" laid out by the report are the religious radicalization of the Muslim world, a belief that terror does not constitute a threat to Israel combined with increased influence of international law, and the need to deal with suicide terrorists operating among a civilian population.

defense budget devoted to labor expenses has declined steadily since the mid-1990s (Central Bureau of Statistics, 2013).

While still a largely conscripted and reserve force, the resulting capital-intensive military has grown increasingly professional. The IDF's air force and intelligence branches, the backbone of an RMA military, largely consist of long-service professionals. In terms of conscription and national service, many middle-class youths no longer participate. Up through the Second Lebanon War reserve units were increasingly excluded from conventional warfare plans.

This process came to a head in 2006 with the IDF's development of a new "operational concept," a phrase (used in the original English) describing the IDF's grandest strategic principles. The new concept emphasized firepower to reduce the need for "deep, large-scale land maneuver" and for "massive takeover of enemy territory." The document continues, "Identifying the aerial medium and its superiority as a central element enables more effective utilization of the maneuver, collection, destruction, and control capabilities (of the area and of the territory across the line) while minimizing friction opposite the asymmetrical elements that the enemy had developed"; that is, airpower was explicitly conceived as countering the enemy's "asymmetrical elements."[7]

The IDF evolved, at least in part, due to changes in its understanding of what is acceptable to the public. As Dan Halutz, CGS at the time of the Second Lebanon War, testified to a post-war investigative committee, "the military system is deeply influenced by long term processes," including "interrelated socio-cultural, budgetary and doctrinaire processes" (Merom, 2008, 2).

7.1.1 Changes in Israeli society

Like much of the world, Israel has profited from and changed through the process of economic globalization. In particular, reduced trade barriers, transportation costs, and communication delays have enabled Israel to shift from a relatively autarkic country in which the state influenced and even ran large swaths of the economy to a more neoliberal, capitalistic, and high technology society (Rivlin, 2011). A concurrent

---

[7] "The General Staff Command's Operational Concept," April 2006, p. 55 quoted in Winograd, 255.

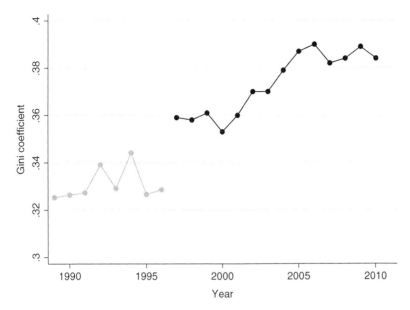

Figure 7.2 Israeli household inequality after transfers, 1989–2010
Source: Central Bureau of Statistics. Household inequality after taxes and redistribution. Inequality for 1989–1996 from Israel National Insurance Institute (in gray) and not comparable to later values.

rise in self-professed individualism has also emerged. In a 2006 survey, only 27 percent of Israeli respondents thought that the interests of the country were more important than the individual's personal ones, compared to 69 percent in 1981 (Arian et al., 2007, 58). Relatedly, the burden of taxation has shifted to the wealthiest segment of Israeli society even as economic inequality has risen steadily over time (Figure 7.2, Israeli Central Bureau of Statistics, 2011).[8]

These factors have enhanced class cleavages amongst Israeli Jews, particularly that between the traditionally elite *Ashkenazim* and the relatively poorer and less politically powerful *Mizrachim*.[9] This divide

---

[8] The top income decile pays 65 percent of all direct taxes in Israel (Even, 2011).
[9] The Israeli Central Bureau of Statistics classifies *Ashkenazim* as "Israeli-born Jews whose fathers were born in Europe or America," but more commonly it refers to Jews of European descent. In 2010, the average monthly salary of urban Ashkenazi Jews was 24 percent higher than that of their Mizrahi counterparts (Swirski and Attias, 2011, 19).

has now been coupled to a rise in influence of two important sections of Israeli society: the *Haredim*, ultra-orthodox (about 10 percent of the Israeli electorate) whose full-time devotion to study is largely subsidized by the Israeli government, and the massive (a 12 percent increase in Israel's population) influx of immigrants from the former Soviet Union. These "Russians" tend to be well-educated but poor, secular yet quite hawkish in their approach to foreign policy. Together, these forces have contributed to a striking increase in economic inequality in Israel and, this chapter suggests, a hawkish shift in its foreign policy (Levy, 2007, 7).[10]

7.1.2 Who shapes Israeli grand strategy?

These simultaneous changes in Israeli society and the IDF have drawn the attention of Israeli social science. Almost all observers believe that Israel's grand strategy and civil–military relations are also changing, but disagree on the direction. Regardless of their ultimate conclusions, much of this research employs military myopia and other elite capture arguments. Rarely do observers claim that Israeli grand strategy takes its form because of voter preferences.

While the formal supremacy of the civilian government has never been questioned, many authors argue that the IDF has myriad ways to "call the shots behind the scenes" (Ben-Meir, 1995, xii). The IDF has historically been largely autonomous in strategic matters and indeed exercises tremendous influence on Israeli politics and society in general. Its massive advantage in planning staff relative to civilian counterparts as well as its monopoly on intelligence gives the IDF tremendous bureaucratic and epistemic power compared to any other Israeli institution (Michael, 2007; Freilich, 2012). This is further enhanced by the high prestige of the IDF within Israel that, while not at the exalted heights of previous decades, remains far higher than that of any other Israeli entity (Levy, 2007).

---

[10] The hawkishness of the *Mizrachim* and FSU immigrants may not rest solely on economic factors. *Mizrachim* have historically resented how the dominant Labor party incorporated them into society in the early decades of Israel, and the Likud party emerged as a consequence. Former residents of the Soviet Union are also suspicious of the political left and on average tend to have harder-line views on race and liberalism.

The head of the IDF has always played a politically visible role, often running for office upon retiring. However, many observers have identified a recent, increased prominence of high-ranking military officers, both retired and active duty, in political life (Peri, 2006). While serving as CGS from 1998–2002, Shaul Mofaz was often described as a "politician in uniform" and almost immediately entered the cabinet upon his retirement. The CGS has at times appealed to the public when disagreeing with civilian leaders, leading one observer to note that, "It seemed as if they [the IDF] claimed the right to conduct direct discourse with the public, as if it were their duty to report to society at large and not to the political echelon" (Peri, 2006, 111). Moshe Ya'alon, Mofaz's successor, quite infamously described himself as "the CGS of the people of Israel, and not just of the political echelon" (Peri, 2006, 139).[11]

Yoram Peri (2006) attributes this growing military involvement in politics to the IDF's increasing attention to counterinsurgency and other low intensity conflicts, where the attitude of the polity is essential to success against the adversary. Kobi Michael (2007) argues, as does Peri, that the IDF has grown in influence mostly because civilian leadership is fragmented, weak, and unwilling to make decisions. According to this analysis, these military leaders, like their American counterparts, share the same myopic obsession with firepower. Letting the generals have their way results in a more aggressive grand strategy; Zeev Maoz (2006) describes an almost "Pavlovian" tendency by the IDF to use force when the opportunity arises.

Not all scholars regard the IDF as continuing to grow in power and influence; others point out the emergence of "civil society" as a counterweight (Shafir and Peled, 2002). The increasing influx of generals into the cabinet no doubt influences their potential successors still in uniform to not rock the boat (Cohen, 2006). Knesset committees appear more willing to scrutinize budget requests (Cohen, 2006). The Supreme Court has recently exercised considerable influence over the nation's security policy on such matters as the "security fence" designed to seal off Israel from Palestinian attacks. The "Four Mothers" movement, centered on (socially well-connected) bereaved parents during the occupation of Southern Lebanon, is often viewed

---

[11] Ya'alon became Defense Minister in March 2013.

as a watershed event where civilian preferences trumped those of the military (Sela, 2011; Helman, 1999). The media has developed an increasingly skeptical view of IDF operations (Lebel, 2007). Stuart Cohen (2006, 771) argues that these various activist groups represent "a process of increasing civilian intrusion into the military domain." Where Peri sees low intensity conflict resulting in increased military influence in society, Cohen argues for the opposite effect: civilians are increasingly involved in unconventional military operations due to their politically sensitive nature.

Regardless of who has the upper hand in civil–military relations, the debate focuses on the role of elites, both military and civilian (Lebel, 2007). Oren Barak and Gabriel Sheffer (2006; 2009) simply describe the entire elite system as a potent "Security Network," made up of actors who have "worked against the systemic differentiation and professionalism of the IDF and the other security agencies and the efficiency of the state's relevant civilian spheres." Empowered by the continuous perception of an existential threat, this network prevents the emergence of "an effective democracy in Israel" (Barak and Sheffer, 2009, 143).

Over an ambitious series of works, sociologist Yagil Levy ties many of these social and strategic developments together by arguing that the citizenship rewards and security gains stemming from serving in the IDF and fighting in war have declined for much of the middle class and elites due to globalization, market liberalism, reduction in threat, and advances in military technology. The IDF responded by shifting its makeup and focus to allow Israel's lower classes to willingly offer a "blood sacrifice" by serving in the military in exchange for social advancement, hawkish policies, ideological satisfaction, or a combination thereof. In turn, the upper classes make a "gold sacrifice" to pay for a high-tech military that reflects Israel's new economy and minimizes the demand for military labor. This "post-materialist militarism" results in an aggressive military seeking to improve its status by fighting fast, violent conflicts in pursuit of overly ambitious war aims (Levy, 2007, 25–26). For Levy, the flawed warfighting of the Second Lebanon War resulted from a "gap of legitimacies," where the use of force is seen as legitimate and desirable but the need for sacrifice by powerful members of society is not.

As Levy observes, large military budgets and civilian control need not be mutually exclusive: "The more the militarization of Israeli society and politics gradually increased, the more politicians were successful in institutionalizing effective control over the IDF" (Levy, 2007, 58). However, where Levy argues that the IDF ultimately reestablished its autonomy through building a heavily capitalized military, I reverse Levy's causal arrow: increased civilian control of the IDF has led to more militarized politics and a higher willingness to employ force. The cost of going to war in terms of either blood or gold is rarely high for the median voter. Those who identify a growing imbalance in military influence over society point to military leaders' appeal to public opinion when in conflict with civilian leaders. If both the government elites and IDF look to the people as the final arbiter in political conflicts, then public preferences must be taken into consideration, something rarely done in Israeli social science (Bar-Or and Haltiner, 2009).

7.2 Israeli public opinion on threats and military force

As in Chapter 3, this chapter's analysis of Israeli public opinion seeks to establish two findings. Showing that SES does *not* affect one's perception of threat undermines an explanation based on elite threat-inflation targeted at the less sophisticated (i.e. less wealthy). Secondly, and more positively, these public opinion data allow the testing of two links of cost distribution theory's causal chain: relative wealth shapes perceptions of the utility of force, as well as an unwillingness to make concessions for peace.

The analysis below will test the same hypotheses found in Chapter 3, as well as a subtly different one. Looking at Israeli respondents' willingness to make concessions to avoid conflict provides an explicit assessment of whether redistribution affects how ambitious a grand strategy one favors:

H_{6a} *Respondents with lower income are less likely to support exchanging territory for peace.*

All data are taken from the 2006 Israeli National Election Study (INES), conducted in the month before Israel's March 28 parliamentary elections. These polls, taken before the Second Lebanon War, give a sense of public opinion prior to the conflict. This chapter analyzes only respondents who identified themselves as Jews, as Arabs are likely to have different attitudes towards the public good provided by the IDF.

As with the American case in Chapter 3, I begin by examining a number of potential measures of *Threat* found in the INES:

- "What rank do you think the country is today, in terms of national security?"
- "To what extent do you consider the establishment of a Palestinian state a threat?"
- "To what extent do you consider war with Syria a threat?"
- "Do you think it is possible to achieve a peace agreement with the Palestinians?"
- Whether respondent answered "the defense situation," to "Which [issue] will have the greatest effect on your voting in the coming elections?"
- "What do you think are the aspirations of the Arabs in the long run?"[12]
- "Are you worried about being injured by Arabs?"
- "What are the odds for a war to break out between Israel and an Arab state in the next 3 years?"

In all of these questions, voters were invited to pick a response from several categories. I have standardized the responses' codings to ensure that higher numbered categories are associated with increased salience of threat or pessimism regarding Israel's security.

Having tested whether SES influences threat perception (i.e. H_5 in Chapter 3), I examine responses to the question, "Should the country spend more money, less money, or the same as it does today on security?" Higher values for *Security Spending* indicate more hawkish preferences.

The second dependent variable is inclination towards military force. The theory predicts that as the cost of a capital-intensive campaign drops for the respondent, one becomes more likely to employ it as a tool of foreign policy. The chapter therefore uses responses to the question, "What should Israel stress in order to avoid war with an Arab state?" Respondents could choose "peace talks," "military might," or the combination "peace talks and military might." A higher value for this variable, *Military Might*, indicates a more hawkish approach. No

---

[12] Possible answers ranged from "To get back some of the territories that we conquered in the Six-Day War" to "conquer the state of Israel and eliminate a significant part of the Jewish population in Israel."

survey question assesses Israeli attitudes towards firepower or military capital, nor does the preference for military might in order to "avoid war" perfectly capture the respondent's predilection for the use of force. Nonetheless, encouraging the respondent to choose between two tools, only one of which is theorized to have redistributive implications, does allow testing of changes to the marginal rate of substitution of diplomacy and military might if the cost of the latter declines with income.

If the cost of an aggressive, militarized grand strategy is lower compared to a diplomatic compromise, then a respondent will favor a less conciliatory approach on providing territorial concessions in exchange for peace. Three INES questions posit the exchange of land for peace, first in a generic reference to "territories," and then in two specific areas. One question reads "Should Israel return to Syria territories in the Golan in return for a peace treaty and security arrangements acceptable to the IDF?" and the other "In a peace agreement with the Palestinians, should Israel agree or disagree to a territorial compromise and to the evacuation of settlements in Judea and Samaria?" Higher values for *Territories*, *Golan*, and *Palestine* indicate a greater willingness to concede territory for peace. Given the categorical nature of the dependent variables, all analyses were performed using ordered logistic regression.

7.2.1 *Explanatory and control variables*

Since the survey does not ask for respondents' income, I use the respondent's assessment of his or her family's monthly expenditure relative to the national average of 9,300 shekels. For the remainder of this section I will use expenditure as a proxy for income and describe it as SES. The responses were recoded so that a larger value for *Expenditure* indicates higher household spending.[13] Since the question asks respondents to compare themselves to an "average" Israeli family, I included the number of people in the respondent's household, or *Household Size*.

---

[13] Results from models using respondents' self-reported "social class" are reported in the online appendix. Many respondents did not answer this question and almost no one described themselves as either upper or lower class. I found coefficients with the expected sign, but not always at statistically significant levels.

For the use of *Threat* as an explanatory variable, I choose the measure most clearly related to the demand for security through military power, whether the respondent assesses "the chances that a war will break out between Israel and an Arab state in the next 3 years" as "High," "Medium," "Low," or "Very low." This is a better measurement of defense spending's public good value than a question that asks the respondent to assess the "security situation," as someone who thinks the security situation is "bad" could conceivably favor more or less military spending.

The statistical models also include potential confounding variables. Respondent *Education* correlates with income and may also exert an independent influence on one's assessment of international politics and the need for defense spending. For similar reasons, I include gender (*Male*), *Age*, and self-placement on a "political spectrum" from left to right (*Politics*). Many argue that the IDF, and Israeli politics more broadly, increasingly reflect the hawkish preferences of religious Jews (who tend to be lower income, especially the ultra-orthodox or *Haredim*); I therefore include variables for how religiously observant respondents describe themselves (*Religiosity*), and whether they identify as *Haredim*.[14] Because many IR realists suggest that militarism correlates to lack of knowledge about foreign affairs, I include a dummy variable for whether the respondent correctly identified the Knesset's chair (*Knesset chair*) and a variable for how often a respondent watches news on television (*TV news*).

Finally, I include a dummy variable for whether the respondent emigrated from the former Soviet Union. Members of this group tend to be relatively poor, well-educated, and secular in outlook. My theory thus suggests that this group would have a more hawkish view than others. However, a group originating from a distinct culture and political regime might have hawkish views for other reasons. I therefore take the more conservative tack and include a former Soviet Union dummy variable (*FSU*) again at the risk of reducing the coefficient of my primary operationalization of SES, household expenditure.

---

[14] The INES, perhaps surprisingly, does not ask whether a respondent is *Ashkenazi* or *Mizrahi*.

7.2.2 Results

SES correlates to willingness to use military force, but not one's assessment of the need for it. A series of models (reported in the appendix) shows that one's SES is unlikely to play a significant role in influencing one's assessment of the likelihood of a war or any other threat. The more highly educated and politically left-leaning find threats less salient and dangerous, while those identifying themselves as "religious" or as Haredim tend to take the opposite stance. Immigrants from the former Soviet Union largely appear to regard security as a very salient issue (and believe that Arabs have quite maximalist aims vis-à-vis Israel). However, they do not appear to differ greatly in their assessment of more specific threats from a Palestinian state, and are less concerned by a war with Syria. The results show that Education and FSU appear to have different relationships to attitudes towards security than SES, and thus must be analyzed separately, even at the cost of underestimating the effects of my explanatory variable.

Figure 7.2 presents graphically the change in predicted probabilities of supporting security spending and military might, while Figure 7.3 does the same for the territorial concession questions. Family expenditure appears to have the predicted effect on grand strategic aims suggested by the theory. Interesting contrasts are apparent in Figure 7.3's two models. Expenditure seems to have a larger effect on the preference for military might than increased defense spending. On the other hand, while older respondents are more likely to support more defense spending, they do not appear to have a higher tendency to prefer might over talks. While one's location on the political spectrum has relatively small effects on spending, it has a large effect on preferences for military might. Curiously, while having little effect on spending, a male is more likely to prefer might over talks. Political knowledge has contrasting effects as well; those correctly identifying the Knesset chair are less likely to support increased spending but there is little effect in terms of preference for might.

Turning to attitudes on territorial concessions in Figure 7.4, we again see support for cost distribution theory. Note that in (a) and (b), the respondent chose how strongly he or she agreed with the statement about land for peace; in (c), respondents chose how much of the Golan Heights to give up (55 percent of respondents did not want to give up

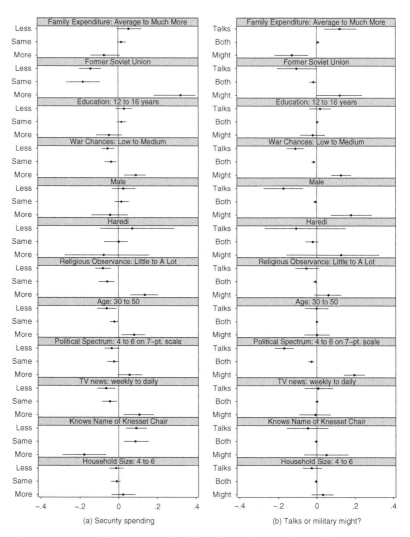

Figure 7.3 First differences, probability of Israeli attitudes on defense.
Ordered logit with 95% confidence intervals depicted. Simulations conducted
using Clarify (Tomz et al., 2001).

any territory). Comparing the Territories ("Judea and Samaria") versus
the Golan Heights (b and c, respectively), many control variables (age,
gender, political knowledge, *Haredi*, household size) have little effect
on responses. On the other, hand, religious observance only affects
attitudes towards the Occupied Territories. FSU immigrants remain

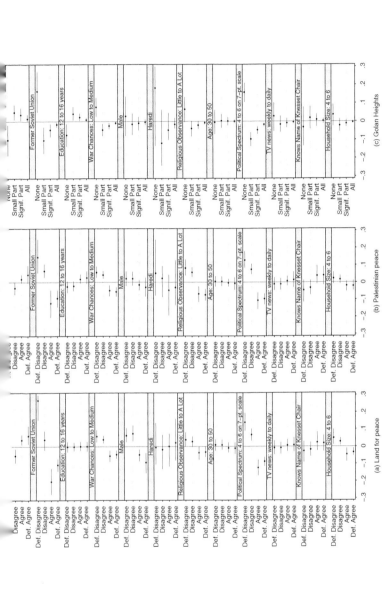

Figure 7.4 First differences, probability of Israeli attitudes on concessions. Ordered logit with 95% confidence intervals depicted. Simulations conducted using Clarify (Tomz et al., 2001)

(a) Land for peace

(b) Palestinian peace

(c) Golan Heights

hawkish on territory regardless of contact, whereas the more educated only have a distinct, dovish preference for the Golan Heights.

Given the support for the theoretically derived hypotheses, we have strong reason to suspect that SES affects grand strategy preferences. However, one's SES does not seem to affect one's assessment of the likelihood of conflict or most other measures of defense's benefit. SES affects respondents' attitudes towards defense spending, and less wealthy people appear more willing to use the military instrument to ensure Israel's security. This same relationship exists for foreign policy goals; people who believe they spend less money per month than the average Israeli household are less inclined to exchange territory for peace. In other words, poorer respondents do not inherently regard the world as a more dangerous place, yet still prefer to invest in military might and are less likely to compromise for peace, suggesting a redistributive component.

7.3 Civilian and military roles in the Second Lebanon War

Israel's security policy reflects these preferences; as predicted by cost distribution theory, a democratic state with a capital-intensive military will engage in small wars in pursuit of ambitious goals while employing a strategy that makes obtaining these goals challenging. Over the course of 34 days in Lebanon during the summer of 2006, Israel pursued a campaign plan that failed to accomplish most of its stated goals, and indeed fought in a manner making the achievement of these goals less likely. The Winograd Report succinctly states the puzzling outcome: "A paramilitary organization composed of thousands of combatants managed to stand up for many weeks to the strongest army in the Middle East which enjoyed complete air superiority and major size and technology advantages" (Winograd, 27). While the best face that Dan Halutz, the IDF Chief of Staff, could put on the operations is that Israel had "won by points," this chapter takes no position on whether Israel "lost" the war. Instead, the conflict represents a clear case of disintegrated grand strategy, in which the military means and the political ends do not appear well connected.

This failure occurred in spite of a massive, capital-intensive effort – flying 15,500 air sorties against 7,000 targets and expending over 100,000 tank and artillery rounds, more ordnance than employed in the conventional 1973 war; 164 Israeli soldiers and 44 civilians were killed, 33 during the brief ground operation in the final two days of the war. By the very end (and only at the very end) about 15,000 Israeli soldiers were operating in Lebanon. The financial costs of the conflict were estimated to be about 1.8 billion US dollars or more than 1 percent of Israel's GDP (Rivlin, 2011, 130). Hezbollah was well-prepared for the capital-intensive onslaught, disabling 45 *Merkava* 4 main battle tanks (10 percent of the armor deployed), knocking the Israeli Navy's most advanced destroyer out of service, and launching a seemingly endless series of *Katyusha* rockets into northern Israel.

The Winograd Report (30) describes a "consensus between the key political echelon and the top brass of the Israel Defense Forces with respect to abstention from a large-scale ground action." Despite the IDF's revamped military doctrine limiting ground operations, favoring standoff fire over maneuver, and giving a central role to air warfare, civilians in the cabinet rejected the uniformed leadership's initial campaign plan. Objecting to, in the words of Transport Minister and former CGS Mofaz, "exposing 40,000 troops to the Lebanese reality" the cabinet ordered an extended air operation. By the fourth day of fighting the IDF Deputy Chief of Staff recommended stopping: "We have exhausted the [aerial] effort; we have reached the peak; from now on we can only descend" (Kober, 2008, 4). Civilians again disagreed and fighting continued (Byman and Simon, 2006). Israel activated only a single reserve division in the conflict's first 11 days, and did not employ significant ground forces until a month after hostilities started, just hours before the signing of the August 11 ceasefire (Kober, 2008, 24).

Despite the decision to avoid a ground war, the Israeli government publicly declared ambitious aims far beyond the release of hostages and the deterrence of further rocket attacks. The Winograd Commission describes the strategic conundrum: "declared goals were too ambitious, and it was publicly stated that fighting will continue till they are achieved. But the authorized military operations did not enable their achievement." The Report acknowledges the government's bind: no "other effective military response to such missile attacks than an extensive and prolonged ground operation" existed, but this "would have a high 'cost' and did not enjoy broad support" (Winograd Partial Report, *Haaretz*, 2007).

Space precludes complete discussion of the many potential causes of poor warfighting.[15] While cost distribution theory helps explain many of these shortcomings, this chapter instead concentrates on what many consider the primary cause of failure: a breakdown in civil–military leadership at the highest levels and the unwillingness to connect preferred means to preferred ends. As in the Vietnam War case, many observers assign much of the blame for this disconnect on a myopic military, given the IDF's bureaucratic or epistemic advantages (Freilich, 2012; Michael, 2007). In this explanation, Prime Minister Ehud Olmert and defense minister Amir Peretz, neither with much military or defense background, were no match for the IDF's pre-dispositions: "The war brought home more than anything else the shortcomings that had developed over the years in all facets of the political level's supervision of the senior military command" (Bar-Or and Haltiner, 2009, 169). Similarly, Charles Freilich (2012, 18) finds that

it is hard to think of another case in which the political leadership provided the IDF with such freedom of action and support. Olmert and Peretz's greatest mistake may have been that they were too supportive, approving virtually everything the IDF sought and letting it decide when, how and, above all, what should be done.

As in the Vietnam case, this chapter disagrees with this finding; in democracies, the military should reflect civilian preferences in equilibrium. The military shared civilian wishes for a firepower-intensive approach limiting casualties; given the IDF's deep connection to the public, this is not surprising (Winograd, 46–50). CGS Halutz presented operational options to Olmert and Peretz that were largely in keeping with this mandate.[16] I locate the sources of this means–ends disconnect within the Israeli cabinet, and the prime minister in particular. Yagil Levy (2010) argues that the civilian government "gave the IDF unprecedented freedom of operation," but civilian control of the military had never been higher than on the eve of the war. Throughout the war, the prime minister clearly was in charge. As with Johnson's

---

[15] Biddle and Friedman (2008) provide a thorough overview in English, with an emphasis on a ground force ill-prepared for small unit operations due to a preoccupation with counterinsurgency in the Occupied Territories.

[16] It is also difficult to describe the CGS, who is the most politically popular figure in Israel, as strictly a military type immune from public pressures.

management of the Vietnam War, all major decisions were made by the prime minister in cabinet, and there was a remarkable amount of micromanagement of operations by even small units of ground forces.

7.3.1 Plans for Lebanon prior to the war

Since withdrawal of Israeli troops from Lebanon in May 2000, Israel pursued a policy towards Hezbollah described as one of "restraint" and "containment," even in the face of serious provocation (Harel and Issacharoff, 2008, 40–43). This restraint was in turn based on the realization that airpower and artillery simply could not eliminate Hezbollah's arsenal of rockets; any attack on Hezbollah would therefore likely escalate into sustained bombardment of northern Israel. Israel was battling the Second Intifada for much of this time period and did not wish to open a second front.

Hezbollah's interest in kidnapping Israeli soldiers (to gain the release of prisoners in Israeli custody) was known to both the IDF and civilian leaders (Interim Winograd Report, quoted in Levine, 2007). Unsurprisingly, the IDF had operational plans in place to respond. Prior to the war's outbreak, Israeli Military Intelligence had not only assessed a kidnapping attempt as "medium to high probability," it also made clear that, in an ensuing war, the only operation likely to prevent short-range rocket barrages into northern Israel was a major ground offensive to occupy southern Lebanon (Bar-Joseph, 2007, 584–586). Nonetheless, in keeping with the IDF's overarching Operational Concept, airpower was envisioned as playing the key role in a Lebanon conflict. The Winograd Report finds that many of the IDF's leaders "entertained" the idea that "precision stand-off fire that would hit strategic Hezbollah targets could decide the battle," but even the Air Force understood prior to the war that it did not have the capability to stop the short-range rocket threat to Israel (Winograd, 15). Additionally, Winograd identifies "political- and military-echelon expectations that special operations would have the power to make a crucial effect on the results of the war" (Winograd, 337).

Focusing on the low-intensity but ongoing Israeli–Palestinian conflict in the West Bank and Gaza Strip, the IDF deliberately deployed a poorly trained, largely reservist contingent on the Lebanon border (Figure 7.5). Should conflict break out, mobilized reserve forces

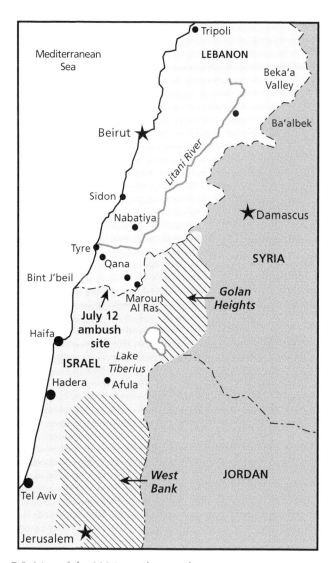

Figure 7.5 Map of the 2006 war theater of operations

would undergo emergency training in a period between the outbreak of hostilities and an escalation into high-intensity war (Levine, 2007). Indeed, the lack of properly trained ground forces resulted in the sloppy small unit operations which made possible the ambush that triggered the war.

The plans formally in place for an IDF operation against Hezbollah had been largely unchanged since 2002, and presented two clear options: one emphasizing firepower and the other the removal of the Hezbollah rocket threat. The first, code-named "Icebreaker," called for a standoff-fire response lasting 48 to 72 hours, while making simultaneous preparation for a "limited land counteroffensive" to follow. The second, called "Supernal Waters," again envisioned several days of firepower-enabled preparation along with a "large-scale call-up of IDF reserve forces for possible imminent commitment." At the end of the preparatory firepower operations, the IDF would be prepared for combined air and ground operations to decisively push Hezbollah out of southern Lebanon (Lambeth, 2011, 28–29). In May 2006, General Halutz reviewed and approved these plans. The following month, the plan was rehearsed in an IDF command-post exercise called "Arm in Arm" that began with an abduction incident much like the one that eventually triggered the war. Interestingly, while a similar June 2004 exercise ("Flint Stone 9") did not include large-scale ground operations in Lebanon, Arm in Arm did. However, because the IDF was still undergoing its doctrinal shift, the General Staff Command did not in effect have a full and updated operative plan for war on the Lebanese front (Winograd, 255–257). In any event, all plans in place were apparently overruled by Halutz (influenced by expectations of civilian reactions) in favor of an improvised, standoff fire-intensive approach.

7.3.2 Overview of "Operation Changing Direction"

On July 12, Hezbollah ambushed an Israeli patrol, killing several soldiers and kidnapping two. In an immediate response, the prime minister approved the bombing of Hezbollah targets. That same day, the cabinet approved a "strong" airstrike and, at the CGS's insistence, a limited attack on Lebanese "dual use" civilian targets such as roads. The three central decision-makers – Prime Minister Olmert, Defense Minister Peretz, and IDF Chief of General Staff Halutz – understood "from the outset that the operation might have to be expanded significantly, but hoped that this would not prove necessary and chose not to raise the matter in the cabinet on July 12." Regardless of which war plan was in effect (and this is not clear from the Winograd Report and elsewhere), all of them envisioned at least a temporary pause in hostilities by July 17, in order "to assess the situation and decide if and how to proceed." Indeed, Halutz apparently considered ending operations as early as July 13 (Freilich, 2012, 210).

On July 14, the "Forum of Seven" – a special wartime decision-making group of cabinet ministers, approved expanding airstrikes to include Beirut's Dahiya neighborhood – a central hub of Hezbollah command-and-control. Within days of the war's start, it was clear that most of the realistic targets for air attacks – the long- and medium-range missiles – had been exhausted.

Small unit raids into Lebanon, largely to prevent exfiltration of the kidnapped soldiers, began shortly after the air campaign. Nonetheless by July 23, two weeks into the war, the IDF had less than a brigade operating within Lebanon (an Israeli brigade roughly consists of three battalions of about 1,000 soldiers each). More importantly, Israel made no effort to mobilize and train the large amounts of reserves needed to make a ground operation in Southern Lebanon even remotely conceivable (Winograd, 30). Only on July 27 did the Cabinet authorize the IDF to mobilize reserves and to prepare – with no decision to go ahead – for an extended ground operation. While continuing its small raids, the General Staff and the Northern Regional Command (the theater commander) began to shift emphasis towards establishing a "special security zone" next to the Lebanese border to be held by non-Hezbollah forces after the war had ceased.

Not until July 31 did the IDF present to the cabinet concrete plans for a large-scale ground operation. It provided the civilians two plans similar in mission but differing in scope. The objectives of "Changing Direction 8" were: (a) significant strikes against Hezbollah along the border, (b) stopping or reducing the short-range surface-to-surface rocket fire in the area Israel envisioned being occupied by third party forces, and (c) "symbolic taking of terrain that was withdrawn from in 2000." The objectives of the alternate plan, "*Gishmei Marom*," differed in magnitude with a larger ground force directed at Hezbollah's operational core and a more aggressive effort to reduce the rocket fire from Lebanon (Winograd, 140). The cabinet approved the more modest Changing Direction 8.

These relatively small ground efforts lasted until early August. "Changing Direction 11," a plan formulated in the first week of August, envisaged a 96-hour operation to take control of Southern Lebanon up to the Litani River, six months of sanitizing and mopping up, and a gradual withdrawal and replacement by the Lebanese Army or multinational forces. On August 9, the cabinet voted in favor of Changing Direction 11 but gave the prime minister and foreign minister the final decision on whether and when to actually embark on the operation (Winograd, 506). While Israeli diplomats furiously negotiated to keep open a window before a ceasefire to allow the IDF to accomplish their objectives, Olmert nonetheless delayed authorizing the operation for another two days after cabinet approval. Once the offensive did begin, the army's advance seemed to peter out of the IDF's own accord 24 hours before the ceasefire was to begin.

The campaign's many plans (11 versions of "Changing Direction" alone) represented a compromise between what the Winograd Report describes as two discrete and separate options: a "pinpoint, major surprise response that would shock Hezbollah and change the price tag for its actions such as abductions," and an "attempt to 'change' the military and political 'reality' in South Lebanon: 'removing the threat' and 'changing the game-rules'." It was clear from "normal Israel Defense Forces expectations, enshrined in operational planning, intelligence documents and military exercises" that the second option would require an extensive and prolonged ground operation requiring several divisions operating in southern Lebanon (Winograd, 512), but both civilian and military leadership refused to address this matter head on.

7.3.3 Civilians leaders set the ends and the means

Civilian leaders, in part anticipating the public's response, played essential roles in the three vital aspects of the war's conduct: the continuation of the air campaign long after its benefits dwindled, the establishment of aggressive goals that were unlikely to be accomplished, and the reluctant use of ground operations. Throughout the deliberations over the war's conduct, the military consistently briefed civilians on what goals could and could not be accomplished. While no official, uniformed or otherwise, relished sending ground forces into Lebanon and the IDF presented no concrete plans, the military consistently acknowledged and stated the limitations of a campaign without them. Furthermore, the military recommended ground forces earlier in the conflict than civilians were willing to consider, and advocated larger numbers of ground forces than the civilians desired or authorized. Throughout the discussion, the role of the public was considered. "With respect to a ground entry to Lebanon, the Minister of Defense and the Head of the Intelligence Branch stated that the public was sure that the Air Force could do the work and gave it priority over embarking on a ground action," although Meir Dagan, Mossad Director, claimed in the same meeting that "the trauma of Lebanon is stronger at the political echelon than at the public."[17] The modest but escalating recommendations for ground forces appears a reasonable strategy on the IDF's part to gradually get the operation it wanted. As Deputy Chief of Staff Moshe Kaplinsky put it on July 28, "if we put the big plan on the table tomorrow, it will not be approved and then we will look bad. The right thing to do is to start with this thing [a smaller operation] and be ready for the big plan" (Freilich, 2012, 211, bracketed text in the original).

While the Winograd Report acknowledges that "supreme responsibility" lies with the political echelon, it assigns "primary responsibility" for avoiding deliberation over the ground campaign to the IDF (Winograd, 538). But this conclusion, shared by several other analyses, is better interpreted as a failure to push back against civilian preferences. As the Report acknowledges, "Senior Israel Defense Forces Officers' assessments that it would be impossible to convince the Prime Minister and the entire political echelon of the need to prepare for a ground operation as an option, was, perhaps, well-founded – but this does not justify refraining from presenting alternatives to the political echelon." Indeed, the fact that "no political echelon approval would be forthcoming" for a ground operation was "explicitly stated by the senior political echelon" (Winograd, 516). Given the civilian's reaction to the one decisive plan proposed by the IDF, one can understand the reluctance of the CGS to go out on limbs too often.[18]

The failure to label the conflict a "war" until well after the cessation of hostilities profoundly affected civil–military relations. This is no semantic matter; in wartime, the IDF gains a great deal of operational leeway. But because "at the General Staff level, peacetime security procedures were observed . . . approvals of the political echelon

---

[17] "Operations and sorties meeting with the Minister of Defense of July 24, 2006," pp. 18–20 (Winograd, 103). Dagan had extensive experience from Israel's previous invasion and occupation of Lebanon.

[18] The civilian leadership also directed the IDF not to attack many Lebanese civilian targets due to the intervention by the United States government, an aspect of the war to which I will return in the conclusion.

were required for wartime operations that would normally require only area commander authority" (Winograd, 300). As a consequence, the Winograd Report notes, "detailed approval was required by the political echelon for each operation," whereas in wartime "the IDF is supposed to be charged with, at its discretion, subject to certain constraints, subject to fundamental political echelon instructions (that could have been as detailed as necessary) – on selecting the means to achieve them" (Winograd, 561). The need for civilian approval applied even to operations by units smaller than a brigade.

Initial decisions on airpower, ground operations, and conflict ends

At the opening of hostilities General Halutz advocated a strong response that included ground operations and bulldozers on the border, and air strikes against civilian infrastructure to put pressure on the Lebanese national government. Halutz did not think the return of the kidnapped soldiers was a realistic objective and recommended against making it an operational goal. Nor did Halutz think that the short-range Katyusha rockets could be mopped up by anything other than a massive ground campaign (Harel and Issacharoff, 2008, 78–81). Halutz briefed the entire cabinet accordingly on the limitations of his recommended strategy: "Don't expect victory or knockouts. I think that what we should do is react harshly enough to cause the international community to intervene by putting pressures [on the Lebanese government]."[19] According to a March 26, 2008 interview with Halutz, he had already "transmitted to the IDF for execution" the following modest (and probably attainable) goals:

- to exact from Hezbollah a grossly disproportionate price for its provocation in kidnapping the IDF soldiers
- to improve the sense of security in northern Israel
- to create conditions for the return of the kidnapped soldiers
- to prevent any escalation of the fighting to include Syria. (Lambeth, 2011, 25–26)

The first afternoon of the campaign (July 12), Peretz and, later, Olmert met with the defense chiefs to hear their plan. The IDF advocated the following goals for the operation: "deal Hezbollah a heavy blow, change the balance of deterrence and lead to a diplomatic process

---

[19] Winograd Interim Report quoted in Levy (2010, 798).

that would provide for the release of the abducted soldiers and implementation of UNSCR [UN Security Council Resolution] 1559," which required the deployment of the Lebanese Army in the south (Freilich, 2012, 204).

To accomplish these ends, the IDF's leader presented three options: (1) a massive air attack on Hezbollah targets and Lebanese civilian infrastructure, but avoiding rocket launch sites to forestall a Hezbollah strike against northern Israel; (2) an air attack focused on the rockets south of the Litani; and (3) a major ground operation. While Halutz recommended the first option, the head of the Mossad recommended the second. The Ministry of Defense's Director of Policy and Political-Military Affairs (a retired general), while not recommending option 3, emphasized that a major ground operation would be required to take on the shorter-range rockets. At the same meeting, the IDF operations chief made it clear to Olmert that no military operation was likely to bring about the return of hostages or the decisive defeat of Hezbollah (Freilich, 2012, 205). According to the IAF's head of operation Planning at the time, from the beginning of the operation the Olmert government made it clear that the IDF should rely exclusively on "standoff attacks by IAF fighters and attack helicopters, supplemented as appropriate by IDF artillery and M270 Multiple-Launch Rocket System (MLRS) fire" south of the Litani (Lambeth, 2011, 28).

The air campaign against Hezbollah's long-range *Fajr* missiles in the first hours of the attack was quite successful, and Halutz again demonstrated awareness of the proper goals given the means available when he informed Olmert on July 12, "all the long-range rockets have been destroyed. We've won the war" (Farquhar, 2009, 14). On July 15 the research unit of Israel's military intelligence branch presented a report to senior Israeli officials that questioned the war plan's ability to achieve the government's goals. The analysis, according to senior Foreign Ministry officials who read it, concluded that the heavy bombing campaign and small ground offensive then underway would show "diminishing returns" within days. It stated that the plan would neither win the release of the two Israeli soldiers in Hezbollah's hands nor reduce the militia's short-range rocket attacks on Israel to fewer than a hundred a day (Wilson, 2006).

Olmert nonetheless delivered a "Churchillian" speech on July 17 to the Knesset advancing ambitious goals in addition to return of the hostages: "a complete cease fire; deployment of the Lebanese army in all of Southern Lebanon; expulsion of Hezbollah from the area; and fulfillment of United Nations Resolution 1559" (Harel and Issacharoff, 2008, 107). Olmert actually added a Palestinian dimension to the speech: "On the Palestinian front, we will conduct a tireless battle until terror ceases, Gilad Shalit [a kidnapped IDF soldier in Gaza] is returned home safely and the shooting of Qassam missiles stops" (Olmert, 2006).

Notwithstanding Olmert's aggressive public statements, Halutz was clearly unwilling to present options for ground forces to the prime minister. Halutz justified this reluctance to his uniformed colleagues in terms of political feasibility. In the July 18 General Staff minutes, the CGS stated that "there is no point planning a ground operation," and that "divisional operations" would be rejected in favor of "smaller, shorter and more focused things." Halutz's Deputy thought the matter of ground forces to be quite urgent: "we must be ready for a deep operation in Lebanon. I do not think that this is a good thing, I know it poses risks; there is a limit to how much longer we can postpone this matter." Halutz concluded "I am not approving a widespread ground operation at this time. It would also be a shame at this time to waste a lot of planning on it, period." The Winograd Report (76–77) adds that "In the opinion of the IDF Chief of Staff, an extensive land portion would occur only when it gained public legitimacy."[20] Halutz may have been anticipating his prime minister's desires, but in a July 20 meeting between Olmert and Halutz, the prime minister left nothing to chance: "So I am telling you as a guideline, if this is raised by the Majors General or in one of these forums that result in operations – I shall not approve an extensive ground operation." Halutz agreed: "Prime Minister, like you, I do not want to go into a [ground] ... operation, moreover, I think that it would be right for us to reach an understanding that that is not the direction we wish to end up in."[21]

But civilians overruled even these limited ground operations planned by the IDF. Responding to a proposed deployment of a few brigades in

---

[20] That same day, Peretz told Halutz that, while it was time to plan an extensive ground action, "We have to start to prepare public opinion for the matter, prepare all of the stuff surrounding it, it is not something simple." "General Staff situation assessment meeting of July 18," p. 26 (Winograd, 76–77).

[21] "Work meeting between the Prime Minister and the IDF Chief of Staff of July 20, 2006," p. 11 (Winograd, 86).

Southern Lebanon, Peretz objected that a brigade was too large to fall "within our decisions about small scale operations." Halutz appears to agree, "maybe at the first stage," but also flatly states that "there is no escaping the use of ground forces too." The Winograd Report continues: "In view of the negative reaction of the Minister of Defense to the planned action, it was decided to continue the discussion as a *limited situation assessment.*"[22] Peretz appears to reluctantly agree: "We should explain to the Prime Minister that these are not small unit operations, but an operation of a number of brigades, each brigade going in at a different time." He postponed discussion of sending any more brigades than the one currently operating until the following day, however. On July 21 the small unit operations were somewhat intensified to include raids of limited time and range against villages near the border, carried out by one or two brigades. According to the Winograd Report (298), "the raids were the operational tool that was adopted by the General Staff, as a kind of compromise between the inability of counterfire to cause sufficient damage to the Hezbollah and stopping or reducing bombardment of the Home Front, and the reluctance of the political and military echelons to perform a major ground operation." Clearly, the civilians ensured that the capital-intensive but ineffective air campaign with few ground forces would continue for the foreseeable future.

Airpower's diminishing returns, "foot-dragging" on ground operations

Senior IDF leaders had been pushing Halutz to formulate an exit strategy for some time. Halutz eventually agreed, and presented the results to Olmert on July 22. According to Charles Freilich (2012, 211), this report concluded that "the IDF had exhausted its target list, that the possible benefits of military action had thus been fully realized, and recommended that Israel agree to end the fighting if an international force was deployed." Apparently, Halutz presented a personal recommendation to continue fighting for 7–10 more days, but Olmert never presented the IDF's exit strategy to the cabinet. As the operations progressed it grew increasingly clear that a significant ground operation would be required to meet all the goals publicly stated by Olmert. For

[22] "Situation assessment in the Ministry of Defense of July 20, 2006," pp. 9–18 (Winograd, 89). Emphasis in the original.

example, on July 26, Peretz was briefed by his Head of the Security Political Division, "Either you go for a broad ground operation that gets the Hezbollah out, or find a way of stopping [the war] ... I explicitly recommend this to you."[23] Disagreements among the military leadership existed; whereas the Head of the Planning Branch preferred the status quo, Brigadier General Ivo Nechushtan, head of the IDF's Planning Directorate, observed: "I think that we made the strategic achievements a week ago.... In my opinion, it has to be said to the political echelon that we shall not be able to reduce [surface-to-surface rocket fire] more than what we have now, unless we occupy the Litani." No general advocated the massive ground operation option, but many forcefully advocated at least preparing for it. Halutz concluded the meeting: "I think that a step, another step and another step will lead us to another place, which while not a total one, will be another place."[24]

Halutz clearly disagreed with the more aggressive ground campaign. On the other hand, he gave civilians all of the options. When Peretz asked Halutz if "military tools had been used in full at this stage," the IDF Chief of Staff replied: "the answer is not yet," and then laid out "the meanings of an extensive ground action." Whereas the Head of the Mossad advocated increasing ground operations in this meeting, the IDF Chief of Staff concluded: "I think that we should continue the operation that we are making today of the pounding in Southern Lebanon, both on the ground, as is being performed, and from the air. I estimate that time will lead to a reduction, will it reduce it to the point that there are no more launches? The answer is no."[25]

Other military leaders pushed Halutz to recommend a larger ground operation. On July 26 Nechushtan (incidentally a fighter pilot) briefed Halutz: "without a major ground campaign, the IDF [cannot] stop the Katyusha rockets. You must bring this before the government. You need to tell them straight that without a major ground operation, we cannot remove the Katyusha threat. If the government does not approve it ... we should tell them that they must stop the campaign

[23] "Situation assessment in the Ministry of Defense of July 26, 2006," pp. 26–27 (Winograd, 117).
[24] "Consultation on the goals of the operation of July 26, 2006," p. 49 (Winograd, 114).
[25] "Situation assessment in the Ministry of Defense of July 25, 2006," p. 24 (Winograd, 108).

now." The same day, Deputy CGS Kaplinsky also went to Halutz and said: "We can't go on like this. You must demand a ground offensive at tomorrow's cabinet meeting" (Lambeth, 2011, 55). At a Security Cabinet meeting the following day, Halutz made the case for at least *preparing* for ground operations: "My recommendation is not to hold a widespread ground operation at this time, but for everyone's sake, I must have it prepared and built up."[26] On July 27, the matter came up again. In a departure from custom, Olmert invited the civilians to talk before the CGS. Of the seven ministers making clear statements on the record, one favored seizing territory in southern Lebanon, one was noncommittal, and the remaining ministers decidedly spoke against a ground operation.[27] The group did approve mobilizing the reserve divisions, however.

In the July 31 cabinet meeting to decide between Changing Direction 8 and *Gishmei Marom*, the prime minister reiterated the primary strategic goal of a multinational force on Southern Lebanon, and that, "The broader our land action, the better the chance for a multinational force."[28] When asked about the difference between the two operations, Peretz and Halutz cited the quantity of short-range rockets eliminated. In a fascinating mandate to his ministers, Olmert continues, "Each of the ministers is requested, after this, to relate to which of the options he recommends to us, if he recommends it. Maybe he will recommend not adopting any of the options." The majority objected to the larger operation, and the IDF embarked on Changing Direction 8 (Winograd, 141).

Late half-measures on the ground
Pressure continued to rise within the General Staff for increased ground operations. When one general asked why the IDF had not recommended it earlier, Halutz stated that "Israeli society was not ready to accept entry to Lebanon on July 12." On August 4, the CGS "announced that he was about to recommend to the political echelon – 'to expand our ground operation' " (Winograd, 153). By August 8, the IDF was mobilizing for a significant escalation of ground forces, Operation Changing Direction 11, and the General Staff expressed concern

---

[26] "Seven Minister Forum of July 26, 2006," p. 28 (Winograd, 120).
[27] "Cabinet meeting of July 27, 2006" (Winograd, 123–124).
[28] "Cabinet meeting of July 31, 2006," p. 21 (Winograd, 140).

that they would ultimately not be allowed by the civilians to proceed. Halutz responded affirmatively: "All of this spring is stretched, it will be released tomorrow." Tellingly, the Air Force's chief added, "And if the Cabinet stops us, then it will stop" (Winograd, 174–175).

The cabinet meeting to consider Changing Direction 11 on August 9 lasted six hours. The IDF's head of operations, Gadi Eizenkot, laid out the plan: four days of positioning the four divisions of soldiers, followed by two to three weeks of fighting in southern Lebanon, and a week to withdraw. Shaul Mofaz, the transportation minister and former CGS, proposed an alternative: a rapid thrust of two divisions and two brigades to the Litani River, lasting a scant 48 hours (Katz, 2008). Halutz protested that the IDF's plan was developed

according to the definition of the objective [by civilians]. If the objective changes, the plan changes. The objective that you set for us is to reduce the volume of short range Katyusha fire. We have brought an answer for this. This is an extension and there is no answer other than it of a shorter length [sic]. This means that we can hold a four day operation, but it does not serve anything. We could hold a three hour operation, but it would not serve anything.

Halutz then presented the cabinet with something of a take-it-or-leave it option: "There are no intermediate ways here – if we do half, or a quarter or a third, for satisfying some of our desires – no, it does not work, it is all or nothing."[29]

This put the officials in the difficult position of "rejecting the only Israel Defense Forces proposal submitted to it or approving it." According to Winograd (521), an

overwhelming majority of Ministers ultimately supported the Israel Defense Forces proposal, so as not to create a situation in which the information emerging the Cabinet meeting – about which it was known that the ground operation was to be discussed – was that it was rejected. This is despite the fact that emerged from the deliberations that the majority of Ministers, including the Prime Minister himself, preferred the proposal that Minister Mofaz raised at the meeting.[30]

---

[29] "Security Cabinet meeting of August 9, 2006," p. 36 (Winograd, 179).

[30] Clearly, Olmert, like Lyndon Johnson before him, did not want to appear to be in control of the process. Olmert again states "I do not remember throughout this month that the military had come with a plan and asked for approval and did not get it." Olmert made a similarly forceful statement to this effect at the

Mofaz later testified: "according to the public's point of view, you can't vote against the security establishment in the middle of a war" (Harel and Issacharoff, 2008, 198).

Peretz, in response to his Security Cabinet colleagues' questions about "why an extensive ground operation had not been conducted until that day," replied, "The military did not submit an operational plan beyond what is being submitted today." Halutz objected force-fully, "But it was explicitly stated that the political system did not want a ground operation. I can read the minutes that came out of here." The Prime Minister intervened in the dispute: "Throughout the war, the military system said: we do not recommend a ground action." And also: "Two days ago the matter was shown for the first time as an operational suggestion of the military command . . . In other words, it was dependent on the readiness of the army." Olmert did not note that he had quashed any preparation for a ground operation that might have increased readiness earlier.[31]

The ground operation appears to be an anomaly for both the war and cost distribution theory. On August 6, with public frustration growing over the ongoing rocket attacks and inconclusive fighting, Vice Premier Shimon Peres warned Olmert that "another week of Katyushas and ten more dead and you will no longer be premier." During the August 9 ministers' meeting Foreign Minister Tzipi Livni stressed that "if we don't approve the (ground) operation we will look like the enemies of the people." On August 11, Minister Ben-Eliezer, "known for his political acumen" according to one analyst, warned Peretz that if the war ended as it then stood, his political career would be over. Peretz asked for an urgent meeting with Olmert and pressed for the ground operation. A primary reason for Olmert finally giving approval was his fear that he would pay the political price if he failed to order an operation approved by the cabinet, with the support of the defense minister and IDF (Freilich, 2012, 214). But the ground

larger cabinet meeting the following day (Winograd, 162) and in front of soldiers during a visit to the theater of operations: "I want you to know that today was the first time, is that right, IDF Chief of Staff? That an operational plan for approval for the Litani area has been submitted to us". "Transcript of the prime minister's visit to the Northern Regional Command of August 7, 2006," p. 5 (Winograd, 166).

[31] "Security Cabinet meeting of August 9, 2006," p. 47–53 (Winograd, 180).

operation's briefness, tardiness, and tepidness does little to undermine the overall interpretation of the case.

Ultimately, the cabinet approved the plan, but left it to the prime minister on when to start its execution.[32] While publicly going along with the general's plan, in a phone call later that day Olmert pushed for a change in the plan akin to Mofaz's suggestion. Halutz initially responded that "We need to go all of the way, all of the way here," but remained open to delays in the start of the operation "if something develops [on the diplomatic front]."[33] The General Staff ordered a second day's delay to Changing Direction 11 the night of August 9. Interestingly, Halutz, trying to force the issue, made the case to Olmert that the ground forces could not be held in place, "taut," for much longer without losing their effectiveness; Olmert actually called the division candidates personally, and was assured by them that "they had no problem waiting" (Freilich, 2012, 212).

Olmert made steps to approve the operation, but cut it down from the originally planned 96 hours to 60. But while the pre-war IDF plan was slated to take two to four weeks (with most fighting in the first five days), the cabinet approved only three days of ground operations, which in practice lasted for only one. For the first time, the IDF employed rocket and artillery-delivered cluster bombs. The final phase of the operation saw a tripling of the number of personnel in Lebanon, but about 45 percent of the sorties flown for the full war occurred in this final phase of the war as well (Lambeth, 2011, 65).

In summary, while both the civilian leadership and the IDF advocated a firepower-intensive strategy that used few soldiers, the civilian leadership was especially reluctant to send troops into combat. Simple casualty aversion is not a sufficient explanation for the Israeli shortcomings of the Second Lebanon War. Despite copious advice from senior military leaders on the limited goals that could be accomplished with the prevailing strategy, Olmert publicly set highly ambitious goals for the operation, and continued the air campaign long after his uniformed advisers thought that anything of value would result.

---

[32] "Security Cabinet meeting of August 9, 2006," p. 91 (Winograd, 183).

[33] "Telephone conversation between the prime minister and the IDF Chief of Staff of August 9, 2006," p. 10 (Winograd, 187).

Eager to signal, reluctant to pay costs

The Winograd Report makes clear that the various decision-makers understood the value of even preparing for a major ground operation as a means of conveying resolve, but did not want to pay the domestic political costs of doing so. Indeed the deliberations display an uncanny resemblance to many aspects of Slantchev's MTM in Chapter 2's appendix. Olmert was unwilling to mobilize large numbers of soldiers and prepare them for a ground operation, and thus "In spite of the fact that at that stage the Army had decided not to prepare for an extended ground operation according to plan, it was decided to mount minor infantry raids into South Lebanon to exacerbate damage to Hezbollah, and to demonstrate determination in dealing with its fighters in a ground operation" (Winograd, 516). The Report acknowledges the dilemma brought on by Olmert's warfighting decisions: "the middle road could cause – and indeed did cause – a lack of resolve. Such lack of resolve subsequently caused the effectiveness of the middle road to be further reduced" (Winograd, 527).

Many observed that showing the willingness to deploy force would produce a better result in the ongoing bargaining over ceasefire conditions in the United Nations. Even as he reluctantly authorized mobilization without deciding to actually fight, Olmert "emphasized the importance of Israel's consciousness of determination, which had to be made apparent to the enemy and countries in the region at the end of the current round of violence."[34] But Peretz told IDF generals on July 26 that "Mobilizing reserves only for threatening somebody looks to me like an adventure that will put the country into stress." The defense minister continued, "If you impress no-one, you shall have to go in."[35]

The lack of consensus over ground forces two days after approving the operation on August 9 conveys the difficulty in sending signals to opponents while minimizing costs:

Some of the political and specialist echelon opponents to the ground operation ... believed, even hoped, that making and publicizing the decision to embark on an extended ground operation would, in itself, bring about a

---

[34] "Summary of security consultation headed by the prime minister of July 29, 2006" (Winograd, 130).

[35] "Situation assessment in the Ministry of Defense of July 26, 2006," p. 28 (Winograd, 118).

rapid end to the war, without the need for implementing the operation. Some feared that initiating the ground operation could disrupt the submission of the diplomatic accord. Supporters of the ground operation felt that it had the ability to change the course of the war and establish a major military achievement. Some believed that the prolonging the diplomatic negotiations was a result of Israel's apparent weakness, that the threat of a ground operation was unreliable – and only embarking upon the operation itself would result in ending the diplomatic process in Israel's favor. (Winograd, 521)

Even once mobilization occurred, an obviously costly decision, debate continued on whether delaying its use undermined the signal Israel was trying to send. On August 11, Halutz and Peretz clearly told Olmert that its effectiveness was diminishing with every delay, leaving the prime minister with a dilemma: "The Prime Minister did not want to initiate [the ground operation], in the hope that it would not be necessary – but neither did he want to lose the implied threat of the ground operation by canceling it in the absence of a reasonable Security Council Resolution" (Winograd, 522). Ultimately, Peretz's fears were realized. According to Winograd (518), the favorable elements of the United Nations "draft accord slowly eroded, to Israel's detriment, due to the awareness that it was neither willing nor able to mobilize a military force capable of changing the situation in South Lebanon."

Lessons learned

This chapter concludes that Israeli doctrine is unlikely to change much because the median voter tends to support an aggressive grand strategy vis-à-vis small wars and a military doctrine that fights them ineffectively. Despite the uproar in the war's aftermath, and the conclusion that the IDF must improve its conventional ground capabilities, Israeli doctrine has not changed significantly. With the exception of some increased training, including the reserves (now under pressure due to budget cuts), not much has changed in terms of IDF combined arms doctrine, which remains fixated on indirect fire, avoidance of casualties, and deterrence by punishment.

While this chapter focused on the ground operations and reliance on firepower, civilians overrode another aspect of IDF's original campaign plan: attacking Lebanese civilian infrastructure in order to "make that country assume national responsibility for Hizballah's operations from its territory" (Winograd, 392). This decision had little to do with cost

distribution theory, but was made after the George W. Bush administration, particularly Secretary of State Condoleeza Rice, repeatedly
urged Olmert to show restraint.

2008's Operation Cast Lead, a punitive operation in the Gaza
Strip, demonstrates which of the war's lessons has been "learned."
Moreover, Northern Command's commanding general threatened in
2008 that "We will wield disproportionate power against every village
from which shots are fired on Israel, and cause immense damage and
destruction. From our perspective, these are military bases," continuing to state that this "is a plan that has already been authorized."[36]

7.4 Society's role in Israeli grand strategy

The Winograd Report (236) observes that "the fear of casualties
among its troops constituted a key component in the planning processes and operational considerations. With all of the sensitivity that
must be attributed to the lives of soldiers and the need to consider
this factor, it is difficult to accept the exceptional effect that this consideration had over the decisions of senior commanders (and of the
decision makers in the political echelon)."[37] But this chapter seeks to
show that casualty aversion is not sufficient to explain how the war
was conducted. As in the Vietnam Case, when substitutability is low,
as it is against unconventional opponents, a high degree of capitalization can result in the prosecution of wars using ill-suited doctrine in
pursuit of (apparently) poorly chosen goals. While this chapter cannot conclusively address every link in the causal chain empirically, cost
distribution theory nonetheless explains more aspects of contemporary Israeli security policy than competing explanations that rest on
elite capture or military myopia.

Among Israeli citizens, one's socio-economic status affects one's
approach to grand strategy; relatively less well-off individuals are

---

[36] Harel (2008); Siboni (2008). Confirmed in interviews with former Israeli
officials; one of whom told me that the chief lesson of the war was that, "Next
time we won't listen to Condi!" (Condoleezza Rice, United States Secretary of
State).

[37] This led to an ironic outcome given my theory: the desire to preserve soldiers'
lives not only led to failure to execute assigned missions, but, perversely, led to
increased civilian casualties (and higher levels of anxiety and terror) for the
civilian population.

more likely to favor military force over negotiations. Less well-off respondents are also more likely to favor increased defense spending as well as a lower willingness to make territorial concessions in pursuit of peace. Israel's conduct of the Second Lebanon War reflected these preferences. It embarked on a firepower-, air-, and capital-intensive campaign in pursuit of overly ambitious goals in an unconventional conflict, a singularly counterproductive combination. Civilians embarked on this course of action – publicly announcing goals, advocating air strikes, and delaying reserve mobilization and ground combat – despite having been briefed by military officers that these tactics would not achieve the stated aims.

More than most democratic militaries, the IDF has a very strong relationship with the public that often bypasses its civilian leaders. Given the IDF's performance in the Second Lebanon War, it seems that even if we cut out the "middle man" of the civilian government, the effect of the average voter on grand strategy remains. The Winograd Report takes the IDF to task for assessing that "the Israeli public was 'not yet ready' for such a [ground] operation" to the point that the "matter was also raised in internal Army deliberations, despite it not being the type of consideration the Army was supposed to have taken into account" (Winograd, 516). The Report does acknowledge that "the Army's professional activity is likewise not carried out in a vacuum. The processes and considerations that influenced the political echelon and the military-political interface have permeated into the Army's activity itself over many years and vice versa" (Winograd, 378). Like this chapter, the Winograd Report also links Israeli society's liberalization to changes in the IDF: "traditional IDF values and the concepts dealing with the Israel Defense Forces and its key position in Israeli society started to be eroded due to the directions of development of Israeli society as a heterogeneous, media saturated one that granted increasing preference to the considerations and interests of the individual, including economic ones, over the considerations and needs of the national collective" (Winograd, 238).

In the end, these findings may not be so surprising; Israel could be considered an easy case for cost distribution theory. Indeed, this chapter helps reconcile the case of Israel with current political economic research regarding redistribution, which suggests that a multiparty, proportional representation, parliamentary system tends to produce "center-left" coalitions that redistribute more than the center-right governments of majoritarian systems (Iversen and Soskice, 2006). Israel has generally been described as trending "rightwards" in the makeup of its governments even as it grows more democratic politically and unequal economically, but this anomaly is solved when one considers that "left" and "right" in Israel politics are generally associated with dovish versus hawkish approaches to security. Security is the highest-priority public good that Israel's government provides and it contains a redistributive element.[38]

While this chapter assigns a pivotal role to the median voter's analysis of the costs of grand strategy, it does not address how grand strategy's benefits are assessed. If security is not seen as a pressing need, the urge to advocate for more will be dampened even if defense does have a redistributive element. All other things equal, economic inequality and capitalized militaries will make increased arming and even conflict more attractive to the median voter. This provokes the question of how the country as a whole construes threats, and the work on Israel's "security network" can shed more light on this process. The chapter's theory also has less to say on the relative attractiveness of offensive and defensive uses of military might. At least in Israel's case, the costs of both have declined for the median voter; Israel engaged in offensive wars in 2006 and 2008 even as it envisions spending several billion dollars on anti-terrorism barriers separating Israelis from Palestinians and on the Iron Dome missile defense system. As IDF spokesman Shlomo Dror recently put it, "there is a bigger issue here than how much it costs. [The Iron Dome system] is going to give us some answers" (Schneider, 2009).

Israel's difficulty in conveying resolve to its opponent illustrates the role that capitalization plays in strategic, militarized bargaining. The effect is clear from two well-known statements by Hassan Nasrallah, the leader of Hezbollah. Prior to the war Nasrallah boasted that "this 'Israel' that owns nuclear weapons and the strongest air force in this region is more fragile than a spiderweb," that its society was not willing to pay the costs of a conflict with Hezbollah (Goldberg, 2002). On the other hand, Nasrallah reflected on the 2006 war that, had Hezbollah known that the kidnapping "would have led to [the war], we would definitely not have done it" (BBC News, 2006). These two statements,

---

[38] Settlements in the occupied territories also tend to have cheap rents, and their defense and support can be considered a middle-class economic subsidy as well.

frequently repeated to me during my interviews with Israeli officials, are not contradictory. In bargaining models of coercion, one side can change its payoff by increasing the punishment it can visit on the opponent, or it can convincingly show that it values the prize at stake and thus will fight with great resolve. Israel's firepower-intensive military may emphasize the former aspect while failing to communicate resolve to the opponent. As the Israeli (and American, and French, and British) way of war continues to evolve, this may lead to considerable instability.

7.A Appendix: statistical results

Table 7.1 *Socio-economic status and Israeli threat assessment*

	(56) Sec. Situation	(57) Pal. Threat	(58) Syria Threat	(59) Sec. Vote	(60) Peace Chances	(61) Arab Goals	(62) Arab Injury	(63) War Chances
Expenditure	−0.0717	−0.0790	0.00241	−0.101	0.0841	−0.159*	−0.0976	−0.0714
	(0.0715)	(0.0772)	(0.0777)	(0.0915)	(0.0737)	(0.0748)	(0.0737)	(0.0733)
FSU	0.656*	−0.0677	−0.900**	1.373***	0.275	0.599*	1.366***	−0.322
	(0.256)	(0.277)	(0.280)	(0.305)	(0.254)	(0.267)	(0.278)	(0.258)
Education	0.0103	−0.0853**	−0.0905**	−0.0352	−0.0863**	−0.0109	0.0116	−0.00750
	(0.0293)	(0.0317)	(0.0323)	(0.0380)	(0.0306)	(0.0307)	(0.0298)	(0.0293)
Male	−0.328+	0.0522	−0.650**	0.0247	0.359+	0.473*	−0.621***	−0.355+
	(0.182)	(0.197)	(0.198)	(0.234)	(0.188)	(0.191)	(0.187)	(0.185)
Haredi	1.275**	0.309	0.693	−0.545	1.522**	0.766	0.524	0.828+
	(0.439)	(0.479)	(0.478)	(0.686)	(0.505)	(0.502)	(0.453)	(0.452)
Religiosity	−0.366**	0.236+	−0.232	0.207	0.301*	0.325*	0.0141	−0.0913
	(0.130)	(0.140)	(0.141)	(0.166)	(0.132)	(0.133)	(0.131)	(0.130)
Age	0.000326	0.0130*	−0.0134*	0.00570	−0.00308	0.00187	−0.00264	−0.0146*
	(0.00592)	(0.00640)	(0.00641)	(0.00760)	(0.00601)	(0.00623)	(0.00609)	(0.00597)
Politics (l. to r.)	0.144*	0.375***	0.0539	0.0289	0.347***	0.351***	0.0848	0.154**
	(0.0567)	(0.0610)	(0.0613)	(0.0732)	(0.0602)	(0.0610)	(0.0585)	(0.0594)

Table 7.1 (*cont.*)

	(56) Sec. Situation	(57) Pal. Threat	(58) Syria Threat	(59) Sec. Vote	(60) Peace Chances	(61) Arab Goals	(62) Arab Injury	(63) War Chances
TV news	−0.150*	−0.0576	0.103	0.246*	0.0413	−0.0727	0.271***	−0.0207
	(0.0722)	(0.0778)	(0.0784)	(0.0991)	(0.0730)	(0.0755)	(0.0749)	(0.0746)
Knesset chair	0.0400	−0.0893	−0.652**	0.208	0.0809	0.0565	−0.112	−0.0806
	(0.203)	(0.220)	(0.220)	(0.266)	(0.210)	(0.214)	(0.206)	(0.204)
Household size	0.0947+	0.132*	0.102+	0.0118	0.0154	−0.00697	0.0450	0.0381
	(0.0548)	(0.0595)	(0.0597)	(0.0745)	(0.0571)	(0.0583)	(0.0561)	(0.0548)
N	450	451	450	453	452	447	454	441
R^2	0.114	0.187	0.142					
pseudo R^2				0.110	0.090	0.078	0.065	0.037

Models 56–58: OLS; Model 59: logit; Models 60–63: ordered logit. Constant coefficients not reported.
Standard errors in parentheses, ***p < 0.001, **p < 0.01, *p < 0.05, + p < 0.1.

Table 7.2 Socio-economic status and Israeli grand strategy attitudes

	(64) Sec. Spend.	(65) Military v. Talk	(66) Generic	(67) Occ. Territ.	(68) Golan Heights
Expenditure	−0.155+	−0.267**	0.209**	0.141+	0.213*
	(0.0834)	(0.0900)	(0.0768)	(0.0775)	(0.0897)
War chances	0.375***	0.567***	−0.406***	−0.423***	−0.361**
	(0.113)	(0.121)	(0.104)	(0.103)	(0.124)
FSU	1.400***	0.564+	−1.380***	−0.873***	−0.881**
	(0.330)	(0.295)	(0.275)	(0.263)	(0.325)
Education	−0.0475	−0.0204	0.00208	0.0471	0.0825*
	(0.0335)	(0.0346)	(0.0299)	(0.0304)	(0.0354)
Male	−0.165	0.736**	−0.599**	−0.199	−0.112
	(0.206)	(0.228)	(0.190)	(0.190)	(0.227)
Haredi	−0.331	0.648	0.112	−0.293	−1.174
	(0.509)	(0.666)	(0.482)	(0.509)	(0.860)
Religiosity	0.552***	0.265+	−0.280*	−0.583***	−0.306+
	(0.151)	(0.158)	(0.136)	(0.136)	(0.161)
Age	0.0171*	−0.0000189	−0.00389	−0.00195	0.00126
	(0.00675)	(0.00724)	(0.00608)	(0.00622)	(0.00739)
Politics (l. to r.)	0.114+	0.473***	−0.429***	−0.416***	−0.394***
	(0.0655)	(0.0760)	(0.0638)	(0.0636)	(0.0747)

Table 7.2 (cont.)

	(64) Sec. Spend.	(65) Military v. Talk	(66) Generic	(67) Occ. Territ.	(68) Golan Heights
TV news	0.224**	−0.0191	0.0331	0.0491	−0.0670
	(0.0820)	(0.0900)	(0.0764)	(0.0750)	(0.0887)
Knesset chair	−0.732**	0.195	0.185	0.333	0.153
	(0.239)	(0.246)	(0.210)	(0.210)	(0.260)
Household size	0.0465	0.0675	−0.159**	−0.0829	−0.0904
	(0.0621)	(0.0704)	(0.0590)	(0.0592)	(0.0729)
N	439	435	432	433	436
pseudo R^2	0.126	0.158	0.132	0.141	0.125

Ordered logit. Constant coefficients not reported.
Standard errors in parentheses, + p < 0.10, * p < 0.05, ** p < 0.01, *** p < 0.001.

8 | Conclusion: strategy wears a dollar sign

War is horror. Small wars, no matter how capitalized, involve death as well as taxes. But the balance of these costs matters greatly to war's initiation and conduct. American forces in Vietnam, which I presented as a model of capital-intensive small warfare, nonetheless sustained over 47,000 combat fatalities. North Vietnam and the Viet Cong lost roughly the same number during the Tet Offensive alone.[1] Approximately a million Vietnamese (many civilians) died in the war. As of early 2013, in Iraq and Afghanistan, the United States suffered 5,242 persons "killed in action."[2] Then again, the Soviets lost 13,310 only in Afghanistan (Taubman, 1988). One relatively conservative estimate places Afghan, Iraqi, and Pakistani civilian deaths in excess of 150,000 (Crawford, 2011).[3] The relative lack of casualties for the third-party force is one of the reasons making these wars possible in the first place, and helps explain why these conflicts have lasted so long. After World War II, George Marshall famously observed that "a democracy cannot fight a Seven Years' War," but the experience of the United States (and its allies) in Vietnam, Iraq, and Afghanistan suggests otherwise.

The copious use of capital in the pursuit of small marginal gains typifies the democratic way of war. British soldiers refer to firing a Javelin, a shoulder-fired anti-tank missile that has been used over 2,000 times in the largely tank-free environments of Afghanistan and Iraq, as

---

[1] See Vickers (1993, 127) for an extensive discussion of the various casualty estimates.

[2] United States Department of Defense. "U.S. Casualty Status." www.defense. gov/NEWS/casualty.pdf (accessed January 8, 2013). Some of these deaths occurred in other locations for Operation Enduring Freedom such as the Philippines or Jordan.

[3] Although only a relatively small percentage of these are directly due to the munitions of the United States, its allies, and the incumbent governments.

"throwing a Porsche" due to its expense (Jacob and Benzkofer, 2012).[4] And of course, the United States has, through the use of Unmanned Aerial Vehicles (UAVs), released ordinance in at least four countries – Libya, Somalia, Yemen, and Pakistan – where there are few if any American combat personnel on the ground.

This book explains these examples of doctrines and the grand strategy they support by focusing on the average voter's assessment of the costs and benefits of arming and aggression. In so doing, I developed a theory to enhance our understanding of, explain important anomalies to, and predict new facts beyond the findings produced by democratic exceptionalism. While the theory's implications force us to reconsider several essential components of liberalism – both the research program and system of government – ironically it does so by appropriating its core mechanism, "where power asymmetries permit groups to evade the costs of redistributing goods, incentives arise for exploitative, rent-seeking behavior, even if the result is inefficient for society as a whole" (Moravcsik, 1997, 517).

I defined an increase in military aggression as the pursuit of conflicts with increasingly smaller expected values – reduced chances of success or lower benefits arising from success. In doing so I called into question most previous work equating victory with policy success; achievement of trivial political gains from a costly "win" is not evidence of sound strategy.

I explained this behavior in democracies using a theory starting with a few broad assumptions: security is a public good; voters weigh security benefits against their personal costs in taxes, conscription, and casualties; the median voter gets her way in a democracy; and economic inequality exists within every state. I then developed a theory in which the median voter can redistribute the cost of arming and war away from herself, creating a condition of moral hazard. I derived a voter preference for a capitalized military doctrine limited by substitutability due to war type and technology. When substitutability is low, as it is against unconventional opponents, a high degree of capitalization can result in non-strategic behavior at the state level, initiating wars for which the doctrine is ill-suited because the costs remain low

---

[4] Raytheon Company, "Javelin Weapons System: Greatest Lethality and Lowest Weight in its Class." www.raytheon.com/newsroom/technology/rtn11_aeroindia/news05/ (February 9, 2011).

for this pivotal voter. When substitutability is high, a democracy is likely to fight an increased number of wars effectively but for trivial stakes. Economic inequality exacerbates these effects, having an independent effect on conflict behavior as well as an indirect effect through its influence on military capitalization. The results do not predict more wars per se, but rather an expensive peace, more aggressive attempts at military compellence, victories for trivial stakes, and a reduced capacity to signal to potential adversaries.

8.1 Empirical summary

To test the microfoundations of militarism, I showed in Chapter 3 that public opinion polling across 37 democracies reveals that the lower a respondent's income, the more supportive he or she will be for increased military spending, suggesting an element of redistribution. Moreover, the average response in any given state grew more hawkish with an increase in state-level inequality, threat, and the ratio of combat aircraft to soldiers.

The chapter continued by looking at polling on US foreign policy, finding that American respondents with a lower income level were more inclined to support the use of the military as a tool for foreign policy. I repeated this analysis with similar results using Israeli data in Chapter 7. Israelis who believed their household expenditure was below average were much less willing to support territorial concessions in exchange for peace. Importantly, in both the American and Israeli cases, wealth was a poor predictor of a respondent's perception of threats to the state, undermining the idea that the less wealthy have systematically different views on threats to or foreign policy goals of the state.

Chapter 4 examines arming and conflict behavior at the state level, first finding that democracies respond to a strategic threat by increasing the percentage of their defense budget devoted to the purchase of equipment. Inequality plays a significant but more complex role in the level of investment in military capital; while at relatively low levels of inequality, a rise in the Gini coefficient correlates to more equipment purchases, the effect reverses at high levels of inequality.

Again in Chapter 4, I found economic inequality and especially military capitalization have a striking effect on democratic aggressiveness. A democracy with a high level of military capitalization is more likely to attempt a militarized revision of the international status quo.

Inequality also appears to have a significant, positive effect on the likelihood of a militarized revision attempt independent of any role it plays in military capitalization (again reversing at high levels of inequality). A one standard deviation increase in inequality, roughly the difference between Germany and the United States, almost triples the likelihood of revisionism. A one standard deviation increase above the mean defense spending per soldier increases the relative risk by a factor of almost four. The analysis of conflict behavior found significant differences between democracies and all other regime types, in keeping with the "strong" version of cost distribution theory presented in Chapter 2.

To explore further the causal mechanism and to show the theory's broad ability to explain significant past conflicts, I applied the theory to three cases. These cases established the links between the voter and foreign policy via democratically elected officials. Moreover, I chose important cases, with a great deal of secondary material and interpretation already associated with them, where dominant explanations largely revolved around capture of the political process by a small elite, military or otherwise. Finding that cost distribution theory helps us understand these "hard" cases suggests the theory's wider applicability.

I found that a rise in the median voter's relative inequality (thanks to the extension of wealth-based suffrage through the Reform Acts of 1868 and 1884) resulted in increasingly aggressive expansion of the British Empire, different goals served by imperialism, and a shift in military doctrine towards more intensive use of "Native" military forces. Instead of a subsidy to provide economic rents for the wealthy, the Empire was a means – expensive for Britain but cheap for the middle-class voter – of maintaining great power status, securing military manpower, and avoiding conscription.

I next looked at the United States' initiation and conduct of the Vietnam War, one of the most costly (and ultimately unsuccessful) counterinsurgencies in history. Increased capitalization of the military, commenced under the auspices of the Kennedy administration, allowed the Johnson administration to pursue and prolong an aggressive, and ultimately failed, campaign whose prospects of success were low from the outset. The United States continued to fight even as the expected value of the conflict clearly dropped. Rather than the hidebound nature of the US military bureaucracy, deliberate decisions by civilian leaders in three administrations based on their assessment of the public's preferences better explain the poor counterinsurgency strategy maintained throughout.

The final case study, on contemporary Israel, examined the increased capitalization and professionalization of the IDF in tandem with an increase in wealth, inequality, and individualism in Israeli society. In addition to the survey analysis noted above, I examined in detail the interaction between civilian and military leaders during the preparation, initiation, and conduct of the Second Lebanon War in 2006. I found that civilians' (and generals') anticipation of the public's reaction strongly affected the prosecution of the conflict, leading to a poorly executed grand strategy.

Do the effects of capitalization mean that democracies can easily build militaries allowing them to act like any other state or does it show a path for democracies to act in ways that systematically differ from other regime types? While much of the book deals exclusively with democracies (in part due to data availability), the book did test for differences between regime types in terms of conflict behavior, allowing me to adjudicate between these weak (realist) and strong (liberal) versions of cost distribution theory. Based on the statistical evidence, democracies with high levels of capitalization and/or volunteer militaries act more aggressively in terms of military conflict. If there is any relationship between these two explanatory variables and arming in non-democracies, it is the opposite.

The book's findings contradict the structural realist tenet that regime type should not affect how a state prepares for war.[5] However, the theory suggests that the role played by democracy is more complex than simple cost aversion. From the perspective of a democratic government, developing the correct military structure gives the executive wide latitude for action by insulating its foreign policy from popular pressure. Military capitalization may provide a liberal path to neorealist behavior. More disturbingly, a median voter who successfully transfers the financial burden of war onto a wealthy minority, while simultaneously minimizing the possibility of casualties and conscription, may be just as susceptible to the temptation of imperial

---

[5] Although it conforms comfortably to the neoclassical realist tenet that domestic forces can often shape the "conduct" of military confrontation "in a manner that may appear puzzling or anomalous from a neorealist perspective" (Dueck, 2009, 139).

overstretch as any other type of political elite. Thus regime type may contribute to the aggressiveness of states, but in ways unanticipated by democratic exceptionalism. If the burden of providing security shifts sufficiently, voters may be non-realists in the "wrong" direction, aggressively pursuing their own interests at the state's expense.

Quantitative analysis using better data, statistical estimators that adhere more closely to the non-monotonic portions of the theoretical model, and better techniques for analyzing near-integrated panel data will help provide a more satisfying answer to this question. Across-case qualitative work is also likely to be essential. An investigation of the Soviet war in Afghanistan as well as Russia's two wars in Chechnya would appear to be a natural series of cases for study given the enticing amount of variation in the explanatory variable of regime type within (approximately) the same state. At first glance, it is not clear that the Soviets fought a war much different in capital-intensity than the Americans in Vietnam. At the very least such an investigation will help to build theory on how different types of non-democracies pursue security, rather than lumping all regime types together in the category "non-democracy," as does this book (and most of the field of IR).

8.2 Adjusting and extending democratic exceptionalism

Whether or not the weak/realist or strong/liberal versions of the theory ultimately carries the day empirically, we are left with some novel and remarkable findings that have important implications for democratic exceptionalism. To evaluate its contribution, I revisit exceptionalism's central conclusions first listed in the Introduction:

(i) Democracies tend to pursue public goods, including security.
(ii) Democracies tend to win military conflicts, largely due to choosing "unfair fights."
(iii) Democracies expend fewer resources on defense in peacetime, but try harder in wartime.
(iv) Democracies employ their resources efficiently in wartime.
(v) Democracies are less likely to fight and more likely to negotiate during crises.
(vi) Democracies are more likely to exit expensive wars and accept a negotiated outcome.

The book's theoretical and empirical work give us a better understanding of how much security democracies will provide, why democracies bother to fight unfair fights, and what wartime effort entails.
Point three only receives partial support; theory suggest that peace can
be quite expensive if the median voter does not feel the costs of arming. The theory adds an extremely important qualification to the fourth
item, noting the importance of technology and war type and the possibility for inefficient war prosecution. The book gives further reason
to be skeptical of item five, often called the monadic democratic peace.
Cases and recent history show that democracies can fight small wars
without agreeing to a settlement.

In this book I have intentionally taken the "hard core" of democratic
exceptionalist theory – rational individuals in a perfect marketplace of
ideas in a democracy located in an anarchic international system – and
added one assumption: economic inequality. In this spirit of progressive research, I suggest avenues of inquiry opened up by this book,
many derived from relaxing the assumptions of its models.

The model of redistribution, arming, and war presented in this book
can be generalized to other types of regimes. Early twentieth-century
Spain's Catholic oligarchy appears to conform to the theory's implications in its own colonial misadventures. Its military served primarily as
a source of oligarchic rents, with an officer for every seven soldiers, and
military pay (mostly for officers) consuming half the budget (compared
to France's sixth). Wealthy Spaniards could pay the equivalent of 300
days of the average laborer's wage to avoid conscription. Despite its
colonial possessions, the metropolitan army consumed 77 percent of
the defense budget yet could not field a division to reinforce Morocco
in 1921 (Balfour, 2002, 10). Although its colonial involvement in
Morocco dated back to 1893, by 1920 Spain controlled less than a
quarter of her "possession" (Woolman, 1994). The under-equipped
and poorly trained conscript force was decimated in 1921 by Rifian
rebel forces at Annual, "the greatest defeat suffered by a European
power in an African colonial conflict in the 20th century" (Alvarez,
1999, 81).

However, it remains unclear where some regime types fall on the
democracy–plutocracy spectrum suggested by cost distribution theory. Not all regimes are necessarily more prone than democracies to
the dangerous cartelization necessary for imperial overstretch (Snyder,
1991). And there are ways for the public to influence non-democratic

leaders. When in 1909 the Spanish government called up draftees to fight in colonial Morocco, rioting broke out, particularly in Barcelona. The government's massive, repressive response, still known as the "tragic week," resulted in the removal of the prime minister in favor of a more liberal one, and the creation of the *Regulares*, a military force consisting of indigenous Moroccan soldiers to replace conscripts, following the long-standing, successful model of democratic France (Alvarez, 1999).[6] One can also imagine that other regimes (or a democracy with specific types of checks and balances favoring the rich) may reflect a broader range of preferences and thus conform more closely to the cost internalization ideal. This may have a dampening effect, similar to the relationship this book identifies in democracies with extremely high levels of economic inequality.

The interaction between two redistributive regimes in conflict suggested in Chapter 2 as well as the subsequent, qualitative chapters should be investigated further. A follow-on model to those presented in Chapter 2's appendix would endogenize the compeller's choice of strategy, for example by allowing a strong state to choose between two strategies (capital- or labor-intensive) and a weak actor to choose between fighting conventionally or unconventionally. Such a model would allow us to further probe the circumstances under which a strong democracy (or any type of actor) would choose a strategy that poorly matches the likely strategic choice of the target.

Cost distribution theory requires the armed forces to provide a pure public good. This assumption is axiomatically violated when the military in a democracy is called to intervene in an internal conflict. I acknowledge this when looking at only Jewish respondents in Israeli public opinion polls. Focusing only on public goods and international politics excludes some of the most interesting examples of democracies at war such as Colombia and India. Fruitful work on the democratic way of civil war lies in the future.

In related logic, given that the military plays a fundamental and often brutal role in preserving non-democratic regimes, an extension of cost distribution theory would expect that fledgling democracies

---

[6] The Army of Africa, consisting of *Regulares* and the Spanish Foreign Legion, would later be used in metropolitan Spain to both crush a miners' revolt and bring Franco to power in the Civil War, something that cannot be said for democratic colonial forces.

should reduce their funding to their potential repressors. This effect should diminish over time as civilians gain confidence in their control of the military (and thus its status as a pure public good). Such an analysis would amount to a competitive test between cost distribution theory and Mansfield and Snyder (2005), which suggests that states undergoing democratic transition are more prone to aggression. For example, while regional military spending dipped significantly with the demise of several South American juntas, the volume of international arms transfers to the Americas increased by 34 per cent between 2003–2007 and 2008–12 (SIPRI, 2013a).[7] This may partly explain the book's finding that support for defense spending and international aggressiveness drop at very high levels of inequality.

What if *nobody* within the state pays for war? Kant (1991, 100) – along with other liberals such as Adam Smith, Cobden, and Hobson – considered war's "crowning evil" to be citizens "having to take upon themselves a burden of debt which will embitter peace itself." Yet contemporary events suggest that, at least in the American case, debt may enable militarism. Deficit spending is a form of temporarily persuading other actors (many outside of the state, particularly in the case of the United States today) to pay for defense and war. It is relatively easy to dismiss this argument in the abstract by arguing for Ricardian equivalence (Barro, 1974); ultimately taxpayers will pay the same amount with interest and thus the Meltzer–Richard logic should hold. However, there is little doubt that government borrowing makes the short-term fiscal pain of militarization smaller for all citizens. Lyndon Johnson certainly made clear his preferences to the Chair of the Federal Reserve, William Martin. Johnson "asked the Secret Service to leave the room. And he physically beat him, he slammed him against the wall, and said, 'Martin, my boys are dying in Vietnam, and you won't print the money I need!'" (Lowenstein, 2008).

Deficit spending may contain an additional element of redistribution if the resulting inflation tends to hurt the wealthy more than the poor. The potentially important role that borrowing abroad may have on

---

[7] Some of this is due to the initiation of and responses to Venezuela's large arms purchases. Identifying the regime type of Venezuela under President Hugo Chávez is a fascinating question in its own right, and also gives the sense of the difficulty in constructing theories about non-democracies.

arming and war does not obviate my theoretical and empirical claims, but it certainly bears investigation.

The United States funds its budget in substantial part through debt rather than taxes. The Chinese government in particular invests heavily in US treasuries in part to keep its exports competitive, at the cost of reduced standards of living for much of its population (Fallows, 2008). It would appear that this would increase American moral hazard over the costs of conflict on top of the mechanism laid out in this book. United States military assertiveness may be funded through a combination of rich Americans and poor Chinese. Indeed, the link between American military protection and debt assumption is quite explicit in the case of Saudi Arabia and other Gulf states (Art, 2009, 20).

International financial ties may play a role in another way. One of the assumptions of the microfoundational model is the inability of capital to leave the country. Future research should examine the interaction of capital mobility and military capitalization. The threat of capital flight may constrain the median voter's ability to tax the rich and build a highly capitalized military or fund expensive wars. Finding a link between the two would deftly incorporate two legs of the "Kantian Triangle" (Russett and Oneal, 2001).

In this sense the book is part of a progressive social science research program, building on the previous theories and findings of democratic exceptionalism. However, the book also proposes a large revision to this program, showing that the median voter is as happy to go to war as any other actor, so long as someone else picks up the tab. Not only that, but the median voter's ability to do so is increasing, and thus this book predicts that we will see increasing levels of democratic aggression in the foreseeable future. The differences are even more stark when comparing my theory to classical liberalism.

8.3 The empirical case against classical liberalism

The most powerful objection to my theory rests on the classical liberal logic that the covariance between inequality, capitalization, and aggression is explained by my argument's inverse: the power of the extremely rich rather than the relatively poor. Why is the evidence of massive (and potentially wasteful) spending on military capital not evidence of the "unwarranted influence, sought or unsought, by the military-industrial complex" (Eisenhower, 1961)? Or, less specifically but more convincingly, perhaps the wealthy have much more to lose in an insecure state than do the poor, for whom even a small amount of taxes may amount to a considerable reduction in one's basic quality of life.

It is helpful to unpack this logic into its two components. The first suggests that the wealthy have more to lose, and therefore a more unequal state will build bigger militaries in peacetime and fight harder in wartime. Second, building a capital-intensive military benefits the wealthy due to their private gains from pork barrel spending.

On the larger point that military expenditure and even aggression tends to favor the wealthy, while several of my empirical findings can be explained by either mechanism, some very important results support my claim and contradict the competing explanation. Both the public opinion data and the curvilinear relationship of inequality to militarism suggest that the wealthy are, on average, more dovish. A recent survey of wealthy Americans ("the top 1 percent or so of US wealth-holders"), finds significantly more enthusiasm for cutting defense spending relative to the broader public (Page et al., 2013).

Turning to a more specific instance of an elite–militarism connection, the so-called military–industrial complex is simply too small to have an effect in a democracy without logrolling. While Eisenhower could report in his 1961 farewell speech that "We annually spend on military security more than the net income of all United States corporations," even the highest estimate of peak post-9/11 US defense spending (including war spending for Iraq and Afghanistan) is about half of the 1.6 trillion dollars in US corporate *profits* for 2007.[8] In 2011, the United States-based companies made up nearly half of the world's top 100 defense and aerospace firms based on revenues. Their combined revenue, $261 billion, was $160 billion less than Wal-Mart's alone.[9]

It is true that defense spending makes up a tremendous portion of the federal government's discretionary spending, but this only shows

[8] Bureau of Economic Analysis, US Department of Commerce.
www.bea.gov/national/Index.htm.
[9] Defense News Top 100 for 2012.
http://special.defensenews.com/top-100/charts/rank_2011.php. Wal-Mart revenue from Fortune 500,
http://money.cnn.com/magazines/fortune/fortune500/. All websites accessed July 6, 2013.

how diffuse the benefits are. The average American voter, or at least the pivotal voter in a great number of congressional districts and states, does quite well from this expenditure. The Defense Department estimates that it has about 20 percent more infrastructure capacity (i.e. buildings and installations) than it requires, but Congress refuses to authorize the base closure procedure necessary to generate these efficiencies (Pincus, 2013). The past few decades have seen a shift in American military spending, as well as all other redistributive federal expenditure, towards the south and west, the so-called "gun belt" (Markusen, 1991). This book suggests this is no coincidence. If some subsection of wealthy elites benefit from defense spending and war, it is only done by logrolling with the median voter.[10]

Consider as another example Israel's economy: 6.7 percent of its GDP went to the domestic procurement of arms and other materiel for the IDF (Zrahiya, 2007).[11] While Israel exports large amounts of arms, it is still a small sector compared to the rest of its booming high-tech economy. The defense industry accounts for 2–3 percent of Israeli GDP, depending on the level of arms exports (Lifshitz, 2010). The bulk of the Israeli arms industry is state-owned. In two of the world's most militarized democratic economies, it is hard to think the owners of defense firms have that much more influence than possessors of other types of wealth.

Finally, I wish to emphasize that this book and its use of median voter theory is not an explanation of what "the poor" want. In the Vietnam case, the steadfast avoidance of reserve mobilization was designed to protect the politically powerful middle class rather than the poor, who were more likely to be drafted.[12] Likewise, the British Empire, given the restrictions on voting that remained in place even

---

[10] Solt (2011) shows the fascinating correlation between economic inequality and nationalism, motivated by a diversionary theory. Nationalism is equally felt across relative income.

[11] This does not count the sizable US subsidies for Israel to buy American military products.

[12] Witness the conversation between Johnson and the segregationist Senator Richard Russell, in which Johnson proposes lowering the IQ standards for draftees in the military, a move that Russell had opposed for years on segregationist grounds. Johnson argues that "It seems to me that you're paying a mighty big price on an Anglo-Saxon white man to make his boy go and fight in Vietnam. But none of the others can because . . . they don't have the exact IQ" (Beschloss, 2001, 212, see also 140–141).

after three Reform Acts, was not a working-class phenomenon. Jingoism – at least during the Boer War, an imperial misadventure par excellence – appeared largely confined to the middle class (Price, 1972), in part because working-class associations were more concerned with social reform at home. Even if one's material condition does affect one's approach to international security, the middle class are likely to both have something to lose and a means for getting someone even wealthier to pay for its defense. Perhaps like unemployment insurance, security may be an impure public good targeting the needs of the politically powerful middle class (Moene and Wallerstein, 2001). Future research should explore defense efforts as a form of "Director's Law" in which those at the median take taxes from those who have more wealth and labor from those who have less (Stigler, 1970).

In Chapter 5 I suggested a reexamination of the classical liberal assumption that imperialism and militarism inevitably lead to tyranny at home based on political developments in Britain compared to those in the European continental states. It seems clear that the flip side of this liberal logic also requires reassessment; under the wrong circumstances, political liberalism at home can produce aggressive behavior abroad. The misplaced confidence of John Hobson at the turn of the twentieth century that democracies eschewed aggression may be even less appropriate now. This book concludes by speculating on possible trends towards increased democratic belligerence in the foreseeable future. Ironically, even as Stephen Brooks (2005) makes the claim that technology has enabled one classical liberal tenet (trade leads to peace) to finally come true, I argue that the same process may make it less likely that another (democracy leads to peace) will continue to remain intact.

8.4 The revolution in military affairs

Early in the Cold War Bernard Brodie (1959) noted that "strategy wears a dollar sign," and Colin Powell's maxim "show me your budget and I will show you your strategy," indicates that not much has changed in 50 years. What has changed over this period is what can be done with this money. As preparing and prosecuting wars becomes increasingly an exercise in fiscal rather than social mobilization, we may very well see some dangerous democracies emerge.

Before its cancellation in 2009, at 15 billion dollars the US Army's Future Combat Systems (FCS) was the largest research program in Department of Defense history. Envisioned to incorporate at least ten unmanned vehicles and sensors, Army briefings claimed the system would reduce logistical support requirements by up to 70 percent, cut a battalion's worth of combat troops by half, and increase survivability by 60 to 80 percent (Feickert, 2005, 152). In its 2010 budget request, the Pentagon cut 700 million dollars in research funding for FCS manned components, deciding to develop a successor ground vehicle with increased armor more suited for conditions in Afghanistan and Iraq. 2.9 billion dollars was still requested for the unmanned portions of the program. Additionally, the Pentagon advocated equipping all 45 of the Army's brigades with this new system rather than the 15 originally planned for FCS, most likely at considerably more expense than the original program. The manned "Ground Combat Vehicle" would equip 22 brigades at an estimated cost of $28.8 billion (Congressional Budget Office, 2013; Feickert, 2013). The FCS and the programs that succeed it represent the largest and latest instance of the continuing attempt to create a "new American way of war," one that increases the speed of warmaking, widens the military power gap between the United States and the rest of the world, minimizes American casualties, and raises the financial costs of defense for American taxpayers (Hoffman, 1996; Boot, 2003; Ferris, 2003).

The United States is not alone in this shift. Democracies as varied as Australia, Great Britain, Israel, and South Korea (Bennett, 2006) are in the midst or have recently completed capital-intensive retoolings of their militaries. For example, France's sweeping 2008 Defense White Paper (Ministry of Defense, 2008) promised to cut personnel by 17 percent (the majority from the Army) with the savings applied to military hardware upgrades – a military space program, improved airlift, and armored platforms designed to protect the remaining soldiers in the force – at a cost of about 300 billion dollars through 2020. Despite the cuts in personnel, the White Paper defines French strategic interests expansively, extending into the Atlantic, Mediterranean, and the Middle East (with a new, permanent naval base established in Abu Dhabi).

Even in austerity, France continues to shift its capital-to-personnel ratio. France's 2013 Defense White Paper operates with very different resource assumptions relative to 2008. 34,000 people will be cut from the defense ministry, but its budget will remain stable. Army personnel will be cut by 25 percent, but special operations forces will increase from 3,000 to 4,000. Helicopter numbers will rise by 21 percent. While fighter aircraft numbers will decline by 25 percent, this is largely because older, less sophisticated aircraft will be retired and UAVs will be used in much greater numbers (Ministry of Defense, 2013).[13]

I argue that such militaries and expansive aims are developed with the average voter's blessing in spite of – indeed because of – the hefty capital investment they require. Military technology can clearly have distributive implications, and allows the median voter to shift the burden of conflict away from themselves *and* simultaneously reduce the state's overall marginal costs for defense. Given the continuing acceleration of the capital-intensive "revolution in military affairs," this effect requires increased attention.

8.4.1 Overweighting of the military option and unilateralism

I have argued that if the costs of creating security are shifted away from the politically powerful, then their demand for security and the ambition of a state's grand strategy will increase. Similarly, as the cost of using the military declines for the politically powerful, its attractiveness rises relative to other means of providing security.[14]

Consider the alternative to increasing one's own defense effort: relying on other states.[15] The arms–allies tradeoff is a classic example of what economists call the "make-or-buy" problem for corporations (Brauer and Van Tuyll, 2008, 312). Both are costly, but in different ways. Arms require the investment of one's own resources but deliver the state near-absolute discretion in their use. Allies do not consume as many resources but, by potentially obligating a state to enter a conflict on behalf of another actor as well as by relying on another sovereign state for defense alliances, entail their own costs (Morrow, 1993; Morgan and Palmer, 2003).

If technology does not allow the substitution of capital for labor, one can use taxes to find an alternate labor source either through

---

[13] The White Paper also emphasized the high priority of supporting the domestic defense industry, a policy with obvious redistributive consequences.

[14] On foreign policy substitutability see Most and Starr (1984) as well as the special volume of the *Journal of Conflict Resolution*, February 2000.

[15] Also known as internal and external balancing (Waltz, 1979).

mercenaries, alliances, or imperialism. Democratic France and autocratic Spain teamed up to fight the Rif Rebellion, and World War
II was largely won through expending Soviet bodies and American
dollars. But this is a second-best option for the median voter; capital-
intensive militaries are preferred over finding alternative labor sources
for a variety or reasons. Allies are uncertain partners, and mercenaries harder to regulate than one's own soldiers. If technology allows
for the relatively easy substitution of capital for labor, and the median
voter pays little of the cost of building this capital-intensive military,
then such a democracy is likely to aggressively use internal balancing and act in an increasingly unilateral manner. Drones operated by
officers who commute from their homes to Creech Air Force Base (a
45-minute drive from Las Vegas) have attacked suspected American
enemies in Afghanistan, Iraq, Libya, Pakistan, Somalia, and Yemen.
While the minimal cost to American lives is obvious, the effectiveness
of such attacks is less apparent.

This make-or-buy logic applies to any kind of institution. International organizations can be an efficient way of achieving security gains,
but a state will always prefer its own way if it is not costly (Keohane,
1984; Glaser, 1994). Similarly, economic sanctions can be a coercive
alternative to military force, but it is also likely to entail domestic costs
for the sender (Drezner, 2003; Lektzian and Sprecher, 2007). As the
costs of the military instrument decline for the median voter relative to
other foreign policy tools, the less relevant institutions and sanctions
become.

Finally, while grand strategy usually requires tough choices and
prioritization, if costs are low enough, or resources large enough,
states may make little effort to develop a coherent grand strategy.
Because of its vast resources, Stephen Biddle (2005, 1) observes, "the
United States can avoid making hard choices and instead pursue ill-
defined goals with limited penalties." When things are not costly, few
choices need be made, especially when threats are low but persistent,
amorphous, or ideological.

8.4.2 *Aggressive democracies in the "age of terror"*

Only after several years of little progress in Iraq did the United States
respond by changing its strategy. Tremendous public attention was
paid to the 2007 "surge" of 30,000 American personnel in Iraq,

representing a 20 percent increase in deployed personnel. Less attention has been given to the *fivefold* increase in Coalition air strikes
over 2006. Simultaneously, in Afghanistan, such sorties nearly doubled from 1,770 to 2,926 (Cordesman, 2008). Yet despite a consensus
that Islamic terrorism remains a threat, particularly in Europe, NATO
cannot find soldiers to prevent Afghanistan from slipping into chaos.

Robert Pape (1996; 2005) argues that while punishment strategies
do not work in general, suicide terrorism can often produce strategic
gains for the weak, especially when targeting democracies. Terrorism
is designed to have an effect disproportionate to the damage it causes.
Indeed, in some cases terrorism is not only designed to engender the
maximum of fear in its target but to provoke the target into extreme
reactions. Whether or not such a response is entirely rational on the
part of the target is beyond this study's scope. With a heavily capitalized military doctrine, one constraint on such responses, the high
cost of military action, has been removed. The combination may prove
volatile.

Cost distribution theory is agnostic about the motivations behind
democracies' coercive behavior, as long as the outcome may provide
a public good. Normative goals, such as the spread of democracy, are
also public goods, albeit ones that Bueno de Mesquita and Downs
(2006) describe as "not remotely equivalent" in value to other more
material gains. But if the costs drop sufficiently, these operations
become more feasible. The suggestion adds an element of irony to
Disraeli's speech to Parliament following the Abyssinian expedition:
"In an age accused, and perhaps not unjustly, of selfishness, and a too
great regard for material interests, it is something, in so striking and
significant a manner, for a great nation to have vindicated the higher
principles of humanity" (Monypenny and Buckle, 1920a, 45). Disraeli's "selfless" invasion of Ethiopia to rescue five hostages was only
contemplated because the private costs for the voter were modest, and
the political gains for the Tories substantial. Linking low costs with the
possibility of achieving vague, normative goals (especially when tied to
security) will likely lead to more aggression.

Creating incentives for powerful democracies to extend deterrence
against a wide variety of threats (material or normative) may actually
result in further instability. In cases of moral hazard by third-party
intervention in civil war (Crawford and Kuperman, 2006), my theory
suggests an additional knock-on effect. The domestic moral hazard

described in this book may lead to more offers of extended deterrence by powerful democracies, which in turn may result in increased international instability due to more moral hazard situations for protégés.

While scholars have speculated that economic inequality can be a source of internal instability in weak states (Boix, 2003; Fearon and Laitin, 2003), cost distribution theory suggests that inequality can also lead to *international* instability instigated by mature, developed democracies. Democracies with a high (but not extremely high) level of inequality, a highly capitalized military, or both (the United States, United Kingdom, and Israel being three examples) will find the costs of any conflict more bearable, particularly as military technology increasingly favors capital.

While I also find that rich democracies probably work differently than poor democracies or rich non-democracies, this does not justify the conclusion that "to advance further the cause of peace, we must encourage increased trade and development along with democratic institutions" (Mousseau et al., 2003, 277), one of the fundamental tenets of American foreign policy. The Clinton National Security Strategy asserted that "the trend toward democracy and free markets throughout the world advances American interests" and this is echoed in the Bush administration's policy that "America will encourage the advancement of democracy and economic openness... because these are the best foundations for domestic stability and international order" (Bush, 2002; Clinton, 1998). The strategic benefits of promoting economic growth and democracy may be less apparent in the absence of concern for the distribution of economic benefits within society.

Many observers argue that most wars of the twenty-first century will be hybrid conflicts involving unconventional opponents such as the Second Lebanon War of Chapter 7 (Hoffman, 2009). Policy-makers in many democracies (not just Israel and the United States) have criticized their militaries' myopic failure to adapt appropriately. This book argues that fixating on reforming the armed services (or even the civilian tools of foreign policy) in an effort to improve democratic performance in small wars is its own form of myopia. My theory gives reason to be skeptical of how much a democracy's military will be allowed to shift by future administrations and the public to which they are held accountable. Dysfunctional organizations can eventually learn and adapt. If the public suffers from foolish preconceptions, it may be dissuaded through public education and the marketplace of ideas. Even positing a powerful strategic culture underpinning American doctrine suggests that "it is at least possible that by deconstructing the standard American 'way' ... some pathways to improved performance may be identified" (Gray, 2006, 30). But if a rational, fully informed electorate views such a military doctrine as its best option, the prospects for change are limited. The calculus is clear in a 2008 *New York Times* op-ed by US Air Force general Charles Dunlap: "the lesson of Iraq is that old-fashioned force works" and that the United States needs an "unapologetically high-tech military that substituted machines for the bodies of young Americans" (Dunlap, 2008). Because of the heavily capitalized nature of its armed forces, the United States and other democracies are likely to fight small wars badly, but continue to fight them all the same. For a democracy's average voter, building a military to fight these wars of choice inefficiently but often is not a bug in the program but a feature.

If democracies can shift the defense burden away from the median voter by developing a certain type of military, one cannot assume that the costs of defense (and ultimately of war) are evenly distributed across society, a crucial assumption of democratic exceptionalism. Scheve and Stasavage (2010) locate the origins of progressive taxation in the effort to distribute fairly the burdens of conflict in the era of mass warfare. This book suggests implications for what happens when the progressive tax system remains, but technology obviates the need to mobilize large, labor-intensive armies. Democracies with large amounts of capital relative to their populations are therefore likely to have an advantage building militaries in which the costs of conflict are relatively low for the median voter. The effect is exacerbated by economic inequality. Wealthy but inequitable democracies with ready access to capital may be quite willing to build large militaries and use them aggressively, because arming and war are, in the minds of many voters, cheap.

Bibliography

1900 (Nov. 17). On the Road to Taxation. *The Speaker: The Liberal Review*, 3, 169–170.

Acemoglu, Daron and Robinson, James A. 2005. *Economic Origins of Dictatorship and Democracy.* Cambridge and New York: Cambridge University Press.

Achen, Christopher. 2000. Why Lagged Dependent Variables Can Suppress the Explanatory Power of Other Independent Variables. Paper presented at the Annual Meeting of the Society for Political Methodology, Nov. 2.

Adams, Paul. 1998. The Military View of the Empire 1870–1899: As Seen through the Journal of the Royal United Services Institution. *The RUSI Journal*, 143(3), 58–64.

Adams, R. J. Q. and Poirier, Philip P. 1987. *The Conscription Controversy in Great Britain, 1900–18.* Columbus: Ohio State University Press.

Adamsky, Dima. 2010. *The Culture of Military Innovation: The Impact of Cultural Factors on the Revolution in Military Affairs in Russia, the US, and Israel.* Stanford University Press.

Alesina, Alberto and Rosenthal, Howard. 1995. *Partisan Politics, Divided Government, and the Economy.* Cambridge University Press.

Alexander, Martin and Keiger, J. F. V. 2002. France and the Algerian War: Strategy, Operations and Diplomacy. *Journal of Strategic Studies*, 25(2), 1–32.

Alvarez, Jose E. 1999. Between Gallipoli and D-Day: Alhucemas, 1925. *Journal of Military History*, 63(1), 75–98.

2001. *The Betrothed of Death: The Spanish Foreign Legion during the Rif Rebellion, 1920–1027.* Westport, Conn.: Greenwood Press.

Anderson, Christopher J. and Singer, Matthew M. 2008. The Sensitive Left and the Impervious Right: Multilevel Models and the Politics of Inequality, Ideology, and Legitimacy in Europe. *Comparative Political Studies*, 41(4–5), 564–599.

Anrig, Christian F. 2009. Neglected Contributors: The Continental European Air Powers. In Joel Hayward (ed.), *Air Power, Insurgency and the*

'*War on Terror*'. Cranwell, UK: Royal Air Force Centre for Air Power Studies, 237–253.

Appy, Christian G. 1993. *Working-Class War: American Combat Soldiers and Vietnam*. Chapel Hill: University of North Carolina Press.

Arian, Asher, Atmor, Nir, and Yael, Hadar. 2007. *The 2007 Israeli Democracy Index: Auditing Israel Democracy, Cohesion in a Divided Society*. June. Israel Democracy Institute.

Arreguín-Toft, Ivan. 2005. *How the Weak Win Wars: A Theory of Asymmetric Conflict*. New York: Cambridge University Press.

Art, Robert J. 2003. *A Grand Strategy for America*. Ithaca: Cornell University Press.

2009. The Fungibility of Force. In Robert J. Art and Kenneth N. Waltz (eds.), *The Use of Force: Military Power and International Politics*. Lanham, Md.: Rowman & Littlefield, 3–22.

Ashcroft, A. C. 2001. As Britain Returns to an Expeditionary Strategy, Do We Have Anything to Learn from the Victorians? *Defence Studies*, 1(1), 75–98.

Asprey, Robert B. 1994. *War in the Shadows: The Guerrilla in History*. New York: W. Morrow.

Avant, Deborah D. 1994. *Political Institutions and Military Change: Lessons from Peripheral Wars*. Ithaca: Cornell University Press.

1996. Are the Reluctant Warriors Out of Control? Why the U.S. Military is Averse to Responding to Post-Cold War Low-Level Threats. *Security Studies*, 6(2), 51–90.

1998. Conflicting Indicators of 'Crisis' in American Civil–Military Relations. *Armed Forces and Society*, 24(3), 375–387.

Bacevich, Andrew J. 2005. *The New American Militarism: How Americans are Seduced by War*. New York: Oxford University Press.

Bailes, H. 1980. Technology and Imperialism: A Case-Study of the Victorian Army in Africa. *Victorian Studies*, 24(1), 83–104.

Balfour, Sebastian. 2002. *Deadly Embrace: Morocco and the Road to the Spanish Civil War*. Oxford University Press.

Bar-Joseph, Uri. 2001. *Israel's National Security Towards the 21st Century*. London: Frank Cass.

2007. Israel's Military Intelligence Performance in the Second Lebanon War. *International Journal of Intelligence and Counterintelligence*, 20(4), 583–601.

Bar-Or, Amir and Haltiner, Karl W. 2009. Democratic Control of the Armed Forces in Israel and Switzerland in Times of Security Threats. In Oren Barak and Gabriel Sheffer (eds.), *Existential Threats and Civil-Security Relations*. Lanham, Md.: Lexington Books, 153–178.

Barak, Oren and Sheffer, Gabriel. 2006. Israel's "Security Network" and its Impact: An Exploration of a New Approach. *International Journal of Middle East Studies*, 38(2), 235–261.

2009. Continuous Existential Threats, Civil–Security Relations, and Democracy: A Comparative Exploration of Five Small States. In Oren Barak and Gabriel Sheffer (eds.), *Existential Threats and Civil–Security Relations*. Lanham, Md.: Lexington Books, 119–152.

Barnett, Correlli. 1970. *Britain and her Army, 1509–1970: A Military, Political and Social Survey.* London: Allen Lane.

Barro, Robert J. 1974. Are Government Bonds Net Wealth? *The Journal of Political Economy*, 82(6), 1095–1117.

Bartels, Larry M. 2008. *Unequal Democracy: The Political Economy of the New Gilded Age.* New York: Russell Sage Foundation.

Baskir, Lawrence M. and Strauss, William. 1978. *Chance and Circumstance: The Draft, the War, and the Vietnam Generation.* New York: Knopf.

Baum, Matthew A. and Potter, Philip B. K. 2008. The Relationship Between Mass Media, Public Opinion, and Foreign Policy: Toward a Theoretical Synthesis. *Annual Review of Political Science*, 11 (June), 39–65.

Baumgart, Winfried. 1982. *Imperialism: The Idea and Reality of British and French Colonial Expansion, 1880–1914.* Revised edn. New York: Oxford University Press.

BBC News. 2006 (Aug. 27). Nasrallah Sorry for Scale of War.

Beck, Nathaniel and Katz, Jonathan N. 1995. What to Do and Not to Do with Time-Series Cross-Section Data. *American Political Science Review*, 89(3), 634–647.

2001. Throwing out the Baby with the Bathwater: A Comment on Green, Kim, and Yoon. *International Organization*, 55(2), 487–495.

2004 (July 26). *Time-Series Cross-Section Issues: Dynamics, 2004.* Working Paper.

Beck, Robert J. 1989. Munich's Lessons Reconsidered. *International Security*, 14(2), 161–191.

Beckett, Ian F. W. 2005. Soldiers, the Frontier and the Politics of Command in British India. *Small Wars & Insurgencies*, 16(3), 280–292.

Ben-Eliezer, Uri. 1998. *The Making of Israeli Militarism.* Bloomington: Indiana University Press.

Ben-Meir, Yehuda. 1995. *Civil–Military Relations in Israel.* New York: Columbia University Press.

Bennett, Bruce W. 2006. *A Brief Analysis of the Republic of Korea's Defense Reform Plan.* Occasional Paper OP-165-OSD. Santa Monica, Calif.: Rand Corporation.

Bennett, D. Scott and Stam, Allan. 1998. The Declining Advantages of Democracy: A Combined Model of War Outcomes and Duration. *Journal of Conflict Resolution*, 42(3), 344–366.

2000. EUGene: A Conceptual Manual. *International Interactions*, 26, 179–204.

Berinsky, Adam. 2007. Assuming the Costs of War: Events, Elites, and American Public Support for Military Conflict. *Journal of Politics*, 69(4), 975–997.

Berman, Larry. 1989. *Lyndon Johnson's War: The Road to Stalemate in Vietnam*. New York: Norton.

Beschloss, Michael R. 2001. *Reaching for Glory: Lyndon Johnson's Secret White House Tapes, 1964–1965*. New York: Simon & Schuster.

Betts, Richard K. 1991. *Soldiers, Statesmen, and Cold War Crises*. New York: Columbia University Press.

2005. The Political Support System for American Primacy. *International Affairs*, 81(1), 1–14.

Biddle, Stephen 2004. *Military Power: Explaining Victory and Defeat in Modern Battle*. Princeton University Press.

2005. *American Grand Strategy after 9/11: An Assessment*. Carlisle, Pa.: Strategic Studies Institute, U.S. Army War College.

Biddle, Stephen and Friedman, Jeffrey A. 2008. *The 2006 Lebanon Campaign and the Future of Warfare: Implications for Army and Defense Policy*. (Sept.). Carlisle, Pa.: Strategic Studies Institute, U.S. Army War College.

Biddle, Stephen and Long, Stephen. 2004. Democracy and Military Effectiveness: A Deeper Look. *Journal of Conflict Resolution*, 48(4), 525–546.

Birtle, Andrew J. 2008. PROVN, Westmoreland, and the Historians: A Reappraisal. *Journal of Military History*, 72(4), 1213–1247.

Black, Duncan 1948. On the Rationale of Group Decision Making. *Journal of Political Economy*, 37, 40–62.

Blackwood's Edinburgh Magazine. 1884. Taxation and Representation Under the New Reform Bill. 135 (June), 794–808.

Blake, Robert. 2010. *Disraeli*. New York: Faber and Faber.

Blyth, Robert J. 2003. *The Empire of the Raj: India, Eastern Africa and the Middle East, 1858–1947*. Basingstoke: Palgrave Macmillan.

Boix, Carles. 2003. *Democracy and Redistribution*. Cambridge Studies in Comparative Politics. Cambridge and New York: Cambridge University Press.

Bond, Brian. 1967. The Third China War, 1860. In Brian Bond (ed.), *Victorian Military Campaigns*. London: Hutchinson, 31–68.

Boot, Max. 2003. The New American Way of War. *Foreign Affairs*, 82(4), 41–59.

Bouton, Marshall M., Kull, Steven, Page, Benjamin, Veltcheva, Silvia, and Wright, Thomas. 2011. *Global Views 2010: American Public Opinion and Foreign Policy.* Ann Arbor: ICPSR.

Brauer, Jürgen and Van Tuyll, Hubert P. 2008. *Castles, Battles, & Bombs: How Economics Explains Military History.* University of Chicago Press.

Brodie, Bernard. 1959. *Strategy in the Missile Age.* Princeton University Press.

Brooks, Clem and Manza, Jeff. 2007. *Why Welfare States Persist: The Importance of Public Opinion in Democracies.* University of Chicago Press.

Brooks, Stephen G. 2005. *Producing Security: Multinational Corporations, Globalization, and the Changing Calculus of Conflict.* Princeton University Press.

Bueno de Mesquita, Bruce and Downs, George W. 2006. Intervention and Democracy. *International Organization*, 60(3), 627–649.

Bueno de Mesquita, Bruce, Morrow, James D., Siverson, Randolph M., and Smith, Alastair. 1999. An Institutional Explanation of the Democratic Peace. *American Political Science Review*, 93(4), 791–807.

Bueno de Mesquita, Bruce, Smith, Alastair, Siverson, Randolph M., and Morrow, James D. 2003. *The Logic of Political Survival.* Cambridge, Mass.: MIT Press.

Burn, William Laurence. 1964. *The Age of Equipoise: A Study of the mid-Victorian Generation.* New York: Norton.

Bush, George W. 2002 (Sept. 17). *The National Security Strategy of the United States.* Washington, DC.

Buzzanco, Robert. 1996. *Masters of War: Military Dissent and Politics in the Vietnam Era.* New York: Cambridge University Press.

Byman, Daniel and Simon, Steven. 2006. The No-Win Zone: An After-Action Report from Lebanon. *The National Interest*, November/December, 55–61.

Cain, P. J. 2007. Capitalism, Aristocracy and Empire: Some "Classical" Theories of Imperialism Revisited. *Journal of Imperial and Commonwealth History*, 35(1), 25–47.

Carter, David B. and Signorino, Curtis S. 2010. Back to the Future: Modeling Time Dependence in Binary Data. *Political Analysis*, 18(3), 271–292.

Caverley, Jonathan D. 2010a. Explaining U.S. Military Strategy in Vietnam: Thinking Clearly about Causation. *International Security*, 35(3), 124–143.

2010b. The Myth of Military Myopia: Democracy, Small Wars, and Vietnam. *International Security*, 34(3), 119–157.

Chapman, John. 1878. India and Our Colonial Empire. *Westminster Review*, 53(2), 569–598.

Chernoff, Fred. 2004. The Study of Democratic Peace and Progress in International Relations. *International Studies Review*, 6(1), 49–77.

Churchill, Winston. 1906. *Lord Randolph Churchill*. Vol. 2. London: Macmillan.

2004. *The River War*. Whitefish, Mont.: Kessinger Publishing.

Clayton, Anthony. 1988. *France, Soldiers, and Africa*. London: Brassey's.

Clerke, Aubrey St. John. 1878. The Military Forces of the Crown: Their Administration and Government. *Quarterly Review*, 146(291), 232–255.

Clinton, William J. 1998 (Oct.). *A National Security Strategy for a New Century*. Washington, DC.

Clodfelter, Mark. 2006. *The Limits of Air Power: The American Bombing of North Vietnam*. Lincoln: University of Nebraska Press.

Cobden, Richard. 1903. *The Political Writings of Richard Cobden*. 4th edn. Vol. I. London: T. Fisher Unwin.

Cohen, Eliot A. 1984. Constraints on America's Conduct of Small Wars. *International Security*, 9(2), 151–181.

Cohen, Stuart A. 2006. Changing Civil–Military Relations in Israel: Towards an Oversubordinate IDF? *Israel Affairs*, 12(4), 769–788.

2008. *Israel and its Army: From Cohesion to Confusion*. Abingdon: Routledge.

Colaresi, Michael P., Rasler, Karen A., and Thompson, William R. 2007. *Strategic Rivalries in World Politics: Position, Space and Conflict Escalation*. Cambridge University Press.

Collier, David, Mahoney, James, and Seawright, Jason. 2004. Claiming Too Much: Warnings about Selection Bias. In David Collier and Henry E. Brady (eds.), *Rethinking Social Inquiry: Diverse Tools, Shared Standards*. Lanham, Md.: Rowman & Littlefield, 75–83.

Commission for the Examination of the Events of the 2006 Campaign in Lebanon [Winograd Commission]. 2008. *The Second Lebanon War*. Final Report [Winograd Report]. Vol. 1. Tel Aviv. Translated from Hebrew by Open Source Center, Reston Va., Feb.

Congressional Budget Office. 2012 (Nov.). *Costs of Military Pay and Benefits in the Defense Budget*. United States Congress, Washington, DC.

2013. *The Army's Ground Combat Vehicle Program and Alternatives*. Washington, DC: Congressional Budget Office.

Cooper, Richard V. L. 1977. *Military Manpower and the All-Volunteer Force*. Santa Monica, Calif.: Rand Corporation.

Cordesman, Anthony H. 2008 (Mar. 11). *Air Combat Trends in the Afghan and Iraq Wars.* Washington, DC: Center for Strategic & International Studies.

Corum, James S. and Johnson, Wray R. 2003. *Airpower in Small Wars: Fighting Insurgents and Terrorists.* Lawrence, Kan.: University Press of Kansas.

Crane, Conrad C. 2002. *Avoiding Vietnam: The U.S. Army's Response to Defeat in Southeast Asia.* Carlisle Barracks, Pa.: Strategic Studies Institute.

Crawford, Neta. 2011 (June 13). Assessing the Human Toll of the Post-9/11 Wars: The Dead and Wounded in Afghanistan, Iraq, and Pakistan, 2001–2011. Available at http://costsofwar.org/sites/default/files/CrawfordAssessingTheHumanToll.pdf.

Crawford, Timothy and Kuperman, Alan J. (eds.) 2006. *Gambling on Humanitarian Intervention: Moral Hazard, Rebellion, and Civil War.* New York: Routledge.

Crosby, Travis L. 2011. *Joseph Chamberlain: A Most Radical Imperialist.* London: I. B. Tauris.

Cunningham, Hugh. 1971. Jingoism in 1877–88. *Victorian Studies*, 14 (June), 429–453.

Darwin, John. 1997. Imperialism and the Victorians: The Dynamics of Territorial Expansion. *English Historical Review*, 112(447), 614–642.

Davis, Lance E. and Huttenback, Robert A. 1988. *Mammon and the Pursuit of Empire: The Economics of British Imperialism.* Cambridge University Press.

De Boef, Suzanna and Granato, Jim. 1997. Near-Integrated Data and the Analysis of Political Relationships. *American Journal of Political Science*, 41(2), 619–640.

Desch, M. C. 2002. Democracy and Victory: Why Regime Type Hardly Matters. *International Security*, 27(2), 5–47.

Dilke, Charles W. 1888. *The British Army.* London: Chapman and Hall.

Dion, Michelle L. and Birchfield, Vicki. 2010. Economic Development, Income Inequality, and Preferences for Redistribution. *International Studies Quarterly*, 54(2), 315–334.

Downes, Alexander B. 2009. How Smart and Tough are Democracies? Reassessing Theories of Democratic Victory in War. *International Security*, 33(4), 9–51.

Downs, Anthony. 1957. *An Economic Theory of Democracy.* New York: Harper & Brothers.

Doyle, Michael W. 1986. Liberalism and World Politics. *American Political Science Review*, 80(4), 1151–1163.

Drezner, Daniel. 2003. The Hidden Hand of Economic Coercion. *International Organization*, 57(3), 643–659.

Dueck, Colin. 2009. Neoclassical Realism and the National Interest: Presidents, Domestic Politics and Major Military Interventions. In Steven E. Lobell, Norrin M. Ripsman, and Jeffrey W. Taliaferro (eds.), *Neoclassical Realism, the State, and Foreign Policy.* Cambridge University Press, 139–169.

Dumbrell, John. 2012. *Rethinking the Vietnam War.* Basingstoke: Macmillan.

Dunlap, Charles J. 2008. We Still Need the Big Guns. *The New York Times,* Jan. 8.

Durrans, P. J. 1982. A Two-Edged Sword: The Liberal Attack on Disraelian Imperialism. *Journal of Imperial and Commonwealth History,* 10(3), 262–284.

Echenberg, Myron J. 1991. *Colonial Conscripts: The Tirailleurs Senegalais in French West Africa, 1857–1960.* Portsmouth, NH: Heinemann.

Edwards, Paul N. 1996. *The Closed World: Computers and the Politics of Discourse in Cold War America.* Cambridge, Mass.: MIT Press.

Eichenberg, Richard C. and Stoll, Richard J. 2012. Gender Difference or Parallel Publics? The Dynamics of Defense Spending Opinions in the United States, 1965–2007. *Journal of Conflict Resolution,* 58(2), 331–348.

Eisenhower, Dwight D. 1961. Farewell Address to the American People. In *Public Papers of the Presidents: The American Presidency Project.* National Archives.

Eldridge, C. C. 1984. *British Imperialism in the Nineteenth Century.* London: Macmillan.

Evans, Rowland and Novak, Robert. 1966. Inside Report... The Vietnam Wall. *The Washington Post,* Aug. 1, A15.

1967. Opposition to the Wall; McNamara Didn't Say Two of the Joint Chiefs of Staff Were Against a Wall in Vietnam. *The Washington Post,* Oct. 8, B7.

Even, Shmuel. 2011. Israel's National Security Economy: Defense and Social Challenges. In Anat Kurz and Shlomo Brom (eds.), *Strategic Survey for Israel, 2011.* Tel Aviv: Institute for National Security Studies.

Fallows, James. 2008. The $1.4 Trillion Question. *The Atlantic Monthly,* Jan.–Feb.

Farnham, Barbara 2003. The Theory of Democratic Peace and Threat Perception. *International Studies Quarterly,* 47(3), 395–415.

Farquhar, Scott C. 2009. *Back to Basics: A Study of the Second Lebanon War and Operation CAST LEAD.* Fort Leavenworth, Kan.: Combat Studies Institute Press.

Fearon, James D. 1995. Rationalist Explanations for War. *International Organization,* 49(3), 379–414.

1997. Signaling Foreign Policy Interests: Tying Hands versus Sinking Costs. *Journal of Conflict Resolution*, 41(1), 68–90.
2002. Selection Effects and Deterrence. *International Interactions*, 28(1), 5–29.

Fearon, James D. and Laitin, David D. 2003. Ethnicity, Insurgency, and Civil War. *American Political Science Review*, 97(1), 75–90.

Featherstone, Donald. 1973. *Colonial Small Wars 1837–1901*. Newton Abbot: David & Charles.

Feickert, Andrew. 2005 (Apr. 28). *The Army's Future Combat System (PCS): Background and Issues for Congress*. Washington, DC: Congressional Research Service.
2013 (June 14). *The Army's Ground Combat Vehicle (GCV) Program: Background and Issues for Congress*. Report No. R41597. Washington, DC: Congressional Research Service.

Ferguson, Niall. 2003. *Empire: The Rise and Demise of the British World Order and the Lessons for Global Power*. New York: Basic Books.

Ferris, John Robert. 1989. *Men, Money, and Diplomacy: The Evolution of British Strategic Policy, 1919–26*. Ithaca, NY: Cornell University Press.
2003. A New American Way of War? C4ISR, Intelligence and Information Operations in Operation 'Iraqi Freedom': A Provisional Assessment. *Intelligence and National Security*, 18(4), 155–174.

Filson, Darren and Werner, Suzanne. 2004. Bargaining and Fighting: The Impact of Regime Type on War Onset, Duration, and Outcomes. *American Journal of Political Science*, 48(2), 296–313.

Fordham, Benjamin O. and Walker, Thomas C. 2005. Kantian Liberalism, Regime Type, and Military Resource Allocation: Do Democracies Spend Less? *International Studies Quarterly*, 49(1), 141–157.

Foster, R. F. 1981. *Lord Randolph Churchill: A Political Life*. Oxford: Clarendon Press.

Freilich, Charles. 2012. *Zion's Dilemmas: How Israel Makes National Security Policy*. Ithaca, NY: Cornell University Press.

French Defense Ministry. 2013. *Livre Blanc: Defense et Sécurité Nationale*.

French Defense. Ministry. 2008. *Livre blanc sur la défense et la sécurité nationale 2008*.

Friedberg, Aaron L. 1988. *The Weary Titan: Britain and the Experience of Relative Decline, 1895–1905*. Princeton University Press.

Friedman, Jeffrey A. 2011. Manpower and Counterinsurgency: Empirical Foundations for Theory and Doctrine. *Security Studies*, 20, 556–591.

Gaddis, John Lewis. 1982. *Strategies of Containment: A Critical Appraisal of Postwar American National Security Policy*. New York: Oxford University Press.

2009. *The Use of Force: Military Power and International Politics.* 7th edn. Lanham, Md.: Rowman & Littlefield. Chapter 8: Implementing Flexible Response: Vietnam as a Test Case.

Galbraith, John S. and al Sayyid-Marsot, Afa Lufti. 1978. The British Occupation of Egypt: Another View. *International Journal of Middle East Studies*, 9(4), 471–488.

Gallucci, Robert L. 1975. *Neither Peace nor Honor: The Politics of American Military Policy in Viet-Nam.* Studies in International Affairs 24. Baltimore: Johns Hopkins University Press.

Gallup/CNN/USA Today. 2006 (Mar.). *Gallup/CNN/USA Today Poll, March, 2006.* iPOLL Databank, The Roper Center for Public Opinion Research, University of Connecticut.

Gartzke, Eric. 2001. Democracy and the Preparation for War: Does Regime Type Affect States' Anticipation of Casualties? *International Studies Quarterly*, 45, 467–484.

Gavin, James M. 1966. The Easy Chair: A Communication on Vietnam. *Harper's Magazine*, 232(1389), 16–18.

Gelb, Leslie H. 1972 (Apr.). The Essential Domino: American Politics and Vietnam. *Foreign Affairs.*

Gelb, Leslie H. and Betts, Richard K. 1979. *The Irony of Vietnam: The System Worked.* Washington, DC: Brookings Institution.

Gelpi, Christopher, Feaver, Peter, and Reifler, Jason. 2006. Success Matters: Casualty Sensitivity and the War in Iraq. *International Security*, 30(3), 7–46.

Gershovich, Moshe. 2000. *French Military Rule in Morocco: Colonialism and its Consequences.* Portland, Oreg.: Frank Cass.

Geys, Benny. 2010. Wars, Presidents, and Popularity: The Political Cost(s) of War Re-Examined. *Public Opinion Quarterly*, 74(2), 357–374.

Gibbons, William Conrad. 1994. *The U.S. Government and the Vietnam War: Executive and Legislative Roles and Relationships.* Princeton University Press.

Gibler, Douglas M. and Sarkees, Meredith. 2004. Measuring Alliances: The Correlates of War Formal Interstate Alliance Database 1916–2000. *Journal of Peace Research*, 41(2), 211–222.

Gifford, Brian. 2006. Why No Trade-off between "Guns and Butter"? Armed Forces and Social Spending in the Advanced Industrial Democracies, 1960–1993. *American Journal of Sociology*, 112(2), 473–509.

Gilens, Martin. 2012. *Affluence and Influence: Economic Inequality and Political Power in America.* Princeton University Press.

Gladstone, William E. 1879. *Political Speeches in Scotland.* London: W. Ridgway.

Glaser, Charles L. 1994. Realists as Optimists: Cooperation as Self-Help. *International Security*, 19(3), 50–90.

Gleditsch, Nils Petter, Wallensteen, Peter, Sollenberg, Margareta, and Strand, Håvard. 2002. Armed Conflict 1946–2001: A New Dataset. *Journal of Peace Research*, 39(5), 615–637.

Goldberg, Jeffrey. 2002. In the Party of God. *The New Yorker*, Oct. 14.

Goldsmith, Benjamin E. 2007. Defense Effort and Institutional Theories of Democratic Peace and Victory: Why Try Harder? *Security Studies*, 16(2), 189–222.

Gooch, John. 1981. *The Prospect of War: Studies in British Defence Policy 1847–1942*. London: Frank Cass.

Goodrich, Caspar F. 1885. *Report of the British Naval and Military Operations in Egypt, 1882*. Washington, DC: Government Printing Office.

Gordon, Michael R. and Trainer, Bernard E. 2006. *Cobra II: The Inside Story of the Invasion and Occupation of Iraq*. New York: Pantheon Books.

Gowa, Joanne. 1998. Politics at the Water's Edge: Parties, Voters, and the Use of Force Abroad. *International Organization*, 52(2), 307–324.

Graff, Henry F. 1970. *The Tuesday Cabinet: Deliberation and Decision on Peace and War under Lyndon B. Johnson*. Englewood Cliffs, NJ: Prentice-Hall.

Gravel, Mike. 1971. *The Pentagon Papers: The Defense Department History of United States Decision-making on Vietnam*. Boston: Beacon Press.

Gray, Colin S. 2006. *Irregular Enemies and the Essence of Strategy: Can the American Way of War Adapt?* Carlisle, Pa.: Strategic Studies Institute, U.S. Army War College.

Greg, W. R. 1878. Foreign Policy of Great Britain: Imperial or Domestic? *The Nineteenth Century and After: A Monthly Review*, 4(19), 393–407.

Griffin, Christopher. 2010. Major Combat Operations and Counterinsurgency Warfare: Plan Challe in Algeria, 1959–1960. *Security Studies*, 19(3), 555–589.

Gurr, Ted Robert, Marshall, Monty G., and Jaggers, Keith. 2002. *Polity IV Project: Political Regime Characteristics and Transitions, 1800–2012*. Available at www.systemicpeace.org/polity/polity4.htm.

Gutteridge, William F. 1970. *Colonialism in Africa, 1870–1960*. Vol. 4: *The Economics of Colonialism*. Cambridge University Press.

Haaretz. 2007. *Main Findings of the Winograd Partial Report on the Second Lebanon War.*

Haaretz. 2007. Nasrallah praises Winograd report. May 5.

Halberstam, David. 2001. *The Best and the Brightest*. New York: Modern Library.

Hamilton, George Francis. 1917. *Parliamentary Reminiscences and Reflections.* Vol. II: *1886–1906.* London: John Murray.

Hanning, Hugh. 1969. *Lessons from the Vietnam War: Report of a Seminar held at the Royal United Service Institution.* London: Royal United Service Institution.

Harcourt, Freda 1980. Disraeli Imperialism, 1866–1868: A Question of Timing. *Historical Journal,* 23(1), 87–109.

Harel, Amos. 2008. Analysis: IDF Plans to Use Disproportionate Force in Next War. *Haaretz,* May 10.

Harel, Amos and Issacharoff, Avi. 2008. *34 days: Israel, Hezbollah, and the War in Lebanon.* New York: Palgrave Macmillan.

Harling, Philip. 2003. Equipoise Regained? Recent Trends in British Political History, 1790–1867. *Journal of Modern History,* 75, 890–918.

Harris, Edward. 2007 (Dec.). *Historical Effective Federal Tax Rates: 1979 to 2005.* Washington, DC: Congressional Budget Office.

Harris, Jose. 1993. *Private Lives, Public Spirit: A Social History of Britain, 1870–1914.* Oxford University Press.

Harris, Walter B. 1927. *France, Spain and the Rif.* London: Arnold.

Harrison, Robert T. 1995. *Gladstone's Imperialism in Egypt: Techniques of Domination.* Westport, Conn.: Greenwood Press.

Hayes, Jarrod. Forthcoming. *Constructing National Security: U.S. Relations with China and India.* Cambridge University Press.

Helman, Sara. 1999. From Soldiering and Motherhood to Citizenship: A Study of Four Israeli Peace Protest Movements. *Social Politics,* 6(3), 292–313.

Hennessy, Michael A. 1997. *Strategy in Vietnam: The Marines and Revolutionary Warfare in 1 Corps, 1965–1972.* Westport, Conn.: Praeger.

Herring, George C. 1986. *America's Longest War: The United States and Vietnam, 1950–1975.* 2nd edn. New York: Knopf.
    1994. *LBJ and Vietnam: A Different Kind of War.* Austin: University of Texas Press.

Heston, Alan, Summers, Robert, and Aten, Bettina. 2006 (Sept.). *Penn World Table Version 6.2.*

Hewitt, Martin (ed.) 2000. *An Age of Equipoise: Reassessing Mid-Victorian Britain.* Aldershot: Ashgate.

Hobson, John A. 1902. *Imperialism: A Study.* London: James Nisbet.

Hoffman, Frank G. 1996. *Decisive Force: The New American Way of War.* Westport, Conn.: Praeger.
    2009. Hybrid Warfare and Challenges. *Joint Forces Quarterly,* 52(1), 34–39.

Holland, Robert F. 1991. *The Pursuit of Greatness: Britain and the World Role, 1900–1970*. London: Fontana.

Home, Alistair. 1984. *The French Army and Politics, 1870–1970*. New York: Peter Bedrick Books.

Honaker, James, King, Gary, and Blackwell, Matthew. 2009 (July 12). *Amelia II: A Program for Missing Data*, Version 1.2-12.

Hopkins, A. G. 1986. The Victorians and Africa: A Reconsideration of the Occupation of Egypt, 1882. *Journal of African History*, 27(2), 363–391.

Horowitz, Michael C. and Levendusky, Matthew S. 2011. Drafting Support for War: Conscription and Mass Support for Warfare. *Journal of Politics*, 73(3), 524–534.

Horowitz, Michael C., Simpson, Erin M., and Stam, Allan C. 2011. Domestic Institutions and Wartime Casualties. *International Studies Quarterly*, 55(4), 909–936.

Hozier, Henry M. 1869. *The British Expedition to Abyssinia*. London: Macmillan.

Hunt, Richard A. 1995. *Pacification: The American Struggle for Vietnam's Hearts and Minds*. Boulder: Westview Press.

Huntington, Samuel P. 1957. *The Soldier and the State: The Theory and Politics of Civil–Military Relations*. Cambridge, Mass.: Belknap Press of Harvard University Press.

India Office. 1900. Return of Wars and Military Operations on or beyond Borders of British India in which Government of India has been engaged since 1849. Page 847 of *House of Commons Papers*. 19th Century House of Commons Sessional Papers, vol. LVIII, no. 13.

1905. East India (Employment of Troops out of India). Page 545 of *House of Commons Papers*. 20th Century House of Commons Sessional Papers, vol. LVII, no. 99.

International Institute of Strategic Studies (IISS). 2013. *The Military Balance 2013*. London: Routledge.

Israel National Election Study. 2006. Tel Aviv: Tel Aviv University.

Israeli Central Bureau of Statistics. 2011 (Sept. 7). *Income Survey, 2010*.

Israeli Central Bureau of Statistics. 2013 (Feb. 2). *Defence Expenditure in Israel, 1950–2011*.

Iversen, Torben and Soskice, David. 2006. Electoral Institutions and the Politics of Coalitions: Why Some Democracies Redistribute More Than Others. *American Political Science Review*, 100(2), 165–181.

Jackson, Matthew O. and Morelli, Massimo. 2007. Political Bias and War. *American Economic Review*, 97(4), 1353–1373.

Jacob, Mark and Benzkofer, Stephan. 2012. 10 things you might not know about the Afghan war. *Chicago Tribune*, Apr. 22.

Jacobs, Lawrence R. and Page, Benjamin I. 2005. Who Influences U.S. Foreign Policy? *American Political Science Review*, 99(1), 107–123.

Jaffe, Greg. 2009. Short '06 Lebanon War Stokes Pentagon Debate. *Washington Post*, Apr. 6.

Jeffrey, Keith. 1982. The Eastern Arc of Empire: A Strategic View 1850–1950. *Journal of Strategic Studies*, 5(4), 531–545.

Jennings, Louis John. 1882. The Justification of Lord Beaconsfield's Policy. *Quarterly Review*, 154(308), 542–570.

Jerusalem Post. 2007. Nasrallah praises Israel's investigation of war. May 12.

Johns, Andrew L. 2010. *Vietnam's Second Front: Domestic Politics, the Republican Party, and the War.* Lexington, Ky.: University Press of Kentucky.

Johnson, Chalmers. 2004. *The Sorrows of Empire: Militarism, Secrecy and the End of the Republic.* New York: Henry Holt.

Johnson, Dominic D. P. 2004. *Overconfidence and War: The Havoc and Glory of Positive Illusions.* Cambridge, Mass.: Harvard University Press.

Justman, Moshe and Gradstein, Mark. 1999. The Industrial Revolution, Political Transition, and the Subsequent Decline in Inequality in 19th-century Britain. *Explorations in Economic History*, 36(2), 109–127.

Kant, Immanuel. 1991. Perpetual Peace. In *Kant's Political Writings*, ed. H. B. Nisbet and H. Reiss. 2nd edn. Cambridge University Press.

Kapstein, Ethan B. 1992. *The Political Economy of National Security: A Global Perspective.* Columbia, SC: University of South Carolina Press.

Katz, Yaakov. 2008. Security and Defense: The Story of 'Changing Direction 11'. *Jerusalem Post*, Jan. 10.

Kaufmann, Chaim D. 2004. Threat Inflation and the Failure of the Marketplace of Ideas: The Selling of the Iraq War. *International Security*, 29(1), 5–48.

Kennedy, John F. 1961a. Special Message to the Congress on the Defense Budget. In John T. Woolley and Gerhard Peters (eds.), *The American Presidency Project [online]*. Santa Barbara, Calif.: University of California (hosted).

1961b. Special Message to the Congress on Urgent National Needs. In John T. Woolley and Gerhard Peters (eds.), *The American Presidency Project [online]*. Santa Barbara, Calif.: University of California (hosted).

Kennedy, Paul M. 1989. *The Rise and Fall of the Great Powers: Economic Change and Military Conflict from 1500 to 2000.* New York: Vintage Books.

Kenworthy, Lane and Pontusson, Jonas. 2005. Rising Inequality and the Politics of Redistribution in Affluent Countries. *Perspectives on Politics*, 3(3), 449–471.

Keohane, Robert O. 1984. *After Hegemony: Cooperation and Discord in the World Political Economy.* Princeton University Press.

Kier, Elizabeth. 1997. *Imagining War: French and British Military Doctrine between the Wars.* Princeton University Press.

Killingray, David. 1979. The Idea of a British Imperial African Army. *Journal of African History*, 20(3), 421–436.

1984. "A Swift Agent of Government": Air Power in British Colonial Africa, 1916–1939. *Journal of African History*, 25(4), 429–444.

1989. Labor Exploitation for Military Campaigns in British Colonial Africa 1870–1945. *Journal of Contemporary History*, 24(3), 483–501.

King, Gary, Keohane, Robert O., and Verba, Sidney. 1994. *Designing Social Inquiry: Scientific Inference in Qualitative Research.* Princeton University Press.

Kipp, Robert M. 1968. Counterinsurgency from 30,000 Feet: The B-52 in Vietnam. *Air University Review*, 19(2), 10–18.

Kisangani, Emizet F. and Pickering, Jeffrey. 2008. International Military Intervention, 1989–2005. Jan. 29. Available at www.icpsr.umich.edu/icpsrweb/ICPSR/studies/21282.

Knaplund, Paul. 1935. *Gladstone's Foreign Policy.* New York: Harper & Brothers.

Knight, Melvin M. 1937. *Morocco as a French Economic Venture: A Study of Open Door Imperialism.* London: Appleton.

Kober, Avi. 2008. The Israel Defense Forces in the Second Lebanon War: Why the Poor Performance? *Journal of Strategic Studies*, 31(1), 3–40.

Komer, R. W. 1973. *Bureaucracy Does Its Thing: Institutional Constraints on U.S. -/GVN Performance in Vietnam.* Santa Monica, Calif.: Rand Corporation.

Krehbiel, Keith. 1998. *Pivotal Politics: A Theory of U.S. Lawmaking.* University of Chicago Press.

Krepinevich, Andrew F. 1986. *The Army and Vietnam.* Baltimore: Johns Hopkins University Press.

Kriner, Douglas L. and Shen, Francis X. 2010. *The Casualty Gap: The Causes and Consequences of American Wartime Inequalities.* Oxford University Press.

Lake, David A. 1992. Powerful Pacifists: Democratic States and War. *American Political Science Review*, 86(1), 24–37.

Lambeth, Benjamin S. 2011. *Air Operations in Israel's War against Hezbollah: Learning from Lebanon and Getting it Right in Gaza.* Santa Monica, Calif.: Rand Corporation.

Lane-Poole, Stanley. 1882. The War in Egypt. *British Quarterly Review*, 76 (Oct.), 388–420.

Laqueur, Walter. 1998. *Guerrilla Warfare: A Historical and Critical Study*. 2nd edn. New Brunswick, NJ: Transaction Books.

Lebel, Udi. 2007. Civil Society versus Military Sovereignty. *Armed Forces and Society*, 34(1), 67–89.

Lektzian, David J. and Sprecher, Christopher M. 2007. Sanctions, Signals, and Militarized Conflict. *American Journal of Political Science*, 51(2), 415–431.

Lenin, Vladimir I. 1987. *Imperialism, the Highest Stage of Capitalism*. In *Essential Works of Lenin : 'What is to be done?' and Other Writings*, ed. Henry M. Christman. New York: Dover Publications.

Leventoglu, Bahar and Tarar, Ahmar. 2005. Prenegotiation Public Commitment in Domestic and International Bargaining. *American Political Science Review*, 99(3), 419–433.

Levi, Margaret. 1997. *Consent, Dissent, and Patriotism: Political Economy of Institutions and Decisions*. Cambridge University Press.

Levy, Yagil. 2007. *Israel's Materialist Militarism*. Lanham, Md.: Lexington Books.

   2010. The Second Lebanon War: Examining 'Democratization of War' Theory. *Armed Forces and Society*, 36(5), 786–803.

Lifshitz, Yaacov. 2010. *The Global Arms Trade: A Handbook*. London: Routledge.

Lin, Eric S. and Ali, Hamid E. 2009. Military Spending and Inequality: Panel Granger Causality Test. *Journal of Peace Research*, 46(5), 671–685.

Lipson, Charles. 2003. *Reliable Partners: How Democracies Have Made a Separate Peace*. Princeton University Press.

Lock-Pulla, Richard. 2004. *U.S. Intervention Policy and Army Innovation: From Vietnam to Iraq*. London: Routledge.

Logevall, Fredrik. 1999. *Choosing War: The Lost Chance for Peace and the Escalation of War in Vietnam*. Berkeley, Calif.: University of California Press.

Lorell, Mark A. (ed.) 1989. *Airpower in Peripheral Conflict: The French Experience in Africa*. Project Air Force. Santa Monica, Calif.: Rand Corporation.

Lorell, Mark A. and Kelley, Charles J. 1985 (March). *Casualties, Public Opinion, and Presidential Policy During the Vietnam War*. Technical Report R-3060-AF. Project Air Force. Santa Monica, Calif.: Rand Corporation.

Lowenstein, Roger. 2008. The Education of Ben Bernanke. *The New York Times Magazine*, Jan. 20.

Lucas, Charles Prestwood. 1921. *The Empire at War*. Vol. 1. London and New York: H. Milford/Oxford University Press/Royal Empire Society (Great Britain).

Lucy, Henry William. 1885. *A Diary of Two Parliaments*. 2nd edn. London: Cassell.

Lyall, Jason 2010. Do Democracies Make Inferior Counterinsurgents? Reassessing Democracy's Impact on War Outcomes and Duration. *International Organization*, 64(1), 167–192.

Lyall, Jason and Wilson III, Isaiah. 2009. Rage Against the Machines: Explaining Outcomes in Counterinsurgency Wars. *International Organization*, 63(1), 67–106.

MacDonagh, Oliver. 1962. The Anti-Imperialism of Free Trade. *Economic History Review*, 14(3), 489–501.

Mack, Andrew. 1975. Why Big Nations Lose Small Wars: The Politics of Asymmetric Conflict. *World Politics*, 27(2), 175–200.

MacKenzie, John M. 1984. *Propaganda and Empire: The Manipulation of British Public Opinion (1880–1960)*. Manchester University Press.

1999. Empire and Metropolitan Cultures. In Andrew N. Porter, Alaine Low, and William Roger Louis (eds.), *The Oxford History of the British Empire*. Vol. 3: *The Nineteenth Century*. Oxford University Press, 270–293.

Mahajan, Sneh. 2002. *British Foreign Policy, 1874–1914: The Role of India*. London: Routledge.

Mahnken, Thomas G. 2013. *Technology and the American Way of War since 1945*. New York: Columbia University Press.

Malkasian, Carter. 2004. Toward a Better Understanding of Attrition: The Korean and Vietnam Wars. *Journal of Military History*, 68(3), 911–942.

Mann, Michael. 2003. *Incoherent Empire*. London and New York: Verso.

Mansfield, Edward D. and Snyder, Jack L. 2005. *Electing to Fight: Why Emerging Democracies Go to War*. BCSIA Studies in International Security. Cambridge, Mass.: MIT Press.

Maoz, Zeev 1989. Power, Capabilities, and Paradoxical Conflict Outcomes. *World Politics*, 41(2), 239–266.

2006. *Defending the Holy Land: A Critical Analysis of Israel's Security Foreign Policy*. Ann Arbor: University of Michigan Press.

Maoz, Zeev and Russett, Bruce 1993. Normative and Structural Causes of Democratic Peace, 1946–1986. *American Political Science Review*, 87(3), 624–638.

Markham, Clements R. 1868. The Abyssinian Expedition. *Macmillan's Magazine*, 106 (August), 289–296.

Markusen, Ann R. 1991. *The Rise of the Gunbelt: The Military Remapping of Industrial America*. New York: Oxford University Press.

May, Ernest R. 2000. *Strange Victory: Hitler's Conquest of France*. New York: Hill & Wang.

McAllister, James. 2010. Who Lost Vietnam? Soldiers, Civilians, and U.S. Military Strategy. *International Security*, 35(3), 95–123.

McIntyre, W. David. 1967. *The Imperial Frontier in the Tropics, 1865–75: A Study of British Colonial Policy in West Africa, Malaya and the South Pacific in the Age of Gladstone and Disraeli*. London: Macmillan.

McMaster, H. R. 1997. *Dereliction of Duty: Lyndon Johnson, Robert McNamara, the Joint Chiefs of Staff, and the Lies that Led to Vietnam*. New York: HarperCollins.

2008. On War: Lessons to be Learned. *Survival*, 50(1), 19–30.

McNeill, William H. 1982. *The Pursuit of Power: Technology, Armed Force, and Society since A.D. 1000*. University of Chicago Press.

Mearsheimer, John J. 1995. The False Promise of International Institutions. *International Security*, 19(3), 5–49.

2001. *The Tragedy of Great Power Politics*. New York: Norton.

Meltzer, Allan H. and Richard, Scott F. 1981. A Rational Theory of the Size of Government. *Journal of Political Economy*, 89(5), 914–927.

Mencken, H. L. 1916. *A Little Book in C Major*. New York: John Lane.

Merom, Gil. 2003. *How Democracies Lose Small Wars: State, Society, and the Failures of France in Algeria, Israel in Lebanon, and the United States in Vietnam*. New York: Cambridge University Press.

2008. The Second Lebanon War: Democratic Lessons Imperfectly Applied. *Democracy and Security*, 4(1), 5–33.

Metcalf, Thomas R. 1994. *Ideologies of the Raj*. Vol. III, Pt. 4. Cambridge University Press.

2007. *Imperial Connections: India in the Indian Ocean Arena, 1860–1920*. Berkeley, Calif.: University of California Press.

Michael, Kobi. 2007. The Israel Defense Forces as an Epistemic Authority: An Intellectual Challenge in the Reality of the Israeli–Palestinian Conflict. *Journal of Strategic Studies*, 30(3), 421–446.

Miller, Benjamin. 2007. *States, Nations, and the Great Powers: The Sources of Regional War and Peace*. Cambridge University Press.

Milne, David. 2006. "Our Equivalent of Guerrilla Warfare": Walt Rostow and the Bombing of North Vietnam, 1961–1968. *Journal of Military History*, 71(1), 169–203.

Milner, Helen V. 1997. *Interests, Institutions, and Information: Domestic Politics and International Relations*. Princeton University Press.

Moene, K. O. and Wallerstein, M. 2001. Inequality, Social Insurance, and Redistribution. *American Political Science Review*, 95(4), 859–874.

2003. Earnings Inequality and Welfare Spending: A Disaggregated Analysis. *World Politics*, 55(4), 485–516.

Monypenny, William Flavelle and Buckle, George Earle. 1920a. *The Life of Benjamin Disraeli, Earl of Beaconsfield*. Vol. 5. New York: Macmillan.

1920b. *The Life of Benjamin Disraeli, Earl of Beaconsfield*. Vol. 6. New York: Macmillan.

Moravcsik, Andrew. 1997. Taking Preferences Seriously: A Liberal Theory of Politics. *International Organization*, 51(4), 512–553.

Morgan, T. Clifton and Palmer, Glenn 2003. To Protect and to Serve: Alliances and Foreign Policy Portfolios. *Journal of Conflict Resolution*, 47(2), 180–203.

Morris, James. 1974. *Heaven's Command: An Imperial Progress*. New York: Harcourt Brace Jovanovich.

Morrow, James D. 1993. Arms Versus Allies: Trade-offs in the Search for Security. *International Organization*, 47(2), 207–233.

Most, Benjamin A. and Starr, Harvey 1984. International Relations Theory, Foreign Policy Substitutability, and Nice Laws. *World Politics*, 36(3), 383–406.

Mousseau, Michael, Hegre, Havard, and Oneal, John R. 2003. How the Wealth of Nations Condition the Liberal Peace. *European Journal of International Relations*, 9(2), 277–314.

Mueller, John E. 1980. The Search for the "Breaking Point" in Vietnam. *International Studies Quarterly*, 24(4), 497–519.

Nagl, John A. 2005. *Learning to Eat Soup with a Knife: Counterinsurgency Lessons from Malaya and Vietnam*. University of Chicago Press.

Narizny, Kevin. 2007. *The Political Economy of Grand Strategy*. Ithaca: Cornell University Press.

NATO. 2011. *Information on Defence Expenditures*. Available at www.nato.int/cps/en/natolive/topics_49198htm.

O'Brien, Patrick K. 1988. The Costs and Benefits of British Imperialism 1846–1914. *Past and Present*, 120, 163–200.

OECD. 2011. *Divided We Stand: Why Inequality Keeps Rising*. Paris: OECD.

2012. *OECD Factbook 2011–2012: Economic, Environmental and Social Statistics*. Paris: OECD.

Offer, Avner. 1985. The Working Classes, British Naval Plans and the Coming of the Great War. *Past and Present*, 107(1), 204–226.

Olmert, Ehud. 2006 (July 17). Address to the Knesset by PM Ehud Olmert. Available at www.knesset.gov.i1/doc.s/eng/olmertspeech2006-eng.htm.

Olson, Mancur. 1982. *The Rise and Decline of Nations: Economic Growth, Stagflation, and Social Rigidities.* New Haven: Yale University Press.

1993. Dictatorship, Democracy, and Development. *American Political Science Review,* 87(3), 567–576.

Omissi, David E. 1990. *Air Power and Colonial Control: The Royal Air Force, 1919–1939.* Manchester University Press.

Owen, John M. 1994. How Liberalism Produces Democratic Peace. *International Security,* 19(2), 87–125.

Preparedness Investigating Subcommittee, Armed Services Committee, US Senate for 90th Cong., 1st sess. 1967. *Air War against North Vietnam.* Washington, DC: US Government Printing Office.

Page, Benjamin I., Bartels, Larry M., and Seawright, Jason. 2013. Democracy and the Policy Preferences of Wealthy Americans. *Perspectives on Politics,* 11(1), 51–73.

Pape, Robert Anthony. 1996. *Bombing to Win: Air Power and Coercion in War.* Ithaca: Cornell University Press.

2005. *Dying to Win: The Strategic Logic of Suicide Terrorism.* New York: Random House.

Peceny, Mark, Beer, Caroline C., and Sanchez-Terry, Shannon. 2003. Dictatorial Peace? *American Political Science Review,* 96(1), 15–26.

Peck, John. 1998. *War, the Army and Victorian Literature.* New York: St. Martin's Press.

Pennell, C. R. 1986. *A Country with a Government and a Flag: The Rif War in Morocco, 1921–1926.* Wisbech: Middle East and North African Studies Press.

Peri, Yoram. 2006. *Generals in the Cabinet Room: How the Military Shapes Israeli Policy.* Washington, DC: United States Institute of Peace Press.

Persson, Torsten and Tabellini, Guido Enrico. 2000. *Political Economics: Explaining Economic Policy.* Cambridge, Mass.: MIT Press.

Peterson, Michael E. 1989. *The Combined Action Platoons: The U.S. Marines' Other War in Vietnam.* New York: Praeger.

Peterson, Susan. 1995. How Democracies Differ: Public Opinion, State Structure, and the Lessons of the Fashoda Crisis. *Security Studies,* 5(1), 3–37.

Pew Center. 2011 (Sept.). *Pew Social Trends Poll.* iPOLL Databank, The Roper Center for Public Opinion Research, University of Connecticut.

Pincus, Walter. 2013. Closing Military Bases: Common Ground on the Wrong Front. *Washington Post,* Mar. 18.

Porch, Douglas. 2008. French Imperial Warfare, 1945–62. In Daniel Marston and Carter Malkasian (eds.), *Counterinsurgency in Modern Warfare*. Oxford: Osprey, 70–90.

Porter, Andrew N. 1988. The Balance Sheet of Empire, 1850–1914. *The Historical Journal*, 31(3), 685–699.

1999. Introduction: Britain and the Empire in the Nineteenth Century. In Andrew Porter, Elaine Low, and William Roger Louis (eds.), *The Oxford History of the British Empire*, vol. 3: *The Nineteenth Century*. Oxford University Press, 1–30.

1987. Lord Salisbury, Foreign Policy and Domestic Finance. In Lord Blake and Hugh Cecil (eds.), *Salisbury: The Man and His Policies*. London: Macmillan, 148–185.

(ed.) 2001. *The Oxford History of the British Empire*, vol. 3: *The Nineteenth Century*. Oxford University Press.

Porter, Bernard. 1987. *Britain, Europe, and the World, 1850–1986: Delusions of Grandeur*. 2nd edn. London: Allen & Unwin.

1996. *The Lion's Share: A Short History of British Imperialism, 1850–1995*. 3rd edn. London and New York: Longman.

2004. *The Absent-Minded Imperialists: Empire, Society, and Culture in Britain*. Oxford University Press.

Posen, Barry. 1984. *The Sources of Military Doctrine: France, Britain, and Germany between the World Wars*. Ithaca: Cornell University Press.

Powell, Robert. 1999. *In the Shadow of Power: States and Strategies in International Politics*. Princeton University Press.

Preston, Adrian. 1978. Wolseley, the Khartoum Relief Expedition and the Defence of India, 1885–1900. *Journal of Imperial and Commonwealth History*, 6(3), 254–280.

Price, Richard. 1972. *An Imperial War and the British Working Class: Working-Class Attitudes and Reactions to the Boer War 1899–1902*. London: Routledge & Kegan Paul.

Rabe, Stephen G. 1988. *Eisenhower and Latin America: The Foreign Policy of Anticommunism*. Chapel Hill, NC: University of North Carolina Press.

Rabe-Hesketh, Sophia, Skrondal, Anders, and Pickles Andrew. 2004 (Oct.). *GLLAMM Manual*. Technical Report 160. U.C. Berkeley Division of Biostatistics Working Paper Series, Berkeley, Calif.

Rama, Martin and Artecona, Raquel. 2002 (June 25). *A Database of Labor Market Indicators Across Countries*.

Rand Corporation. 2011. *Rand Database of Worldwide Terrorism Incidents*.

Rauchhaus, Robert. 2006. Conflict Management and the Misapplication of Moral Hazard Theory. In Timothy Crawford and Alan J. Kuperman (eds.), *Gambling on Humanitarian Intervention: Moral Hazard, Rebellion, and Internal War*. New York: Routledge, 64–73.

Ray, James L. 2003. Explaining Interstate Conflict and War: What Should Be Controlled For? *Conflict Management and Peace Science*, 20(2), 1–31.

2005. Constructing Multivariate Analyses (of Dangerous Dyads). *Conflict Management and Peace Science*, 22(4), 277–292.

Record, Jeffrey. 2007. *Beating Goliath: Why Insurgencies Win*. Washington, DC: Potomac Books.

Rego, Robert D. 2000. Anti-Infiltration Barrier Technology and the Battle for Southeast Asia (1966–1972). M.Phil. thesis, Air Command and Staff College, Air University, Maxwell Air Force Base, Alabama.

Reiter, Dan. 2003. Exploring the Bargaining Model of War. *Perspectives on Politics*, 1(1), 27–43.

Reiter, Dan and Stam, Allan C. 2002. *Democracies at War*. Princeton University Press.

Rivlin, Paul. 2011. *The Israeli Economy from the Foundation of the State through the 21st Century*. Cambridge University Press.

Robinson, Ronald Edward and Gallagher, John. 1968. *Africa and the Victorians: The Climax of Imperialism*. Garden City, NY: Doubleday.

Robson, Brian. 1991. Mounting an Expedition: Sir Gerald Graham's Expedition to Suakin. *Small Wars & Insurgencies*, 2(2), 232–239.

Rodgers, Nini. 1984. The Abyssinian Expedition of 1867–1868, Disraeli's Imperialism or James Murray's War? *Historical Journal*, 27(1), 129–149.

Rogowski, Ronald. 2004. How Inference in the Social (but Not the Physical) Sciences Neglects Theoretical Anomaly. In Henry E. Brady and David Collier (eds.), *Rethinking Social Inquiry: Diverse Tools, Shared Standards*. Lanham, Md.: Rowman & Littlefield, 75–83.

Rosato, Sebastian. 2003. The Flawed Logic of Democratic Peace Theory. *American Political Science Review*, 97(4), 586–602.

Rosen, Stephen P. 1982. Vietnam and the American Theory of Limited War. *International Security*, 7(2), 83–113.

Rostow, Walt W. 1972. *The Diffusion of Power: An Essay in Recent History*. New York: Macmillan.

Rowe, David M. 1999. World Economic Expansion and National Security in Pre-World War I Europe. *International Organization*, 53(2), 195–231.

2005. The Tragedy of Liberalism: How Globalization Caused the First World War. *Security Studies*, 14(3), 407–447.

Rowe, David M., Bearce, David H., and McDonald, Patrick J. 2002. Binding Prometheus: How the 19th Century Expansion of Trade

Impeded Britain's Ability to Raise an Army. *International Studies Quarterly*, 46(4), 551–578.

Russett, Bruce M. and Oneal, John R. 2001. *Triangulating Peace: Democracy, Interdependence, and International Organizations*. New York: Norton.

Select Committee on Duties Performed by British Army in India and Colonies. 1867–1868. *Report, Proceedings*. House of Commons Parliamentary Papers Vol. VI. 789.

Saturday Review of Politics, Literature, Science and Art. 1868 (May 9). Taxation and Expenditure, 25(654), 600–601.

1869 (Mar. 20). The Income-Tax. 27(699), 369–370.

Samatar, Abdi Ismail. 1989. *The State and Rural Transformation in Northern Somalia, 1884–1986*. Madison: University of Wisconsin Press.

Samuelson, Paul A. 1954. The Pure Theory of Public Expenditure. *Review of Economics and Statistics*, 36(4), 387–389.

Sandler, Todd and Hartley, Keith. 1995. *The Economics of Defense*. Cambridge University Press.

Saunders, Christopher and Smith, Iain R. 1999. Southern Africa, 1795–1910. In Andrew Porter, Alaine Low, and William Roger Louis (eds.), *The Oxford History of the British Empire*, vol. 3: *The Nineteenth Century*. Oxford University Press, 597–623.

Saunders, Elizabeth N. 2011. *Leaders at War: How Presidents Shape Military Interventions*. Ithaca: Cornell University Press.

Scales, Robert H. 2010. Small Unit Dominance: The Strategic Importance of Tactical Reform. *Armed Forces Journal*, 148(3), 14–16.

Schandler, Herbert Y. 1977. *The Unmaking of a President: Lyndon Johnson and Vietnam*. Princeton University Press.

Scheve, Kenneth and Stasavage, David. 2010. The Conscription of Wealth: Mass Warfare and the Demand for Progressive Taxation. *International Organization*, 64(4), 529–561.

Schneider, Howard. 2009. Israel Finds Strength in Its Missile Defenses. *Washington Post*, Sept. 19.

Schuessler, John M. 2010. The Deception Dividend: FDR's Undeclared War. *International Security*, 34(4), 133–165.

Schulimson, Jack, Blasiol, Leonard, Smith, Charles R., and Dawson, David A. 1997. *US Marines in Vietnam: 1968, The Defining Year*. History and Museums Division, United States Marine Corps.

Schultz, Kenneth A. 1999. Do Democratic Institutions Constrain or Inform? Contrasting Two Institutional Perspectives on Democracy and War. *International Organization*, 53(2), 233–266.

2001. *Democracy and Coercive Diplomacy*. Cambridge University Press.

Schultz, Kenneth A. and Weingast, Barry. 2003. The Democratic Advantage: Institutional Foundations of Financial Power in International Competition. *International Organization*, 57(1), 3–42.

Sechser, Todd S. 2007. *Winning Without a Fight: Power, Reputation, and Compellent Threats in International Crisis*. PhD thesis, Stanford University.

2011. Militarized Compellent Threats, 1918–2001. *Conflict Management and Peace Science*, 28(4), 377–401.

Sechser, Todd S. and Saunders, Elizabeth N. 2010. The Army You Have: The Determinants of Military Mechanization, 1979–2001. *International Studies Quarterly*, 54(2), 481–511.

Sela, Avraham. 2011. Civil Society, the Military, and National Security: The Case of Israel's Security Zone in South Lebanon. *Israel Studies*, 12(1), 53–78.

Shafir, Gershon and Peled, Yoav. 2002. *Being Israeli: The Dynamics of Multiple Citizenship*. Cambridge University Press.

Shannon, Richard. 1982. *Gladstone*, vol. II: *1865–1989*. London: Hamilton.

Shapiro, Robert Y. 2011. Public Opinion and American Democracy. *Public Opinion Quarterly*, 75(5), 982–1017.

Shaw, Martin. 1991. *Post-Military Societies: Militarism, Demilitarism, and War at the End of the Twentieth Century*. London: Polity.

Sherry, Michael S. 1995. *In the Shadow of War*. New Haven, Conn.: Yale University Press.

Siboni, Gabi. 2008. Disproportionate Force: Israel's Concept of Response in Light of the Second Lebanon War. *INSS Insight*, Oct. 2.

Signorino, Curtis S. 1999. Strategic Interaction and the Statistical Analysis of International Conflict. *American Political Science Review*, 93(2), 279–297.

Signorino, Curtis S. and Tarar, Ahmer. 2006. A Unified Theory and Test of Extended Immediate Deterrence. *American Journal of Political Science*, 50(3), 586–605.

Stodeholm International Peace Research Institute (SIPRI). 2013a. *SIPRI Arms Transfer Database*.

2013b. *SIPRI World Military Expenditure Database*.

Siverson, Randolph M. 1995. Democracies and War Participation: In Defense of the Institutional Constraints Argument. *European Journal of International Relations*, 1(4), 481–489.

Slantchev, Branislav L. 2004. How Initiators End Their Wars: The Duration of Warfare and the Terms of Peace. *American Journal of Political Science*, 48(4), 813–829.

2005. Military Coercion in Interstate Crises. *American Political Science Review*, 99(4), 533–547.

2010. *Military Threats: The Costs of Coercion and the Price of Peace.* Cambridge University Press.

Smith, Paul. 1996. Ruling the Waves: Government, the Service and the Cost of Naval Supremacy, 1885–99. In Paul Smith (ed.), *Government and the Armed Forces in Britain 1856–1990.* London: Hambledon Press, 21–52.

Snidal, Duncan. 1979. Public Goods, Property Rights, and Political Organizations. *International Studies Quarterly*, 23(4), 532–566.

Snyder, Jack L. 1984. *The Ideology of the Offensive : Military Decision Making and the Disasters of 1914.* Ithaca: Cornell University Press.

1991. *Myths of Empire: Domestic Politics and International Ambition.* Ithaca: Cornell University Press.

2003. Imperial Temptations. *The National Interest*, Spring, 29–40.

Sobel, Richard. 2001. *The Impact of Public Opinion on U.S. Foreign Policy since Vietnam: Constraining the Colossus.* New York: Oxford University Press.

Solt, Frederick. 2008. Economic Inequality and Democratic Political Engagement. *American Journal of Political Science*, 52(1), 48–60.

2009. Standardizing the World Income Inequality Database. *Social Science Quarterly*, 90(2), 231–242.

2011. Diversionary Nationalism: Economic Inequality and the Formation of National Pride. *Journal of Politics*, 73(6), 821–830.

Sorley, Lewis. 1999. *A Better War: The Unexamined Victories and Final Tragedy of America's Last Years in Vietnam.* New York: Harcourt Brace & Co.

2011. *Westmoreland: The General Who Lost Vietnam.* Boston, Mass.: Houghton Mifflin Harcourt.

Spectator, The. 1878. The Summons to the Sepoy, 51(May 4), 556–557.

Spiers, Edward M. 1992. *The Late Victorian Army, 1868–1902.* Manchester University Press.

Spruyt, Hendrik. 2005. *Ending Empire: Contested Sovereignty and Territorial Partition.* Ithaca: Cornell University Press.

Stanley, Henry M. 1874. *Coomassie and Magdala: The Story of Two British Campaigns in Africa.* New York: Harper & Brothers.

Starry, Donn A. 1980. *Armored Combat in Vietnam.* New York: Arno Press.

Steele, E. David. 1999. *Lord Salisbury: A Political Biography.* London: UCL Press.

Stempel, John Dallas. 1966. Policy/Decision Making in the Department of State: The Vietnamese Problem, 1961–1965. Ph.D. thesis, University of California, Berkeley.

Stern, Robert W. 1988. *The Cat and the Lion: Jaipur State in the British Raj*. Leiden: Brill.

Stigler, George J. 1970. Director's Law of Public Income Redistribution. *Journal of Law and Economics*, 13(1), 1–10.

Strachan, Hew. 1980. The Early Victorian Army and the Nineteenth-Century Revolution in Government. *English Historical Review*, 95(377), 782–809.

Sullivan, Patricia L. 2007. War Aims and War Outcomes: Why Powerful States Lose Limited Wars. *Journal of Conflict Resolution*, 51(3), 496–524.

Summers, Harry G. 2007. *On Strategy: A Critical Analysis of the Vietnam War*. Mineola, NY: Dover Publications.

Swartz, Marvin. 1985. *The Politics of British Foreign Policy in the Era of Disraeli and Gladstone*. New York: St. Martin's Press.

Swirski, Shlomo and Attias, Etty Konor. 2011. *Israel: A Social Report, 2011*. Tel Aviv: Adva Center.

Taubman, Philip. 1988. Soviet Lists Afghan War Toll: 13,310 Dead, 35,478 Wounded. *New York Times*, May 26.

Taylor, Maxwell D. 1960. *The Uncertain Trumpet*. New York: Harper. 1972. *Swords and Plowshares*. New York: W. W. Norton.

Taylor, Miles. 1991. Imperium et Libertas? Rethinking Radical Critique of Imperialism during the Nineteenth Century. *Journal of Imperial and Commonwealth History*, 19(1), 1–23.

Taylor, Robert G. 1975. *Lord Salisbury*. New York: St. Martin's Press.

Thayer, Thomas C. (ed.) 1975. *Pacification and Civil Affairs: A Systems Analysis View of the Vietnam War: 1965–1972*. Vol. 10. Office of the Assistant Secretary for Defense (Systems Analysis). 1985. *War without Fronts: The American Experience in Vietnam*. Boulder: Westview Press.

Themnér, Lotta and Wallensteen, Peter. 2012. Armed Conflict, 1946–2011. *Journal of Peace Research*, 49(4), 565–575.

Thomas, Martin. 2005. *The French Empire between the Wars: Imperialism, Politics and Society*. Manchester University Press.

Thompson, Andrew S. 2000. *Imperial Britain: The Empire in British Politics, c.1880–1932*. Harlow: Longman. 2005. *The Empire Strikes Back? The Impact of Imperialism on Britain from the Mid-Nineteenth Century*. Harlow: Pearson Longman.

Thompson, George Carslake. 1886. *Public Opinion and Lord Beaconsfield, 1875–1880*. London: Macmillan.

Thompson, Robert. 1966. *Defeating Communist Insurgency: The Lessons of Malaya and Vietnam.* St. Petersburg, FL: Hailer Press.
1969. *No Exit from Vietnam.* New York: D. McKay Co.
Thompson, W. Scott and Frizzell, Donaldson D. 1977. *The Lessons of Vietnam.* New York: Crane, Russak.
Tinker, Hugh. 1988. The Construction of Empire in Asia, 1945–48: The Military Dimension. *Journal of Imperial and Commonwealth History,* 16(2), 218–233.
Tomz, Michael and Weeks, Jessica L. P. Forthcoming. Public Opinion and the Democratic Peace. *American Political Science Review.*
Tomz, Michael, Wittenberg, Jason, and King, Gary. 2001 (June 1). *CLARIFY: Software for Interpreting and Presenting Statistical Results. Version 2.0.*
Toronto, Nathan. 2005. *Military Recruitment Data Set, Version 2005.1.*
UK Government. 1867. *Hansard Parliamentary Debates.*
United Nations Office for Disarmament Affairs. n.d. *United Nations Report on Military Expenditures.*
Utley, Rachel E. 2000. *The French Defence Debate: Consensus and Continuity in the Mitterand Era.* Basingstoke: Macmillan.
Vagts, Alfred. 1959. *A History of Militarism: Civilian and Military.* New York: Meridian Books.
Valentino, Benjamin A., Huth, Paul K., and Croco, Sarah E. 2010. Bear Any Burden? How Democracies Minimize the Costs of War. *Journal of Politics,* 72(2), 528–544.
Van Evera, Stephen. 1999. *Causes of War: Power and the Roots of Conflict.* Ithaca: Cornell University Press.
2001 (July). Militarism. Available at http://dspace.mit.edu/handle/1721.1/5534.
Van Staaveren, Jacob. 1966. *USAF Plans and Operations in Southeast Asia, 1965.* Technical Report. USAF Historical Division Liaison Office, Washington, DC.
Vasquez, Joseph Paul, III. 2005. Shouldering the Soldiering: Democracy, Conscription, and Military Casualties. *Journal of Conflict Resolution,* 49(6), 849–873.
Vickers, George. 1993. U.S. Military Strategy. In Jayne S. Werner and Luu Doan Huynh (eds.), *The Vietnam War.* Armonk, NY: M. E. Sharpe, 113–129.
Waltz, Kenneth Neal. 1979. *Theory of International Politics.* Reading, Mass.: Addison-Wesley.
2001. *Man, the State, and War: A Theoretical Analysis.* New York: Columbia University Press.
West, Francis J. 2003. *The Village.* New York: Pocket Books.

Westmoreland, William C. 1989. *A Soldier Reports.* New York: Da Capo Press.

Whitten, Guy D. and Williams, Laron K. 2011. Buttery Guns and Welfare Hawks: The Politics of Defense Spending in Advanced Industrial Democracies. *American Journal of Political Science*, 55(1), 117–134.

Williams, Rhodri. 1991. *Defending the Empire: The Conservative Party and British Defence Policy, 1899–1915.* New Haven, Conn.: Yale University Press.

Wilson, Scott. 2006. Israeli War Plan Had No Exit Strategy. *Washington Post*, Oct. 21.

Wilson, Sven E. and Butler, Daniel M. 2007. A Lot More to Do: The Sensitivity of Time-Series Cross-Section Analyses to Simple Alternative Specifications. *Political Analysis*, 15(2), 101–123.

Winters, Jeffrey A. and Page, Benjamin I. 2009. Oligarchy in the United States? *Perspectives on Politics*, 7(4), 731–751.

Wlezien, Christopher. 2004. Patterns of Representation: Dynamics of Public Preferences and Policy. *Journal of Politics*, 66(1), 1–24.

Wolfers, Arnold. 1962. *Discord and Collaboration: Essays on International Politics.* Baltimore: Johns Hopkins University Press.

Woolman, David. 1968. *Rebels in the Rif.* Stanford, Calif.: Stanford University Press.

1994. In Spanish Morocco, Two Berber Brothers Became a Legend in their Guerrilla War against Two European Powers. *Military History*, 10(6).

World Bank. 2006. World Development Indicators Dataset. Available at http://data.worldbank.org/data-catalog/world-development-indicators.

Yingling, Paul. 2007. A Failure in Generalship. *Armed Forces Journal*, May.

Zrahiya, Zvi. 2007 (Dec. 28). Another Record Year for Defense Spending in 2008. *Haaretz*, Dec. 28.

Index

Cambridge Studies in International Relations